Sams Teach Yourself in 24 Hours

Sams Teach Yourself provide qui[...] proven step[...] approach that works for you. In just 24 sessions of one hour or less, you will tackle every task you need to get the results you want. Let our experienced authors present the most accurate information to get you reliable answers—fast!

GIMP

The GIMP Toolbar

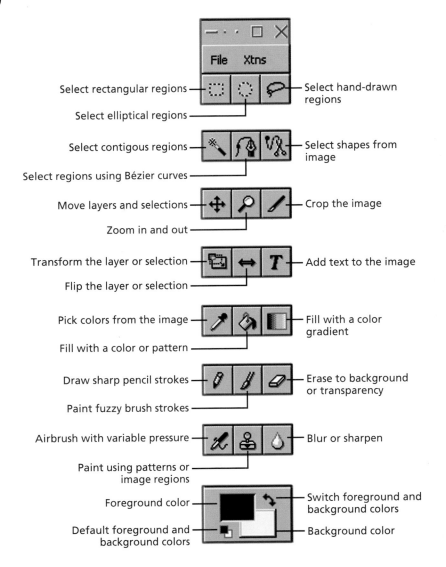

Select rectangular regions

Select elliptical regions

Select hand-drawn regions

Select contiguous regions

Select regions using Bézier curves

Select shapes from image

Move layers and selections

Zoom in and out

Crop the image

Transform the layer or selection

Flip the layer or selection

Add text to the image

Pick colors from the image

Fill with a color or pattern

Fill with a color gradient

Draw sharp pencil strokes

Paint fuzzy brush strokes

Erase to background or transparency

Airbrush with variable pressure

Paint using patterns or image regions

Blur or sharpen

Foreground color

Default foreground and background colors

Switch foreground and background colors

Background color

GIMP Keyboard Shortcut Quick Reference—Tools & Dialogs

TOOLS

Rectangle Select	R	Color Picker	O
Ellipse Select	E	Bucket Fill	Shift+B
Free Select	F	Blend	L
Fuzzy Select	Z	Paintbrush	P
Bézier Select	B	Pencil	Shift+P
Intelligent Scissors	I	Eraser	Shift+E
Move	M	Airbrush	A
Magnify	Shift+M	Clone	C
Crop	Shift+C	Convolve	V
Transform	Shift+T	Default Colors	D
Flip	Shift+F	Swap Colors	X
Text	T		

DIALOGS

Brushes	Shift+Ctrl+B
Patterns	Shift+Ctrl+P
Palette	Ctrl+P
Gradient Editor	Ctrl+G
Layers and Channels	Ctrl+L

GIMP Keyboard Shortcut Quick Reference—Menus

FILE MENU

New	Ctrl+N
Open	Ctrl+O
Save	Ctrl+S
Close	Ctrl+W
Quit	Ctrl+Q

EDIT MENU

Cut	Ctrl+X
Copy	Ctrl+C
Paste	Ctrl+V
Clear	Ctrl+K
Fill	Ctrl+.
Undo	Ctrl+Z
Redo	Ctrl+R
Cut Named	Shift+Ctrl+X
Copy Named	Shift+Ctrl+C
Paste Named	Shift+Ctrl+V

LAYER MENU

New Layer	Ctrl+N
Raise Layer	Ctrl+F
Lower layer	Ctrl+B
Duplicate Layer	Ctrl+C
Delete Layer	Ctrl+X
Scale layer	Ctrl+S
Resize Layer	Ctrl+R
Anchor Layer	Ctrl+H
Merge Visible Layers	Ctrl+M

SELECT MENU

Toggle	Ctrl+T
Invert	Ctrl+I
All	Ctrl+A
None	Shift+Ctrl+A
Float	Shift+Ctrl+L
Sharpen	Shift+Ctrl+H
Feather	Shift+Ctrl+F

VIEW MENU

Window Info	Shift+Ctrl+I
Toggle Rulers	Shift+Ctrl+R
Toggle Guides	Shift+Ctrl+T

CHANNEL MENU

New Channel	Ctrl+N
Raise Channel	Ctrl+F
Lower Channel	Ctrl+B
Duplicate Channel	Ctrl+C
Delete Channel	Ctrl+X
Channel to Selection	Ctrl+S

CHANNEL OPS

Duplicate	Ctrl+D
Offset	Shift+Ctrl+O

FILTERS

Repeat Last	Alt+F
Re-show Last	Shift+Alt+F

Joshua Pruitt and Ramona Pruitt

SAMS
Teach Yourself

GIMP

in 24 Hours

SAMS

A Division of Macmillan Computer Publishing
201 West 103rd Street, Indianapolis, Indiana 46290

Sams Teach Yourself GIMP in 24 Hours

Copyright © 1999 by Sams Publishing

International Standard Book Number: 0-672-31509-2

Library of Congress Catalog Card Number: 98-87919

Printed in the United States of America

First Printing: March 1999

01   00   99   3   2   1

Trademarks

Warning and Disclaimer

EXECUTIVE EDITOR
Brad Koch

ACQUISITIONS EDITOR
Dustin Sullivan

DEVELOPMENT EDITOR
Tom Dinse

MANAGING EDITOR
Brice Gosnell

PROJECT EDITOR
Gretchen Uphoff

COPY EDITOR
Pamela Woolf

INDEXER
Bruce Clingaman

PROOFREADER
Billy Fields

TECHNICAL EDITOR
Zach Beane

SOFTWARE DEVELOPMENT SPECIALIST
Jack Belbot

INTERIOR DESIGN
Gary Adair

COVER DESIGN
Aren Howell

LAYOUT TECHNICIANS
Branden Allen
Stacey DeRome
Timothy Osborn
Staci Somers

Contents at a Glance

Contents

About the Authors

Joshua Pruitt is an administrator/digital-graphic artist residing in Nashville, Tennessee. He works for a local college and also teaches UNIX there. He is part of a Web design and hosting firm known as Mid-TN Network. He sets up local area networks for small businesses, and he is also Webmaster for the Nashville Linux User's Group (www.nlug.org). Joshua spends way too much of his spare time with his books and computers, follows the politics of the tech industry soap opera, and will never pass up an opportunity to extol the virtues of Linux and the GIMP. If you don't believe that, write him at joshua@mid-tn.com.

Ramona Pruitt is a self-taught graphic artist, cutting her first graphic teeth on Windows-based programs such as Photoshop and Paint Shop Pro, and then applying that knowledge to explore the GIMP. Like Joshua, she lives in Nashville, Tennessee, and is a part of the Web design team at Mid-TN Network, using her computer as a tool for her creative abilities. In her spare time, she enjoys sewing, reading, hiking, and spending time with a beautiful new German Shepherd pup. She welcomes email addressed to wildflower@mid-tn.com.

Dedication

We dedicate this book to you, our readers, whether aspiring or accomplished artists. It is our hope that in writing this book, we have provided you with a diverse look at how the GIMP functions, and practical applications for its use.

Acknowledgments

It's amazing how many people are involved in a project such as this one. We'd like to thank, first and foremost, the two men responsible for the GIMP itself, Peter Mattis and Spencer Kimball. Thanks guys, for creating such a cool and inspiring program. Next we'd like to thank David Fugate, our agent at Waterside Productions, for helping us get the gig. A very special thanks goes to our two favorite editors at Macmillan Publishing, Dustin Sullivan and Tom Dinse, and of course to all the other folks at Macmillan who were involved in bringing the project to completion. Also, many thanks to Zach Beane, for taking on the task of technical editing. And finally, a big thank you to Robert Pruitt, for his support and encouragement throughout, and to Jasari, our favorite lion at the Nashville Zoo, who was kind enough to stand still and be photographed for book illustration purposes.

Tell Us What You Think!

As the reader of this book, *you* are our most important critic and commentator. We value your opinion and want to know what we're doing right, what we could do better, what areas you'd like to see us publish in, and any other words of wisdom you're willing to pass our way.

As the executive editor for the operating systems team at Macmillan Computer Publishing, I welcome your comments. You can fax, email, or write me directly to let me know what you did or didn't like about this book—as well as what we can do to make our books stronger.

Please note that I cannot help you with technical problems related to the topic of this book, and that due to the high volume of mail I receive, I might not be able to reply to every message.

When you write, please be sure to include this book's title and author as well as your name and phone or fax number. I will carefully review your comments and share them with the author and editors who worked on the book.

Fax: 317.581.4663
Email: opsys@mcp.com
Mail: Executive Editor
        Operating Systems
        Macmillan Computer Publishing
        201 West 103rd Street
        Indianapolis, IN 46290 USA

Introduction

Because you're doubtlessly wondering by now, GIMP is an acronym for *GNU Image Manipulation Program*. And it's more than just its name that sets this application apart from the norm. The GIMP itself is a tremendously sophisticated and powerful image editing program written for UNIX and the X Window environment. It is used for editing and creating digital graphics, and is similar in function and design to Adobe Photoshop, Corel Draw, Paint Shop Pro, and other popular applications, with the added benefit that it happens to be free, and it runs on the world's greatest PC operating system, Linux. Furthermore, its modular design allows for the continual addition of functionality—it will never become an abandoned project. It has an unequivocally fantastic laundry list of features that tend to make even the most hardened hacker puzzle and delight at just how incredibly functional and polished GIMP really is. It is extremely utilitarian, fast, feature-laden, stable, expandable, and is possibly the greatest thing since sliced bread (and the Linux kernel). In short, prepare to be astounded and amazed!

A Little Background

The GIMP began in 1995 as a small class project by two students at the University of California, Berkeley: Peter Mattis and Spencer Kimball. It was released to the public under the GNU GPL (General Public License), and, due to the contributions of many coders and thousands of testers, has subsequently evolved beyond a simple class compiler project into the fully-fledged graphics-editing suite it is today. GIMP is a relatively young program, just now developing into maturity, and now that it has truly arrived, its development is occurring at an increasingly accelerated rate. In fact, by the time this book hits the presses, there will likely be new features, additional functionality, and perhaps an entirely updated version of the GIMP available for download from FTP sites around the globe. Welcome to the wonderful world of Open Source software! (May the source be with you!)

The most important aspect of the GIMP is not necessarily its power or utility as a graphics application, (although that is, of course, what you want and expect from well-coded software), but that it is in fact *free* software—released under the GPL as defined by the Free Software Foundation. This means that it is free not merely in terms of *free of cost*, but also in the sense of freedom—end users are at liberty to alter and distribute the source code as they see fit. This is because the GNU GPL ensures that the source code to the application is always freely available, without restriction, to anyone with the inclination to take a peek. This adds tremendous momentum to the development of software projects such as Linux, the many FSF projects, Apache, KDE, GNOME, Mozilla, and the

GIMP. It allows developers from all over the Internet to view, study, alter, revise, and improve the code in a dynamic way, with celerity and quality that is simply unmatched by private companies alone, which are staffed with limited numbers of developers and motivated only by immediate marketability. In short, Open Source software generates the most stable and easily improved software in the world. And, GIMP stands as a shining testament to this fundamental truth.

GIMP binaries are currently available for Solaris, SunOS, HP-UX, IRIX, Linux, and FreeBSD, and probably most any other relatively modern UNIX variant you can name. There is also an OS/2 port available, a Microsoft Windows port that is workable, but still in heavy development, and a BeOS port is churning around the rumor mill. As of yet, there are no plans to port GIMP to the Macintosh. (Sorry, guys.)

Who This Book Is For

This book assumes that you are running and are comfortable using the Linux operating system. (Most modern UNIX variants will work as well, but they're not as much fun as running Linux, in the author's most humble opinion). It is suggested that you take the time to familiarize yourself with your computer's operating system before attempting to tackle the GIMP for the first time.

As far as learning the GIMP goes, the process is the same as with any other robust application: the best way to learn is simply to play with it! I suggest that you take time between hours to push all the buttons, try new things out, and get a feel for the software (who could resist doing that anyway?). This book is designed as an addendum and an aid to the learning process, and with some time and effort, you'll be a GIMP guru by the time you're finished.

Conventions Used in This Book

This book is designed to teach you topics in one-hour sessions. All the books in the *Sams Teach Yourself* series enable you to start working and become productive with the product as quickly as possible. This book will do that for you!

Each hour, or session, starts with a quick overview of the topic to inform you of what to expect in that lesson. The overview helps you determine the nature of the lesson and whether the lesson is relevant to your needs.

Each hour has a main section that discusses the topic in a clear, concise manner by breaking the topic into logical parts and explaining each component clearly. You'll also find examples and illustrations to help you understand and master the material under consideration.

Interspersed in the lessons are special elements called Notes, Tips, and Cautions, which provide additional information for you.

Notes provide supplemental information about the topic or feature being discussed.

Tips offer time-saving advice and suggest ways to help you achieve more professional results.

Cautions warn you about pitfalls, traps, and mistakes to avoid.

HOUR 1

Installation and Configuration

Bring Out the GIMP

This hour is designed to assist you through the mundane task of getting GIMP (GNU Image Manipulation Program) v.1.0 successfully installed and running smoothly on your system—if you haven't done so already. It is primarily geared for those of you who are running Linux 2.0+ on PC architecture (Intel and clones), although the steps laid out here can easily apply to the other UNIX variants and hardware platforms as well, with generally little or no alteration involved (most of the time).

I'm assuming that you have Linux or some UNIX variant and an implementation of the X Window System up and running already. However, if this is not the case, this hour also briefly touches on getting Linux installed on a PC. There's really no excuse not to try this stuff out.

Preparation and understanding are essential to install new software such as this, especially if you have little experience with UNIX. It is by no means difficult, but there are many variables involved along the way, any one of which can conceivably cause issues. Therefore, in order to prevent any difficulties before they arise, you should take stock of the following criteria carefully:

- You should have administrative privileges on the machine in question.
- Check over the required packages and take note of what you have installed and what you do not have installed—as well as the versions of the software.
- You should know exactly how your system is set up and what is installed. That way, you can be aware of any idiosyncrasies your setup might possess (for example, those who run Red Hat 5.1 should be aware that it uses glibc). Now let's get started.

Installing Linux—A Primer

This book is primarily geared for those who already have Linux (or another UNIX variant) installed and running, and possess some working knowledge of how to run and use it. However, if you are new to GNU/Linux or UNIX in general, but would like to get started right away using GIMP and other great Open Source software, don't fret; Linux is available from several vendors (see the list of web sites below), and with a little research, you can be up and running a fine Linux box in no time. The CD-ROM has the GIMP and many other fantastic applications to assist you in your expedition into the wonderful world of free software. The following list briefly outlines what you'll find:

- The GIMP source code in gripped format
- The GIMP source code in RPM format
- GIMP binaries in RPM and gripped format for various platforms
- Everything else GIMP needs to run smoothly (libraries, extra filters, and so on)

In order to install Linux, you will need the following:

- An Intel-clone PC running anything from a 386 to a PII. (Linux is also readily available for other platforms, such as the PowerPC, Alpha, and Sun Sparc.
- At least 8MB of RAM (Linux can technically run on a 386 with 4MB of RAM, and while this is sufficient for many applications, running such applications as X and the GIMP tends to require a little more horsepower in order to be productive. I recommend at least a Pentium 100 with 16MB of RAM to work comfortably, regardless of software.)

- A CD-ROM drive (or at least a floppy drive, a fast Internet connection—something 56K or better, if you want to keep your sanity—and a lot of patience, depending on how you choose to approach Linux installation.)
- A desire to learn and tinker

Basic instructions for successfully installing Linux are included with title distribution you select from any of the companies listed below. You will find the basic instructions for doing things such as creating a boot disk, partitioning your hard drive, installing Linux, setting up X, and so on. It is probably a good idea to print title instructions for reference during the installation and setup process. There are also many great Linux books out there available to help you get started, (such as *Sams Teach Yourself Linux in 24 Hours*). More information about Linux can be found at the following Web sites:

- The Linux documentation project—`http://sunsite.unc.edu/mdw/linux.html`
- Red Hat (versions available for Intel, Alpha, and Sparc machines)—`http://www.redhat.com/`
- Caldera (Open Linux)—`http://www.caldera.com/`
- Slackware Linux—`http://www.slackware.org/`
- Debian Linux—`http://www.debian.org/`
- S.u.S.E. Linux—`http://www.suse.de/`
- Linux for the PowerPC—`http://www.linuxppc.org/`
- Yellow Dog Linux (Another Macintosh distribution—based on LinuxPPC)—`http://www.yellowdoglinux.com/`
- MKLinux (Linux for the Power Macintosh; an alternative to LinuxPPC)—`http://www.mklinux.apple.com/`
- Linux-m68k (supports older m68k Macintoshes)—`http://www.linux-m68k.org/`
- The Linux laptop help page—`http://www.cs.utexas.edu/users/kharker/linux-laptop/`
- The Linux/Sparc help page—`http://www.geog.ubc.ca/s_linux.html`
- The semi-official Linux home page—`http://www.linux.org/`
- Linux Now!—`http://www.linuxnow.com/`
- All about X Window Managers—`http://www.PLiG.org/xwinman/`
- More X Window System Information—`http://www.x11.org/`
- Customizing your X environment—`http://themes.org/`

System Requirements for Running GIMP

In order to successfully install and run GIMP 1.0, the following items are required:

- A working UNIX variant (Linux, Solaris, HP-UX, FreeBSD, OpenBSD, AIX, DEC UNIX, IRIX, and so on)
- A working implementation of the X Window System (X11R5 or better—preferably X11R6)
- The GNU C compiler or equivalent
- GTK 1.0.1 or higher
- The latest graphics libraries (libjpeg, libgif, libpng, libtiff, libxpm, libmpeg, libz, and so on)
- Sufficient hardware (on a PC, this would probably mean at the very least a 486 with 16+MB of RAM)
- At least 20MB of hard drive space for minimal installation (100MB for a full compile and debugging session) with room to spare (if you plan on getting any work done)

About GTK

GTK is short for the GIMP ToolKit. It is a vital and required component of the GIMP—as it is the GUI toolkit on which the GIMP is built. (In case you're wondering, a *toolkit* is more or less any library that draws the "widgets" for a graphical application—scrollbars, buttons, menus, check boxes, and so on. UNIX traditionally has had many different toolkits to choose from, with varying degrees of simplicity or robustness, depending on the needs of the programmer.) Originally, the GIMP used Motif as the toolkit library of choice, but the creators of GIMP created GTK as a more modern and workable alternative to the commercially licensed and developmentally repressed Motif. GTK is very clean, powerful, efficient, and aesthetically pleasing (to me, at least). It is now also being used for many other applications, as well as the GNOME desktop project.

As of this writing, it is best to install only the *stable* series of GTK for use with the GIMP (that is, the stable 1.0 series as opposed to the developmental 1.1 series). You cannot compile GIMP 1.0 with GTK 1.1+ (which is needed for the latest releases of GNOME). Of course, as with anything in the Open Source community (or free software community, if you prefer), this is likely to change very rapidly—perhaps even by the time this book hits the shelves this will no longer be an issue, because GNOME is fast reaching the completion stage, the next release of GIMP might likely use the currently developmental version of GTK. So, you will want to check out http://www.gtk.org/ and http://www.gimp.org/ for the most current, up-to-date details.

Graphics Libraries

Your operating system (OS) installation, if installed recently or well maintained, is likely to have fairly up-to-date graphics libraries already available, but you will want to make sure you have installed them all from the latest versions—to make for more stability and less headaches in the installation process. The most recent libraries, in source form and in various packaged formats, are provided on the CD-ROM. Otherwise, you can find them at many FTP mirror sites worldwide, such as `ftp://ftp.x.org/contrib/libraries/` and `ftp://ftp.gimp.org/pub/gimp/libs/`. Here is a checklist:

- aalib 1.2 or later.
- xdelta .20 or later.
- libpng 1.0.1 or later.
- libxpm 4.7 or later.
- libtiff 3.4 or later.
- libmpeg 1.2.1 or later.
- libjpeg 6b or later.
- zlib 1.1.2 or later.
- ImageMagick (not really required, but it includes support for many file formats, and some very handy utilities as well). It can be found at `http://www.wizards.dupont.com/cristy/ImageMagick.html`.

Other Things

In addition to what is required, you will likely want to have these things installed as well:

- **XV**—XV is an image viewer/editor that is a good tool for use in concert with the GIMP. Being nearly a staple of most any standard X environment, XV is probably already installed. If not, you can grab it at nearly any Linux-centric FTP site.
- **SANE**—You'll need this if you want to use a scanner from within the GIMP. SANE can be found at `http://www.mostang.com/sane/`. Using a SANE supported scanner within GIMP is a real joy.
- **gzip and bzip2**—Enables internal file compression.

  GNU zip and bzip2 are file compression formats, such as zip or StuffIt files. The GIMP allows for the direct compression/decompression of graphics files from within the GIMP environment. This is a really handy feature, especially if you find yourself passing unfinished files around online or over SneakerNet (carrying floppies around on foot). They can be snagged at `http://www.gnu.org/` and `http://www.muraroa.demon.co.uk/`.

If you choose to compile, GIMP has been designed to be as compiler-friendly (ANSI C) as possible. However, in reality nothing compiles the GIMP as painlessly as the trusty GNU C compiler (and variants), as the proprietary compilers might not have all the features necessary to compile the GIMP, though most should. You might want to check and see if you have the gcc compiler installed. (Issue a gcc -v). If not, you might need to ask yourself why the heck not! Obtain it from http://www.gnu.org/software/gcc/gcc.html.

Installing GIMP

The following sections contain instructions for installing GIMP on your system. The first thing to do in approaching GIMP installation is to determine which installation method you want to use. Depending on your situation, there are a few different ways to go about installing GIMP.

Binary Installation

New Term If you want to get the GIMP up and running as quickly and painlessly as possible, *binary* installation is by far the best way to go. (Binary is another term for an executable program.) This means that you will install the program into its proper place, and then run it.

 Note that the binaries on the CD-ROM are for Linux 2.0+, Solaris, and IRIX only. If you are running another platform, you will need to get the binaries elsewhere, or compile the source code on your machine.

There are generally two main ways to go about a binary installation: the standard way or by using a package manager.

The Standard Way

The standard way to go about a binary installation is to grab the program in the form of a compressed archive (usually a tar.gz file), decompress the archive (tar -zxvf *.tar.gz), and put the files where they need to go according to the documentation. The GIMP binary for Solaris on the CD-ROM is packaged in this manner.

Using RPM

Another popular way to do this is by using RPM—the Red Hat Package Manager. This program, which is available by default on the Red Hat, Caldera, and S.u.S.E distributions and available for any UNIX platform, takes care of installation issues for you. It takes any file compacted into RPM format, installs it, and puts everything where it needs to go. Installation and upgrading are thereby greatly simplified, because all the details as to where things belong are taken care of for you. (This is particularly handy for uninstalling software.) It can also retain your configuration files, so that customizations are not lost during upgrades. One little command and you're finished.

(There are other good package managers out there as well, such as the Debian distribution's DEB format and Stampede's SLP format. These should work much in the same way as RPM.)

Binary Installation for RPM Enabled Systems

You can find GIMP binaries on the CD-ROM in the RPM format under the /gimp/RPMS/ directory. As root, simply change into the directory reflecting your platform of choice (that is, /mnt/cdrom/gimp/RPMS/) and type the following at the prompt:

```
rpm -Uvh gimp-1.0.2.i386.rpm
rpm -Uvh gimp-devel-1.0.2.i386.rpm
rpm -Uvh gimp-data-extras.1.0.2.i386.rpm
rpm -Uvh gimp-plugins-unstable.-1.0.2.i386.rpm
```

This will be followed by a succession of hash marks (#) indicating the installation is in progress. Pending no error messages, you should be ready to run the GIMP. Nice and simple, wouldn't you say?

RPM Troubleshooting Quick Reference

Q I get a `dependency not found` error.

A This means that the installing package was looking for a required file or library that was not there. You will need to install/upgrade any packages containing the files you need. This might require a little investigation on your part. For example, if the error says `missing libjpeg.so.1 - dependency not found`, you can deduce from this that there is a problem with the libjpeg package. It's probably misplaced, not installed, or is an outdated version. You should then go to any one of many Linux FTP site mirrors and download/install the latest libjpeg package to reconcile the problem.

Although most of the time these dependency issues are pretty easy to resolve, sometimes it is not quite so easy to deduce what package contains the missing file at merely first glance. But, not to worry; most of the time you can find out where the file beckons from by way of a little research. Chances are that after checking the newsgroups or mailing lists, someone will have run into the same thing and can tell you what you are missing. These resources are always timely, accurate, and quick to respond. (You'll be surprised.)

Q That didn't work. After installing the latest necessary packages, I still get the same error.

A Assuming that the problem is associated with library dependencies (lib*.so), you might need to add the directory containing the said lib to the library path. You do this by editing /etc/ld.so.conf and adding the string `/usr/local/lib` (or wherever the library resides). Then run ldconfig and you should be set.

Otherwise, you might need to add the directory to your `LD_LIBRARY_PATH` variable in your .bashrc (or equivalent) if you do not have administrative privileges.

Every once in a while, older versions of libs might be installed in a different directory, such as /usr/lib, thereby causing confusion. You might need to completely uninstall all the older library packages before installing the new ones.

Q I get `undefined symbol: register frame info` errors when trying to run the GIMP.

A This is caused by running a gcc-compiled GIMP with egcs-compiled graphics libraries (as can be the case when upgrading the GIMP in Red Hat 5.1). You will need to recompile GIMP with egcs, or update *all* the RPM packages, including graphics libraries and gtk, for consistency (The binaries in /gimp/RPMS/ on the CD-ROM are compiled uniformly).

Source Installation

The other way to install any Open Source application is to compile the *source code* from scratch. Source code is the programming text that compiles into an executable application file. On more traditional PC operating systems, source code is rarely available to the public, so the concept does sometimes cause confusion for new users. You will want to compile source code from scratch if

- You are running a UNIX platform for which there are no precompiled binaries available.
- You have a home-rolled custom installation and you want to make a really clean and fully compatible installation.
- You want to apply patches (updates) without downloading the entire installation source tree over and over again.
- You want to hack on this stuff for fun.

For a beginning Linux user, compiling the GIMP is probably not the easiest undertaking there is. (It is usually best to start on small compiles to familiarize yourself with dealing with source code). The GIMP is quite a large and complex application. However, you don't have to be a hardened UNIX hacker in order to compile GIMP successfully...you simply need to follow the instructions carefully, read the READMEs, and be willing to do a little research if you happen to run into trouble.

The source code on the CD-ROM is available in tar.gz format as well as in RPM format. The *source RPMs* allow you to compile the source code from scratch, and then *build binary RPMs* for installation (to keep things nice and tidy, and easy to upgrade/uninstall).

This section describes the basic steps needed to compile and install the GIMP from the source packages—it should be pretty uniform across platforms. However, if you do run into trouble compiling GIMP on a non-Linux platform, you should consult the GIMP mailing lists and newsgroups. There have been a few mild issues with different compilers on different platforms, although they are usually fairly simply to remedy.

Installing and Compiling from the Source Packages

Installing and compiling the GIMP from the source distribution should work roughly the same in all UNIX-like platforms. To compile the sources, you must do the following as the root user:

- Compile and install GTK:

  ```
  cp /mnt/cdrom/gtk/src/gtk-1.0.7.tar.gz /usr/local/src
  ```

  (or snag it from `ftp://ftp.gimp.org/pub/gtk/`)

  ```
  tar -zxvf gtk-1.0.7.tar.gz
  ```

  ```
  cd ./gtk-1.0.7
  ```

  Read the Readme file: `vi README`.

  (Substitute pico, emacs, or whatever text editor you use for vi if necessary.)

  ```
  ./configure
  ```

  ```
  make
  ```

  ```
  make install
  ```

- Make sure all the appropriate graphics libraries are installed (Updates can be found in /mnt/cdrom/gimp/libs/src. Unpackage them and read the appropriate README files).

- Copy the source package of GIMP from the CD-ROM to a suitable compiling spot.

  ```
  cp /mnt/cdrom/gimp/src/gimp-1.0.2.tar.gz /usr/local/src
  ```

  Alternatively, you can grab the latest version of the GIMP from `ftp://ftp.gimp.org/pub/gimp/`

- Decompress the source package.

  ```
  tar -zxvf gimp-1.0.2.tar.gz
  ```

  ```
  cd ./gimp-1.0.2
  ```

- Read the Readme file.
- Do the standard compile as the root user.

  ```
  ./configure
  make
  make install
  ```

- Install the GIMP data package; repeat preceding steps for `gimp-data-extras-1.0.2.tar.gz`.
- Compile and install the GIMP extra filters package—`gimp-plugins-unstable-1.0.2.tar.gz`. This is completely optional, but you'll most likely want these fantastic plug-ins. Read the Readme file—included in the filters package—thoroughly for more details concerning installation and specifically the source compilation. You will save yourself much time and many headaches by doing so.

Given a smooth compile session, everything should be in order for you to run the GIMP for the first time.

Although the preceding instructions might seem to indicate otherwise, installation of the GIMP will, in all likelihood, proceed smoothly and without incident. However, there are always exceptions to the rule. If you happen to find yourself in such a situation, take advantage of the world's most reactive and reliable technical support system available anywhere—Linux newsgroups and mailing lists.

Source Installation for RPM-Enabled Systems

Even if you are running an RPM-enabled system, you might still want to compile the source tree from scratch. This can be handy in situations where your system might be employing an idiosyncronous directory tree, or where system libraries might be slightly different or customized. Sometimes there's nothing better than to have something custom built for your system.

If you are installing from the CD-ROM, you will want to install the GIMP sources via RPM from the /gimp/RPM/src directory like this:

```
rpm -ivh gimp-1.0.2-1.src.rpm
rpm -ivh gimp-data-extras-1.0.2-1.src.rpm
rpm -ivh gimp-plugins-unstable.src.rpm
```

This decompresses the source files into the /usr/src/redhat/ directory, under which the source and spec files (building parameters) are unloaded into the ./SOURCES and ./SPECS directories, respectively. You will need to cd into the /usr/src/redhat/SPECS directory and issue the following commands in order to build the source according the spec files:

```
rpm -bb gimp-1.0.2-1.spec
rpm -bb gimp-data-extras-1.0.2-1.spec
rpm -bb gimp-plugins-unstable.spec
```

This compiles the source and packages the binaries into tidy RPM packages for you. Be forewarned: The GIMP consists of over 300,000 lines of code, so expect this compilation to take a while, depending on your machine. After it finishes, you can then install these RPMs just like you would any other.

```
cd /usr/src/redhat/RPMS
rpm -Uvh gimp-1.0.2.i386.rpm
rpm -Uvh gimp-devel-1.0.2.i386.rpm
rpm -Uvh gimp-data-extras.1.0.2.i386.rpm
rpm -Uvh gimp-plugins-unstable.-1.0.2.i386.rpm
```

Source Installation Troubleshooter

Q I keep getting errors about not finding libgtk.

A First of all, make sure you have GTK installed! Then, make sure it is in your search path. Add the line /usr/local/lib to /etc/ld.so.conf with your favorite text editor, and then run ldconfig.

Q I keep getting `glibconfig.h - not found` errors.

A Make sure that the header files glib.h and glibconfig.h are in their proper places. On most systems, glibconfig.h should go in /usr/(local)/lib/glib/include, and glib.h in /usr/(local)/include.

Q GIMP won't compile correctly on Solaris, HP-UX, and so on.

A Every platform has its own little quirks. For non-Linux platform specific issues, it is best to consult newsgroups and Web sites for answers. The GIMP Developer's FAQ—`http://www.rru.com/~meo/gimp/faq-dev.html`—has a lot of really good, solid answers for these kind of issues.

Summary

Hopefully, installation has proceeded smoothly and without incident. Again, if you do run into snags, there are a lot of people out there willing and able to help. If this is the case, you will likely find that the answers are frequently quite simple. Fortunately, GIMP is, for the most part, well behaved for installation.

Q&A

Q   I run Windows 95/98/NT. Am I just out of luck?

A   Not necessarily. There is not a *full* GIMP port available for Windows; although a Windows port is in the works, it is not ready for prime time just yet, but running the GIMP is not out of reach. You can either wait for a full Windows version (you might be waiting quite a while… but who knows?) or, you can partition your hard disk for a dual-boot Linux solution, which is much more fun anyway. And the good news is that installing Linux shouldn't in any way interfere with the software that is already installed. It can happily coexist with any other operating system you might be running now. Instructions on how to do this are in the CD-ROM documentation (D:\Docs\Rhmanual\Manual\index.htm). There are also a lot of really good Linux books out there worth checking out if you are interested in trying it.

Exercise

If you haven't guessed it already, the exercise for this hour is to install GIMP (and Linux) if you haven't already done so!

Hour 2

Getting Started

In Hour 1, "Installation and Configuration," you covered GIMP installation in detail. Now that the installation issues are taken care of, you are ready to begin learning how to use the GIMP effectively. Because it is a graphics application, the first logical thing to do in this hour is to open, manipulate, and save some graphics, and learn about the various file formats and options in the process.

Although it is a very robust program, and might work a little differently than you're used to, the GIMP is actually pretty easy to learn. If you are somewhat familiar with graphics applications already, you should feel right at home with the GIMP. You might want to browse these next two hours (2 and 3) just long enough to get a feel for the application, and then dive right in to the really fun stuff.

Your First GIMP Session

In order to start the GIMP (making sure that X is up and running), type the executable's name at an Xterm (or create an icon or menu item within your favorite Window Manager), and watch the magic begin.

```
gimp &
```

An installation dialog box will appear, as shown in Figure 2.1, containing a paragraph about the GNU General Public License, and prompting you for the go-ahead to create your various local GIMP files in your home directory (in a hidden area labeled .gimp— viewable with the `ls  -a` command). These files contain all the custom preferences you will store, as well as personal files—brushes, palettes, patterns, plug-ins, scripts, and so on). This dialog box occurs *only once*—when any user starts the GIMP for the first time. You should click the Install button and let it create the necessary directories for you.

FIGURE 2.1

This is the first screen you will see in the GIMP. It will occur only once.

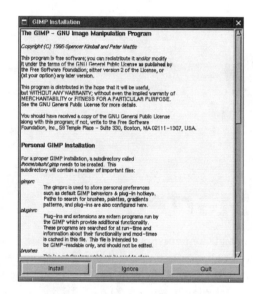

This will soon be followed by a confirmation dialog box (see Figure 2.2). Click Continue here.

FIGURE 2.2

The confirmation dialog box. This tells you exactly which files GIMP has installed into your home directory.

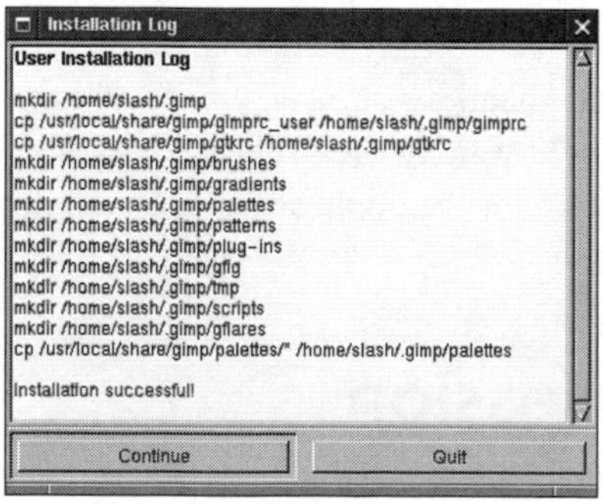

If all goes well, a splash-screen appears, along with a startup progress indicator as shown in Figure 2.3. This will appear every time the GIMP initializes from now on.

FIGURE 2.3

The progress indicator represents the various plug-ins, scripts, and extensions that are being loaded into memory.

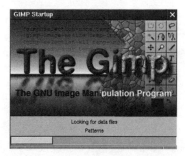

In the event that the shell returns `gimp: command not found`, you will want to make sure that the GIMP executable is in fact in your *path*. For example, if your GIMP binary is located in a somewhat non-standard place such as /opt/gimp/bin, you will want to add that directory to your PATH variable in your .bashrc file (or equivalent).

After a few short moments of startup, the initial GIMP toolbar and Tip dialog box will appear (see Figure 2.4). Now you're ready to begin using the GIMP productively.

FIGURE 2.4

This is the normal GIMP palette on startup.

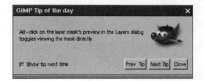

After the GIMP has finished initializing, you will be greeted by the happy face of the GIMP mascot Wilber, in the Tip of the Day dialog box. If you happen to be a refugee from the Windows/Macintosh camps, you might groan at the sight of yet another happy little dialog message, but I implore you, don't disable this one just yet! I have personally found this dialog box to be very insightful. Put another way: The GIMP authors have actually put some useful information in there! You might want to read all the tips before disabling it. (The dialog box can be disabled at any time by unchecking the Show Tip Next Time box.)

You should now also see the GIMP toolbox on your desktop. This is the dialog box that contains icons representing the 21 most common image editing tools.

The GIMP Interface

Before beginning on an image, one of the first things you will want to do is familiarize yourself with the basic interface.

The GIMP toolbox dialog, as pictured in Figure 2.5, is the single most important element in the entire program. From it, you will gain access to all your graphics files and the most essential controls. The first thing you'll notice, if you've used other popular graphics applications, is that this toolbox works much in the same way you'd expect. The GIMP toolbox contains the controls for 21 of the most basic and essential of graphics editing tools, as well as the two main menus (File and Xtns) and the Foreground/Background Color Selection box.

FIGURE 2.5

The GIMP toolbox contains the most essential tools and menus.

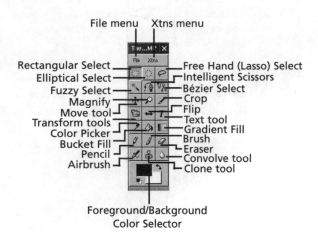

File menu   Xtns menu

Rectangular Select — ⌐ Free Hand (Lasso) Select
Elliptical Select — ⌐ Intelligent Scissors
Fuzzy Select — ⌐ Bézier Select
Magnify — ⌐ Crop
Move tool — ⌐ Flip
Transform tools — ⌐ Text tool
Color Picker — ⌐ Gradient Fill
Bucket Fill — ⌐ Brush
Pencil — ⌐ Eraser
Airbrush — ⌐ Convolve tool
⌐ Clone tool

Foreground/Background
Color Selector

Creating a New File

Obviously, the most common task in dealing with graphics is to create, open, and edit files. In fact, the GIMP doesn't even automatically open a new blank image for you; it assumes that you will primarily be altering existing graphics. So this is where you'll begin. The first thing to do is go to the File menu and click New. You will then be greeted with the New Image dialog box, as shown in Figure 2.6.

FIGURE 2.6

*The New Image
dialog box creates
an empty canvas
from which to work.*

2

File Size

NEW TERM In the top portion of the New Image dialog box, the width and height options are visible. You can specify the size for your new image here. The GIMP *always* measures image sizes in *pixels*, which are, of course, the singular *picture elements* that make up your digital display.

Image Type

The middle portion of the dialog box consists of two image types pertaining to color depth. RGB (referring to full color) and grayscale. It is almost always wise to create an image in full color, because it can be reduced to any number of colors or grayscaled later on. (Certain GIMP functions will only work on full color images.)

Fill Type

Fill type refers to the background color of the image you are working with. *Background* is the color that is the second one in the Foreground/Background Color Selector on the toolbox. This usually defaults to white, but it can be any color you choose. Next, the White option is pretty self-explanatory. And finally, the Transparent option allows you to create an image with a transparent (invisible) background, such as the kind found in transparent GIFs.

After you click OK, your new canvas will appear. You can, of course, have more than one image open in the GIMP at any given time.

Opening Files

Opening files works in much the same way as creating new ones. First, go to the File, Open menu. The file selector box is pretty easy to follow (see Figure 2.7). Essentially, listings of your directories are on the left, and files are listed on the right. You will notice that at the top, three option buttons allow you to create directories, and delete, or rename files as well. (This can come in handy sometimes.)

FIGURE 2.7

*The Load Image dia-
log box shows you a
listing of the files on
your disk.*

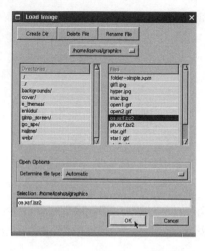

In the directories listed on the left, you will see two directory representa-
tions you might be unfamiliar with: ./ and ../. ./ refers to the directory
you are currently in. Double-clicking it will allow the contents of the working directory to be refreshed, which is good if you happened to have
changed the contents of the directory while the dialog box is open. The ../
option, even more importantly, allows you to go back one directory into the
one containing the directory you're in. Sound confusing? You will just have
to try it out and see. (For reference, if you're from a Windows background,
../ functions exactly the same way as the Up icon in Windows Explorer.)

Below the directory listings, you will see an Detect File Type drop-down menu. Most of
the time, this can be left on Automatic with no problems. However, in the event that
GIMP fails to recognize the file you are trying to open, you might need to tell GIMP
exactly what type of file it is by selecting it in the Detect File Type menu.

File Formats

So, what kind of files can the GIMP deal with? The GIMP can open and save just about
any file format you could ever care to use, and then some.

A Word About UNIX and File Format Extensions

Because you're no longer working in Windows, I should mention that Linux deals with file formats and extensions a little differently than you might be accustomed to. For the most part, you should follow the standard naming conventions for graphics files, appending the usual three or four letter extension to the end of the name, such as .gif for GIF files, .eps for post-script files, .tif or .tiff for TIFF graphics, and so on. You do this in order to stay compatible with your friends, as well as a convention of habit, so that you can remember what kinds of files you're dealing with. But you should keep in mind that in UNIX files are not *defined* by their filename extension. It is entirely possible to save a GIF file with no extension whatsoever, as long as you specify to the application that opens it what kind of file it is. So if, for the sake of obfuscation, you have a GIF file named picture.jpg, you can still easily open it with GIMP. In the Determine File Type menu in the open dialog box, the Automatic option is selected by default. Nine times out of ten, the GIMP will not be fooled and will open it for the GIF it really is. It does this by more or less looking at the file data itself, not at the filename extension. If, for some reason, GIMP does not autodetect the type of a file with no extension (or a mislabeled one) correctly, you must then select the correct file type from the menu to tell the GIMP directly what kind of file you're dealing with.

2

Take a laundry-list look at what file formats GIMP can handle by default.

TABLE 2.1 FILE FORMATS IN GIMP

Format	Open	Save	Information
ASCII	X	X	ASCII text (such as those nifty BBS, for example).
bitmap	X	X	Windows and OS/2 bitmap. A popular uncompressed format.
bzip2	X	X	bzip2 is a compression utility. GIMP allows you to open and save compressed images directly from within the program.
CEL	X	X	KISS indexed file format.
Fax G3	X		The format used by fax machines.
FITSX	X		The Flexible Image Transport system.
FLC, FLI	X		Popular animation formats.
GBR	X	X	GIMP Brush (GIMP's native brush format).

continues

TABLE 2.1   CONTINUED

Format	Open	Save	Information
GIcon	X	X	GIMP's native icon format. Use this to make custom toolbar icons.
GIF	X	X	Graphics Interchange Format. The popular indexed format used frequently for Web graphics.
Header	X		C Header file for programmers who want to include graphics in applications.
HRZ	X	X	Slow scan television (256∞240 RGB images).
HTML		X	No, this isn't really a graphics format, but it does render HTML tables out of pixels. (Handy for drafting up quick tables, or just playing with large graphics for fun—likely to crash your browser though.)
JPEG	X	X	Joint Photographic Experts Group—A popular image format, especially for the Web, as it possesses small file size and full color support. It is, however, a *lossy* format, which means that some measure of quality is lost in translation.
MPEG	X		Motion Picture Experts Group. A popular animation format.
PAT	X	X	GIMP's native pattern format.
PCX	X	X	Zsoft format.
PIX	X	X	Alias/Wavefront Power Animator format.
PNG	X	X	Portable Network Graphics. An image format designed for use on the Web. It combines the best features of both GIF and JPEG (Lossless image compression, and the ability to use millions of colors). One caveat: Not everyone's browsers support format just yet. (Hopefully, this will not be an issue in the near future.)
PNM	X	X	Portable Anymap.
PSD	X		Photoshop's native file format. This is really convenient if you happen to have a lot of Photoshop files laying around. GIMP reads all the preserved layering information, too!
SGIX	X		The Silicon Graphics image format.
SNP	X		The MicroEyes animation format.

Format	Open	Save	Information
SUNRAS	X	X	Sun Rasterfile.
TDI	X	X	TDI Animation Software format.
TGA	X	X	The Targa file format.
TIFF	X	X	The Tagged Image File format.
URL	X		The GIMP allows you to open files directly from the Internet. You enter the URL as you would in any browser (`http://path/file`, or `ftp://path/file`).
XBM	X	X	X bitmap format.
XCF	X	X	GIMP's native file format. Use this format to save all the layering and selections information between editing sessions.
XV Thumbnail	X		Loads XV's .xvpic thumbnail files.
XWD	X	X	X Window Dump—X Window's screen dump file format.
XPM	X	X	X Pixmap. Used frequently in X Window Manager icons and such.
gzip	X	X	GNU Zip format. The GIMP allows you to save files in compressed format directly; this saves a lot of upload time.

Now that you've seen the various file formats that GIMP supports, you will no doubt want to experiment with them and discover their strengths and weaknesses for yourself.

Closing and Saving Files

Since you have opened a file, you will probably want to do something to it, and then save it to your disk. The procedure is simple. You get to the dialog box by right-clicking the image you want to save, and selecting File, Save as (see Figure 2.8). This right-click pulls up the additional menu items that ultimately add a tremendous amount of functionality to the GIMP by letting you access filters, scripts, and many other options. (These are discussed in full detail in the following hours.)

To save a file, bring up the Save Image dialog box, enter the name of the file in the text area, name your file (with the common three letter extension), and click OK, as shown in Figure 2.9.

FIGURE 2.8

You pull up the Save as menu by right-clicking on the image.

FIGURE 2.9

The Save Image dialog box is where images are saved to disk. Remember to use the correct file extension, or choose the file format from the menu when saving.

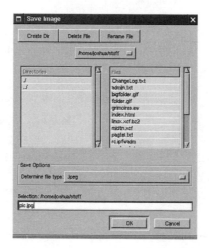

When saving files to your local disk, make absolutely sure that you have write *permissions* to the directory to which you are attempting to save. Otherwise, your attempt will fail, and the image will not be written to disk. (Permissions are an intrinsic concept to UNIX. You should familiarize yourself with them, if you haven't done so already.) Of course, saving to your own home directory should present no problems.

Other Toolbox Menu Options

The File menu on the Toolbox dialog box also has a few other options you should be aware of.

About

The About item pulls up a dialog box that lists the GIMP development team, the version you're running, and so on.

Tip of the Day

This option pulls up the Tip of the Day dialog box anytime you want to look at it.

Dialogs

These items give you the dialog boxes for various features and options—brushes, patterns, palettes, gradient editor, and tool options. These will be covered in the Hour 3, "Basic GIMP Tools."

Preferences

This option brings up the Preferences dialog box, as in Figure 2.10. As you become more familiar with the GIMP, you will likely want to customize the application in terms of look, feel, and performance. For now, the main preference you might want to alter is the *Levels of Undo* (how many steps back you can go in the editing process) on the Interface tab. The GIMP can accommodate a tremendously large amount of undos, as this is limited not by software, but by hardware. If you do not have loads of memory in your machine, you might want to lower this setting. However, if your workstation is crammed with RAM, I see no reason not to bump this up to 15 or more (if you'd really use it, of course.) Also, note that this can be dependent on the size of the image you are working with. If you are editing an extra large image, you might want to bump the setting down a couple of notches to conserve memory.

FIGURE 2.10

You can customize your GIMP installation in the Preferences dialog box.

The Xtns Menu

The Xtns menu (an abbreviation for Extensions) contains many plug-ins and Script-FU items supplementing the GIMP, which are written by various talented authors. These items extend the functionality of the GIMP, enabling it to acquire many more features than it has by default. These very numerous and powerful extensions are covered in Hours 19–22.

Exiting the GIMP

Exiting the GIMP is as straightforward as any application. You can either

- Click on the Close button in your favorite Window Manager.
- Or, Go to File, Quit on the Toolbox dialog box or right-click the image itself (see Figure 2.11).

FIGURE 2.11

Exiting the GIMP.

If you have unfinished changes open while exiting the GIMP, you will be asked if you want to exit the GIMP anyway, or cancel the exit in order to save your changes first. (This has saved me from a lot of mistakes many times.)

Summary

In this hour, you became acquainted with the GIMP interface—getting around, finding files, and so forth. Yes, the GIMP interface can be a little tricky at first, but stick with it! It will make a whole lot more sense as you go along. In truth, the lack of readily visible menu items (remember right-clicking on the images?) in many graphics applications can actually be great after you get used to it. Being graphic-centric in nature does make for a very space-efficient and logical approach—in my opinion, but, then again, I am a little biased.

Q&A

Q Why doesn't the GIMP support _____ format?

A If the format is indeed popular enough, chances are, it will be. The great thing about GIMP is that you don't have to wait for a newer version to be released in order to take advantage of new features. The GIMP does this by incorporating plug-ins. So far, however, the GIMP supports those formats that 99 percent of us ever really care to use.

Q **When I try to save a GIF, the GIMP tells me that my save has failed, although I know for a fact that I do have write permissions to this directory.**

A On indexed formats (reduced color depth) such as GIF, you need to make sure that the image is in fact in Indexed mode before you attempt to save it. You can do this by right-clicking the image and going to Image, Indexed, and selecting the 256 color palette.

Exercise

This hour was admittedly pretty easy. It was intended to help familiarize you with the GIMP interface. However, the best way to do this effectively is to experiment. Go now, put down this book, and play with GIMP! Push all the buttons, select all the menu items, and see what they do. And there's no need to worry; the GIMP won't bite.

Hour 3

Basic GIMP Tools

By now, the interface has become a little more familiar to you, and you can get around in the GIMP well enough to open and save images in various file formats. You are now well on your way toward achieving full GIMP apprenticeship. In this hour, you begin to learn more about the basic tools, so we can illustrate the essential concepts well enough to proceed into creating and editing images (which is why this book was written, after all). We will also begin going into a little more detail about some of the tools, and continue this trend into the next few hours, thoroughly illustrating specific techniques for using the tools productively and creatively.

Using the Basic Tools

As a GIMP user, you will have at your disposal a tremendous library of various effects, plug-ins, and scripts to help you do amazing things with graphics. The GIMP will doubtlessly acquire many more of these in the future as the program continues to evolve. And yet the standard tools are the ones you will likely rely on most for your creative tasks. Master these, and you will be surprised at the level of sophistication your images can achieve with relative ease. And ultimately, what you will be able to accomplish using this knowledge in concert with the intense effect capabilities the GIMP has to offer will be no less than astounding.

The 21 basic tools, as shown briefly in the Hour 2, "Getting Started," are essential to creating nearly any image. These tools often have more than one function, and many options available as well. To access the additional options and functions of any tool in the toolbox, double-click on the Tool Button icon. This will pull up that particular tool's Option dialog box, as shown in Figure 3.1.

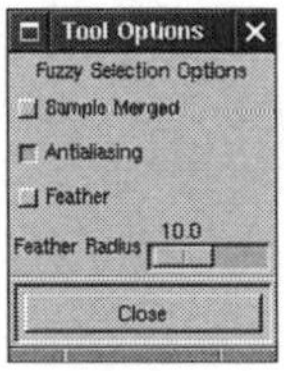

FIGURE 3.1

Additional options and functions can be invoked by double-clicking a tool icon, or by going to File, Dialogs, Tool Options on the Toolbox menu.

In the interest of continuity and organization, these tools will be grouped here by function into five basic categories—Selection tools, Transformation tools, Artistic tools, Color tools, and the Text tool.

Selection Tools

NEW TERM
Selection tools are a way to mark a portion of the image apart from the rest of the composition. This allows the program to apply any functions or changes you specify *only* to that which you have selected, without affecting the rest of your work. Changes can include, but are not limited to, alterations in color, size, shape, composition, orientation, and so on.

The six tools at the top of the toolbox deal with creating and editing selections (see Figure 3.2). Selections enable you to select any part of an image, marked by a blinking border, called the *marching snts* or *marquee* (see Figure 3.3). (This marquee is animated, and to some people resembles blinking marquee lights or ants on the move, depending.

FIGURE 3.2

The Selection tools are valuable for affecting change on only certain portions of your image.

FIGURE 3.3

A selection is made. Any changes applied by any tool or menu item would happen only *within the confines of the marching ants.*

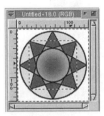

> You can change the rate of the blinking marquee (or ants) by going to File, Preferences, clicking the Interface tab, and changing the value in the Marching Ants Speed text box.
>
> Also, you can toggle the marquee on or off by right-clicking the image, and going to Select, Toggle.

When you make a selection, you will need to use the proper select tool for the job. With these six tools at your disposal, you will have the ability to set apart any shape, size, and color portion of an image for alterations. Later in this book, you will go over selections in greater detail, and learn how to utilize them to do new and interesting things to your images.

Transformation Tools

 A *transformation* is anything that alters the perspective of the image, whether it is by size, position, rotation, mirroring, or plain distortion.

You have a good image to begin with, but something just isn't right with it somehow. Perhaps you could position it a little better, rotate it, or get a closer look at it. That's what the Transformation tools are for (see Figure 3.4). These tools are great at altering the perspective, size, position, ratio, or orientation of an image, as in Figure 3.5.

FIGURE 3.4

The Transformation tools alter your image in terms of shape, size, and position.

FIGURE 3.5

Transformations in actions. Transformations can make elements in your graphics more interesting.

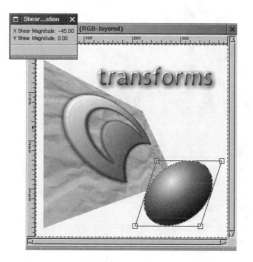

Artistic Tools

The Artistic tools do exactly what their name implies—they enable you to draw, paint, erase, and brush your images with colors and patterns. The tools used to do these things resemble the tools you'd find in any artist's tool collection—pencils, brushes, erasers, airbrushes, and so forth (see Figure 3.6). And they work in much the same way as the real things (see Figure 3.7).

The three last Artistic tools are unique, and worth mentioning here. The Airbrush works just like a can of spray paint, thickening the paint the longer you use it in one place or enabling a thin spray of color to be applied with a sweeping motion. The Clone tool will paint with an exact duplicate of any image or pattern (which will come in handy for photo retouching). And the Convolve tool works like a paintbrush, but will blur or sharpen an image instead of painting it with color.

FIGURE 3.6

The Artistic tools resemble the equipment used by the artists who work with analog media.

FIGURE 3.7

The Artistic tools in action. This example illustrates the many effects you can create with these tools.

3

The Color Tools

The Color tools, as you've probably guessed, have to do with color, and the way it is applied to your images. With these tools, shown in Figure 3.8, you can choose and fill selections with color in ways that would be difficult to do using physical art equipment. But thanks to the wonders of technology, changing and altering colors is as simple as moving a mouse. We will go ahead and touch on some of their aspects here, as they will be vastly useful when working with the other tools.

FIGURE 3.8

The Color tools are used for selecting, filling, and creating effects with color.

Color Select Tool

The Color Select tool, also known as the Eyedropper, can select any color in your image. By clicking on the Tool icon, your cursor will be transformed into a little cross-hair, at which point you can *pick up* a color from any pixel in your image (see Figure 3.9). By way of a mouse click, this tool will change the selected toolbox color in the toolbox

Color Selector, either foreground or background, to the same color as the pixel located under your cursor. This is a handy tool for color matching, which is very important for doing things such as print and Web graphics.

FIGURE 3.9

One click, and that color is loaded into the foreground. You can now use it in conjunction with any tool.

Bucket Fill

The Bucket Fill tool (shown in Figure 3.10) fills your image or selection with any active color or pattern (via the Pattern dialog box). The Fill tool has a few options worth noting here (accessed by double-clicking the tool icon, which brings up the Fill Tool Option dialog box, shown in Figure 3.11).

FIGURE 3.10

The Bucket Fill in action. Experimenting with different fills on selections can alter the entire composition of an image.

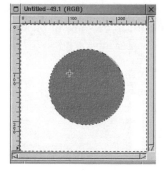

3

FIGURE 3.11

The Fill Tool Option dialog box enables you to use the tool in many ways.

- **Opacity**—Refers to the see-through quality of the color or pattern used as a fill. You can adjust this incrementally to let more or less of the background seep through.

- **Fill threshold**—Approximates the area to fill by looking at the surrounding pixels and determining if they are close enough to the one selected and deciding whether or not to fill them as well. So, for example, a setting of 1 would mean that only the color you specifically click on will be filled. The maximum setting of 255 will fill the whole image or selection regardless of color.

- **Fill type**—Lets you select what you want to fill your selection with, a color or a pattern. You can select any color using GIMP's Color Selection dialog box by double-clicking the Foreground color on the toolbox.

NEW TERM *Patterns* are accessible from File, Dialogs, Patterns, in the toolbox menu. Patterns are interesting, repetitive designs that can be used to fill in a selection or background to add texture. You can select a pattern in the Pattern dialog box, and then fill an image with that pattern to create interesting effects. Using and creating your own patterns will be discussed at length in Hour 4, "Using Brushes and Patterns in Depth."

Gradient Tool

The Gradient tool will enable you to draw a gradient (transition between two or more colors) into your image or selection (see Figure 3.12). It can do this in many different patterns and color combinations. You can also create custom gradients using the Gradient Editor, which will be thoroughly detailed in Hour 7, "Working with Color."

FIGURE 3.12

Gradient fills can add a lot of tone and realism to your images.

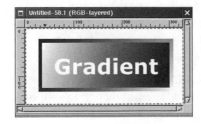

The Foreground/Background Color Selector

As long as you're covering the topic of color, you should go ahead and learn how to use this tool, shown in Figure 3.13, because it is a vitally important one.

*The Foreground/
Background Color
Selector is primarily
what you will use to
deal with color when
working in the
GIMP.*

The *foreground* color is used by your tools—Paintbrush, Pencil, Airbrush, Bucket Fill, and Gradient (as the first color). The background color is used by the Erase tool when cutting a selection from an image, and acts as the endpoint of gradients.

You can access the GIMP Color Selection dialog box by double-clicking on either the foreground or background color icons in the box (see Figure 3.14). Now you can select any color available by either dragging the cursor through the spectrum and color boxes, or by specifying any value with the sliders and text boxes. The sliders control Hue, Saturation, Value, Red, Green, and Blue. By clicking the Close button, you have made your color the active selected color, which you can now use with any tool.

FIGURE 3.14

*The Color Selection
dialog box lets you
pick any color to use
with your tools.*

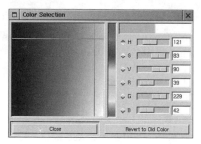

The little arrows on the Foreground/Background Color Selector tool allow you to swap the foreground and background colors. And the little black-and-white boxes in the lower-left corner bring the colors back to the default black and white.

Text Tool

The GIMP Text tool is very useful, especially in regards to creating graphics for use on the Web. It enables you to insert type anywhere into your image. And because text is treated essentially as a selection, you can insert it into anything as you would a selection—fill it with patterns, gradients, or alter it any number of ways (see Figure 3.15).

FIGURE 3.15

The Text tool could arguably be one of the most useful tools available in the GIMP. With it, you can not only create simple text, but used in conjunction with the other tools and plug-ins, it can help you create some really neat effects, which is almost essential in creating a look for your Web site.

3

Using the Text Tool

Clicking on the Text Tool icon will change the cursor over the image into an I-beam. To insert some text, click the mouse with the I-beam over the image. This brings up the Text Tool dialog box, as in Figure 3.16.

FIGURE 3.16

The Text Tool dialog box.

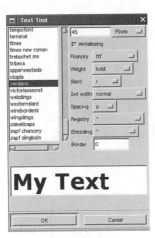

Near the bottom of the Text Tool dialog box, you will see a blank text space. This is where you need to type in your text. After this has been done, look toward the left side of the dialog box to see a listing of the fonts that are available to the X Window System. By clicking on any one of these, your text will be previewed, in that font, right where you typed it.

At the top of the dialog box, you will see an option for text size. The implication here is obvious. Type in any text size, click Enter, and your preview will be updated.

Foundry refers to the maker of the font. This can be important when dealing in fonts that have the same name but are made by different individuals or companies.

Other Options are available on the dialog box as well, such as Slant (Italics), Weight (Bold), Set Width (Spacing), and so forth.

After your text appears how you want it, click OK, and your text will appear on the image canvas, as an active selection. The color of the text will be the active foreground color in the Foreground/Background Color Select box in the toolbox. You can now move it using your cursor to any position in the page. Or, because it is an active selection, you can apply any pattern, fill, gradient, or effect to it. You will practice many of these effects as you continue throughout the hours in this book.

Using X Fonts with the GIMP

X supports many styles of fonts. In using the GIMP, you will likely want to increase the volume of fonts available to use on your system. (The fonts that come with X are admittedly pretty dull). On the CD-ROM, in the Fonts directory, there are two font packages: sharefonts.tar.gz and freefonts.tar.gz. You should look into installing these. Uncompress them into the /usr/X11R6/include/X11/fonts directory, read the READMEs, and follow the directions. (These font packages can also be downloaded from many Linux FTP repositories, such as Red Hat's pub/contrib directory).

You will find that all your native X fonts are located in subdirectories of /usr/X11R6/ lib/X11/fonts (or variant thereof, on different systems). So if you ever want to add or remove fonts in the future, you'll know where to go. I've also found it helpful to remove extraneous fonts by deleting certain font files and editing out the reference to them in the file fonts.dir. The Far Eastern ones are good candidates for deletion (unless you really need them), and they *do* tend to take a long time to render.

Although these fonts are pretty good, I am still itchin' to utilize my vast collection of TrueType fonts with the GIMP. Fortunately, X can be supportive of those too—with a little assistance. In order to use TrueType, you have to install and run a TrueType Font Server. This isn't too difficult, either. All you need to do is acquire the xfstt TrueType Font Server application and install it. It, too, is available on the CD-ROM in the font directory as Xfstt.tar.gz. Unzip it into your directory, compile it, and install it as follows:

```
make && make install
```

Create the directory /usr/ttfonts, and copy your favorite TrueType TTF files there. Then run `xfstt sync` to load the fonts.

Start `xfstt` as a background process:

`xfstt &`

Tell the running X11 server about the new font service:

`xset +fp unix/:7100`

Add the new font path to the X11 config file (probably `/etc/X11/XF86Config`):

`FontPath "unix/:7100"`

You should now be able to bring up the GIMP Text dialog box and see your TrueType fonts there. After installing xfstt, you might then want to get it to start automatically every time Linux boots (not that Linux ever needs rebooting) by adding a reference to it in /etc/rc.d/rc.local. This keeps you from having to start the TrueType Font Server every time you start X. One caveat: If you do this, make sure that you add the *full* pathname to rc.local, as in /usr/X11R6/bin/xfstt &, *especially* if you use xdm to start a graphical login automatically on startup.

3

Also, you might not want to load in every single TrueType font you own, but instead be selective with the TrueType fonts you want to use with Linux. Xfstt is a handy application, but it can suck up a little RAM if left to load 200+ fonts. I've found it's best to use only 30 or so of the very best fonts instead. And finally, there are other TrueType font servers out there as well, although I have not personally used them yet. One such server is called xfsft, which uses the Free Type library and has had a lot of positive review. It's available online everywhere xfstt is, so you might want to check it out. You can grab a RPMs of Xfree86 with integrated TrueType font support via xfsft from `http://www.darmstadt.gmd.de/~pommnitz/xfsft.html`.

Summary

The essential concepts in dealing with a graphics application such as the GIMP have been covered during the first three hours. Before any real techniques can be applied, you must have an understanding of the basic tools illustrated here. In the next few hours, you will move on to mastering these concepts in order to create some interesting images and effects. You might be surprised at what can be accomplished using only these simple tools. And, gaining mastery over them will give you an edge when confronted with specific graphics issues, such as image restoration or simple manipulation.

Q&A

Q When selecting fonts, the GIMP freezes up and won't do anything.

A It is likely that you have inadvertently selected one of the Far Eastern fonts that
come with Linux. The GIMP isn't really locked up, but if your video card is like
mine, it is taking its sweet time rendering these fonts. (The glyphs are quite complex in these fonts). You might want to avoid these fonts in the future, or delete
them altogether.

Exercise

You might be wondering just how much you can accomplish using these ordinary tools.
Well, in order to gain an understanding of them, you must use them. I suggest that you
start experimenting right away. Try opening up a new palette, and begin to paint simple
shapes and textures with the tools outlined here. You can start off with simple things,
such as geometric shapes, logos, buttons, or even hand-crafted text. Then try emulating
some real-world objects and textures—the Gradient Fill to create metal, or the Airbrush
to create mist. As you move along in the hours ahead, you will come across easier and
more efficient ways of doing these things, which will in turn increase your mastery at a
faster pace. Then the really fun stuff begins.

Hour 4

Using Brushes and Patterns in Depth

Congratulations! You've put in some time and learned the elementary GIMP basics during the first three hours. At this point, you are probably starting to understand the interface and recognize the many tools you have to work with.

Now it's time to graduate to some of the fun stuff, really focus on the various aspects of the program, and learn how wonderful and versatile it can be for creating and editing graphics.

This hour concentrates on the wide array of brushes and patterns—including the Brush and Pattern dialog boxes, the options, and even how to turn your very own creations into custom brushes and patterns—and look at different ways they can be put to work in your graphics.

Using Brushes

In Hour 3, "Basic GIMP Tools," you were introduced to the tools in the GIMP toolbox. For the first part of this hour, I'll direct your attention to the tools that will more than likely become some of your favorites—the painting and drawing tools.

By activating any one of these tools, you'll have at your disposal an entire collection of brushes containing a variety of appearances and textures.

The Brush Settings

Begin by going to File, Dialogs, Brushes, and bring up the brush Selection window, as shown in Figure 4.1. Your choice of brush settings can be applied using any of the painting and drawing tools (Pencil, Paintbrush, Eraser, Airbrush), the look and feel being dependent on the characteristics of the particular tool. The Paintbrush yields a much softer appearance, for instance, whereas the pencil gives a hard-edged look.

FIGURE 4.1

The Selection window offers many brush choices.

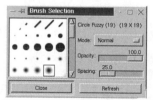

In the left area of the window, you can see an assortment of preinstalled brush tips, ranging in size and shape from a tiny circular tip to textured tips, and even tips that are made from images.

When you select a brush by clicking on it, notice that the brush name and size (in pixels) show in the right area of the window. The GIMP works a little differently than most other graphics programs in relation to brush size. There is no sizer where you can adjust the size via a slider or numerical value. You simply choose a brush in the size you want to use. By clicking and holding on the thumbnail image of each brush, you can see the size as it appears when used.

Large brushes cannot easily be seen in the browsable brush thumbnails of the brush select dialog box. If you can't find a particular brush, try clicking and holding on the thumbnails that appear to be blank.

Underneath the brush name is an option called Mode. This is where you can change the blend mode. Blend modes are primarily used in conjunction with layers and are discussed in depth in Hour 9, "Hands-on Layering." For now, leave the mode setting on Normal.

Opacity

The next setting is the opacity, which is controlled by a slider with values ranging from 0–100. Setting the slider to 0 enables total transparency in the brush, whereas the 100 setting is totally opaque. Think of the opacity slider as paint thinner, diluting your paint to the point of transparency when applied to an image.

Spacing

This setting is also controlled by a slider and is used to determine the space between brush strokes. If you look at Figure 4.2, you can see that if you want to paint in a smooth continuous line, you should set the spacing low. A higher setting separates the strokes of the brush by the desired amount, resulting in a totally different look. You might want to experiment with the Spacing slider using different brush tips.

FIGURE 4.2

The top line shown here was drawn with the spacing set to 0, and the spacing was gradually increased in the following lines.

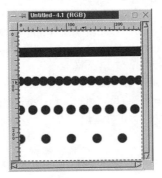

4

Tool Options

Double-click on the Paintbrush tool to bring up the options box, as in Figure 4.3. You'll take a more in-depth look at what these two options can accomplish, now that you're familiar with the brush settings.

Fade Out

This option is used to create a gradually diminishing color effect, as shown in Figure 4.4. By setting the numerical fade out value, you can choose how many pixels are colored in with the brush before the fading effect actually begins. To fade entirely out uses approximately three times the amount of the set value. Setting the fade out value to 0.0 (which is the default setting) disables the effect.

FIGURE 4.3

The Paintbrush also has some unique options you can set in the tool option box.

FIGURE 4.4

Shown here are several different brushes with the fade effect applied.

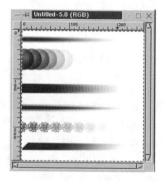

Incremental

When you drag the Paintbrush swiftly across an image, it appears to be painting in a continuous line. However, if you drag it across *very* slowly, you'll notice that it is actually adding one increment at a time of the shape of your chosen brush tip. Choosing the Incremental function in the tool options enables you to see the overlap of these increments in the painted line, as in Figure 4.5. This function is visible only when you are painting with the brush settings at a reduced opacity. The following steps show you how this feature works:

- Open a new image with a white background.
- Set the foreground color to black.
- Open the Brush dialog box. Choose a large brush, such as the circle(19). Set the opacity to around 50 and spacing to around 70 or so.
- Double-click the Paintbrush, set the fade to 0, and leave the Incremental option *un*checked. Paint a line across your image.
- Now *check* the Incremental box and paint another line under your first one, and you'll see how the Incremental option functions.

FIGURE 4.5

The Incremental option at work.

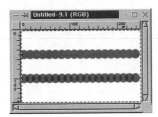

Making Custom Brushes

As you play and experiment with the numerous brushes that are included in the GIMP, you will find that the uses for these brushes are virtually unlimited—from creating textures to making matching sets of brush images that you can use over and over in your graphics.

Because basically any image can be resized, grayscaled, and saved as a brush (thereby gaining access to the varied brush options), the capability to create custom brushes presents some interesting ideas on various ways to put them to use. You'll explore two possibilities here.

A Custom Graphic Brush

Find or draw a small simple graphic on a white background that you would like to make into a brush, such as in Figure 4.6.

FIGURE 4.6

Simple images make the best brushes.

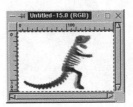

The first step is to grayscale the image. Right-click on the image and go to Image, Grayscale. Your image now appears in shades of gray, as if you were looking at it on a black-and-white television set.

Next you need to invert the colors by right-clicking on the image and going to Image, Colors, Invert. This causes your image to show up as a negative, but when it's saved as a brush, it reverts back to positive.

Now you are ready to save it as a brush. Right-click and go to File, Save As. Here you need to give your image a name and GBR (GIMP Brush) extension. Save it in your personal folder or somewhere you can remember.

After you have saved it as a GBR, you then have to move it into the brush dialog by opening the GIMP directory and moving the file into .gimp/brushes.

Open the brush dialog and press the button called Refresh; your new brush is now accessible for use.

> There is a Script-Fu script that can convert a selection into a brush directly. Select the desired area, right-click, and go to Script-Fu, Selection, To Brush. A pop-up box then appears where you can give your brush a descriptive name.

Check out Figure 4.7 to see how an entire look can be pulled together in a few minutes by using a custom brush.

FIGURE 4.7

Your custom brush makes it easy to create a matched set of Web graphics.

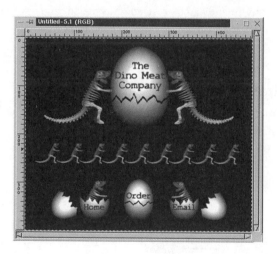

Signature Brush

Unless you are extremely dexterous with a mouse or have a graphics pen, you will either want to scan an image of your signature or use the text tool and a font that is similar to your handwriting to create a signature brush, as shown in Figure 4.8.

After you have the signature, follow the same steps you used previously to create and save the graphics brush.

> You can use a small signature brush with a low opacity setting to add a sort of digital watermark to graphics you have created.

FIGURE 4.8

A signature brush can come in handy.

Using Patterns

You will spend the second part of this hour concentrating on patterns. Through the composition of color, design, and special effects, you'll be able to create mind-blowing patterns with a minimum of effort.

Patterns can be useful in many graphics tasks. The capability of the Bucket Fill tool to perform pattern fills in selections can help you easily and quickly achieve a cool patterned look to your graphics and text, and using of GIMP's Seamless Tiling function enables your patterns to become beautifully tiled backgrounds.

The Pattern Dialog

Open the Pattern Select dialog box, shown in Figure 4.9, by going to File, Dialogs, Patterns.

FIGURE 4.9

The pattern dialog box is a great place to browse for inspiration.

Notice that the GIMP comes with an abundance of preloaded patterns. To choose a pattern, left-click on the thumbnail image. The pattern name shows at the top of the pattern dialog window. Take a few minutes to click on the patterns in turn, and note that if you hold down the mouse button, you can get a full size view of the chosen pattern, as in the brush dialog box.

4

Using the Fill Tool with Patterns

Patterns can be used to fill any selected area, whether it is a text or other defined selection or an entire image area. Let's do a simple pattern fill to see how it works.

- With the pattern selection dialog box open, select a pattern that you like.
- Open a new blank image with a white background.
- Double-click on the Bucket Fill tool to activate it and also pull up the Options box.
- In the Options box, set the fill opacity to 100 and check Pattern Fill.
- Now merely left-click once on your image and watch your pattern choice fill the area, as shown in Figure 4.10.

FIGURE 4.10

A built-in GIMP pattern fills a blank image.

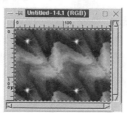

Custom Patterns

Now that you have the general idea of how pattern fills operate, you will no doubt want to create some patterns of your own.

Follow the steps outlined here to build your first simple GIMP pattern from the ground up.

Open a new blank image, background color of your choice. I've chosen a dark color for my illustration purposes.

Set the foreground color to a color you'd like to see in your pattern. Because my background is dark, I'm going to use bright colors for the pattern. Open the Brush dialog box, pick any brush, and randomly place bits of color in the image. Repeat this procedure several times using different brushes and changing colors until you have something similar to Figure 4.11.

Now for the fun part. This gives you an introduction to what special filters can do. Right-click on the image and go to Filters, Distorts, Whirl and Pinch. Play around with the sliders until you have a look that you like (see Figure 4.12).

FIGURE 4.11

Play with colors and brushes to form the beginnings of a pattern.

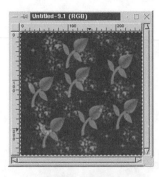

FIGURE 4.12

The whirl creates a colorful vortex effect.

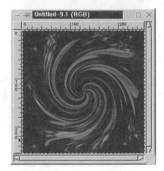

4

Seamless Tiling

After you have a pattern look that you are satisfied with, you should make it *tileable*, meaning that when you use it as a background or pattern fill on a large area, the seams or edges blend smoothly together with no visible lines.

This is relatively easy to achieve with a function called Make Seamless. Right-click the image you want to tile and go to Filters, Map, Make Seamless. Your pattern now magically unites with no seams showing when saved and tiled. See Figure 4.13 and notice how the edges have been changed so that the pattern tiles correctly.

FIGURE 4.13

Your seamless pattern is now ready to be saved.

Saving Patterns

After creating a pleasing pattern, you can save it in the Pattern Select dialog box for future use.

- Right-click the finished image and select File, Save, to bring up the save options.
- Name your pattern and save with a PAT (pattern) extension.
- A small window called Save as Pattern appears and prompts you to give your pattern a simple name description. This is the name that shows up when you view the pattern in the pattern selection dialog box.
- The pattern can now be moved to the GIMP pattern directory (.gimp/patterns).
- In the Pattern Select dialog window, click Refresh and your pattern is now ready for use.

For a unique pattern look, you can select an area of a photograph and convert it to a Seamless Tile, as shown in Figure 4.14. Shown first is the original photo, then a portion of the photo converted to a seamless pattern, and even a step further with a few special effects.

FIGURE 4.14

The resource possibilities are endless for making great patterns.

Summary

As you work more and more with graphics, you will come to think of brushes and patterns as your basic tools of the trade.

In this hour, I covered the essentials to get you started working with these artist's little helpers.

The capability to create and save your own custom brushes and patterns will, without a doubt, enhance your understanding of the intricacies involved in the creation of great graphics.

Q&A

Q Can I make custom brushes in full color?

A No. All images must be grayscaled before becoming custom brushes. When you paint with them, they then use your chosen foreground color.

Q Do I have to save my pattern as a PAT file before I can use it to fill an image or selection?

A Yes. Although some programs enable you to use any open image as a pattern fill, the GIMP requires that the image first be saved with a PAT extension and placed in the Pattern Selection dialog box.

4

Exercise

Look out your window or take a walk and have a good look around at various things: the trees, the grass, the water, everything that surrounds you. Examine the textures and patterns in these everyday items from an artist's viewpoint. Isolate small areas of color and texture and try to imagine how you could re-create the look using brushes and patterns. If you have a flatbed scanner, try scanning some simple textures, such as a leaf or a piece of fabric and turn them into patterns.

HOUR 5

Working with Selections

In the preceding hours, you learned the basics of how the image editing tools work, and how to create, open, and save images in different file formats. Your next step is to learn how to utilize the various selection tools to *select*, or identify a certain portion of an image.

In essence, a *selection* is a specifically chosen area of an image that can be moved, edited, or manipulated without affecting the non-selected areas of the same image.

There are many different methods of making a selection. For instance, you can select an area by color alone, by using a shape tool—such as a square or circle, or by drawing freehand around the area you want to modify.

The GIMP contains six handy selection tools that will be covered in this hour, along with the options for these tools.

- Rectangle/Square tool
- Ellipse/Circle tool
- Lasso/Free Select

- Fuzzy Select
- Bézier Select
- Intelligent Scissors

The Selection Tool Icons

The first six tools in the toolbox, as shown in Figure 5.1, are the selection tools.

FIGURE 5.1

Familiarize yourself with these important tools.

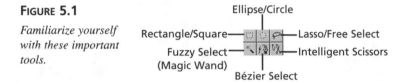

Ellipse/Circle

Rectangle/Square——————Lasso/Free Select

Fuzzy Select————————Intelligent Scissors
(Magic Wand)

Bézier Select

Tool Options

Before you start making selections, spend a few minutes going over the options that are available for the different kinds of selections. Bring up the options window for each of the six tools to acquaint yourself with the choices offered by each (see Figure 5.2).

FIGURE 5.2

Each tool has an options box.

As with all tools in the toolbox, there are two ways you can bring up the options windows. You can either double-click the icon of the tool you want to use, or you can go to the top of the toolbox window, and click File, Dialogs, Toolbox options, and the options window will automatically show for any tool you click on.

Setting the Basic Options

Antialias and Feather are two basic options available for all the tools, with the exception of the Rectangle/Square tool, which has no antialiasing option.

Antialias Is Your Friend

Antialiasing is an effect used to produce a smooth-edged selection by filling in pixels just along the edge of the selection with similar colors, thereby softly blending it in with adjacent colors. If antialiasing is not used, a selection might tend to appear jagged around the edges, especially along curves. This is a condition commonly known among graphic artists as *the jaggies.* By using the Antialiasing option, you'll end up with a much softer and smoother appearance to your selection edges, as shown in Figure 5.3 (which has been magnified somewhat to enable you to see the difference).

FIGURE 5.3

Compare the difference in the edges of these two filled text selections; one is antialiased, and the other is not.

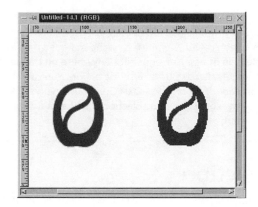

Feather Effects

The Feathering option produces an even smoother transition between the selection and the surrounding area. It works by fading the pixels into the background along the edge by a chosen amount, called the *feather radius.* You control the feather radius by a slider in the Tool Options window. The higher you set the slider (0–100), the farther the pixels of your selection will feather out and blend in. This is an invaluable effect, particularly when working with photo manipulations.

5

Sample Merged

This option is only available when using the Fuzzy Select tool. When activated, this option causes the selection to be made based on the composite image created by all layers, instead of the contents of the current layer alone. (This will be easier to understand when you get to Hours 8, "Introduction to Layers," and 9, "Hands-on Layering.")

Viewing a Selection

When a selection is made, it is identified as such by a border of flashing black-and-white dashes known in most graphics programs as a *marquee*. In the GIMP, this flashing border is also referred to as *marching ants*, but I will just keep things simple and refer to it here as the marquee. After it is selected, the area within the marquee is now the only part of the image that is *active*, meaning that it is the only part of the image that will be affected by the administration of tools or applications.

 Sometimes the flashing marquee can be in the way when trying to view changes in your image. However, once you've made your selection, you can use an option called *Toggle* to turn the marquee on or off while keeping the selection intact. Just right-click anywhere on the image and select File, Select, Toggle. Repeat to reverse the action. You can also toggle the marquee on and off by pressing Ctrl+T on your keyboard. When you use the toggle, just remember your selection is still active, even though you cannot see the marquee.

Making a Selection

Get started by making a simple selection with the Rectangle/Square tool.

1. Open a new image (size doesn't matter at this point, but make it a large enough area to work in easily).
2. Activate the Rectangle tool by clicking the icon.
3. Place the mouse cursor at the corner of the area you want to select.
4. Left-click, and while holding down the button, drag across the image in the direction you want your selection to go. As you move the mouse, you'll see a line appear, designating where the border of your selection will be.
5. When you release the button, the marquee will indicate your selected area, as shown in Figure 5.4.

FIGURE 5.4

A simple rectangular selection.

Extra Selections

If you need to have more than one selected area in the same image, you can do this in a couple of easy steps:

1. Make the first selection and release the mouse button to show your marquee.
2. Press and hold the Shift key while making the additional selection.

As long as the selections do not touch one another or overlap, they will become individual selections within the image (see Figure 5.5).

FIGURE 5.5

You can have many selected areas in one image.

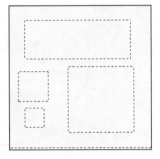

Adding to a Selection

Sometimes you might want to attach additional sections to a selected area to create a unique shape. This is also easily to achieve. Just follow the same steps you used to create an extra selection, but this time, you'll want to touch or overlap the two sections, and as you release the mouse button, they will then become one single selection, as in Figure 5.6.

FIGURE 5.6

Two selections can be merged into one.

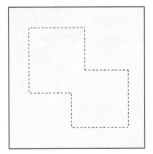

5

Subtracting from a Selection

In a similar way, you can use the Ctrl key to subtract an area from a selection.

1. Make an active selection; try another rectangle.

2. For the next step, do something a little different and switch over to the Ellipse tool by clicking the Ellipse icon in the toolbox.

3. Now press and hold the Ctrl key while you drag over the area you want deleted from your active selection. As you release the mouse button this time, you will see, as in Figure 5.7, that the area where the ellipse overlapped the rectangle has been subtracted from that selection.

FIGURE 5.7

The ellipse area has been removed from the rectangle.

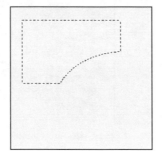

Intersecting the Selections

By using the Shift and Ctrl keys together, you can choose the intersection (the overlapping region) of two areas as your active selection.

1. Make a selection.

2. Press and hold Shift and Ctrl at the same time and drag as if you were making an addition to a selection, but notice where the two areas overlap. When you release the mouse button, the overlapping region will become the only active selection (see Figure 5.8).

FIGURE 5.8

The intersection of a rectangle and ellipse becomes the selected area.

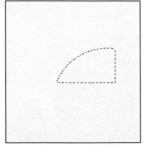

Deactivating a Selection

An active selection can be deactivated in three different ways. You can begin making a new selection, and the first one will disappear automatically. Another way to deactivate is to left-click once on your image while in the Rectangle/Square tool mode, Ellipse/Circle tool mode, or Lasso tool mode. The third method is to right-click on your image to bring up the menu options, and then click Select, None.

Shape Tool Extras

Specifically, the shape tools are the Rectangle/Square and Ellipse/Circle tools, because they are the only tools limited to forming only those shapes. However, you have already learned that by using the Shift and Ctrl keys to add, subtract, and so on, you can use the shape tools to make a variety of uniquely shaped selections. There are also a few extra tricks that you can play with using the Shift and Ctrl keys, giving them dual functionality when used in combination with the shape tools.

1. You can achieve geometrically perfect squares and circles by keeping the Shift key held down as you make the selection.

2. Pressing and holding Shift and Ctrl together while selecting will cause your perfect squares and circles to begin at the point where you place the cursor and radiate out from there, rather than starting at the corner.

3. Holding down only the Ctrl key as you select will make rectangles and ellipses also form from the center of the shape, rather than from the corner.

You'll notice that when working with the shape tools, the dual functionality of the Shift and Ctrl actions can conflict with one another in certain circumstances. Luckily, you can separate these functions or combine them in different ways by a well-timed key release.

For instance, let's say you want to make a selection, and then attach an addition to it (requiring the use of the Shift key). But, the addition you want to make is an ellipse, and because you're holding down the Shift key, it becomes a perfect circle. What you have to do in this situation is to *set* one action and *release* the key before you begin the next action. For example

1. Make an active selection in a shape of your choice.

2. Press and hold the Shift key. The *pressing* of the Shift key has told the GIMP that you want to make an additional selection.

3. Left-click the mouse button and hold.

4. Release only the Shift key, but continue holding the mouse button as you drag in your additional selection. The release of the Shift key before actually forming the added selection freed it from having to make only perfect circles or squares.

5

The difference in the timing of the Shift and Ctrl keys can also permit two actions to be mingled in the same selection. For example

1. This time, let's say you want to subtract from the first selection (requiring the use of the Ctrl key), but you want to do it with a perfect circle (requiring the Shift key). You would follow these steps:

2. Make your first selection as normal.

3. Press and hold the Ctrl key and left-click and hold the mouse button. The pressing of Ctrl has told GIMP that you want to subtract with the next selection.

4. Now release the Ctrl key while still holding down the mouse button. The release of Ctrl has freed you to make another choice.

5. While still holding the mouse button down, you can now use the Shift key to form the perfect circle.

It might seem a little confusing at first, but after you've worked with these functions a couple of times, it will begin to make sense and you'll see how easy it really is!

Lasso Selections

To make a lasso, or freehand selection, activate the Lasso tool, and place your mouse cursor at the point where you'd like the selection to begin. Now left-click and drag, and as you move your cursor you'll notice a line forming your shape. After you have the desired selected area and you're back at the starting point, release your mouse button and you'll see the marquee designating your selection. If you release the mouse button before you get back to your starting point, the Lasso tool will automatically close the ends of your selection with a straight line between the two points. You can add, subtract, and intersect lasso selections using the same methods you learned with the shape tools.

Fuzzy Select

This tool is similar to the Magic Wand tool, which is familiar in most other graphics programs. It is unique in comparison to the other selection tools in that it makes selections based on color value. It's a handy tool to use for making selections that are essentially one color, such as selecting a background out of a picture. All you have to do is click on a pixel in the color you want selected and all adjacent pixels that are the same color are included in the selection area. If you want your selection area to expand, including several colors in the same range, click and drag the cursor over all the colors you want to incorporate, and the adjacent pixels of all those colors will be included. By using your Shift and Ctrl key methods along with the Fuzzy tool to add or subtract areas of color, you can quickly modify a selection to the color specifications you like.

The Bézier Tool

This gadget, although probably the most challenging to learn of the six selection tools, can be remarkably useful once you master it.

It works by the placement of a number of points which, when clicked on by turn, develop two handles that are then used to manipulate the shape. By moving the handles, you can form curves and angles out of what began as a series of straight lines.

The Bézier tool can be a lot of fun to play with, and that's probably the best way to learn to use it, so you can jump right in with this one.

1. Create a new image large enough to work in comfortably.
2. Activate the Bézier tool by clicking the icon in the toolbox.
3. Place your cursor over the area where you want your selection to begin, and click it once to create a starting point.
4. Now move your cursor over a little and click again. You will notice you have added another point, connected to the first by a straight line. Repeat the moving and clicking until you've made a basic shape consisting of the straight lines. Connect back to your starting point by clicking your ending point into it.
5. You will now have a selection area that resembles a connect-the-dots picture, as in Figure 5.9.

FIGURE 5.9

A Bézier selection in the first stages.

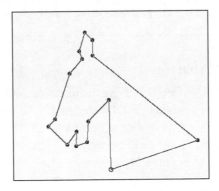

5

And the fun begins. Let's make some curves...

Click on any point and you will see an additional line appear. This new line consists of your point in the center (marked by a small circle), and a tiny square at each end. These are your *handles*, as seen in the lower-right corner of Figure 5.10. By manipulating them in different directions, you'll see that they give your selection line the capability to form a curve. It will probably seem awkward at first, but you'll get the feel of maneuvering the curves as you go.

FIGURE 5.10

*The handles appear
when the point is
clicked on.*

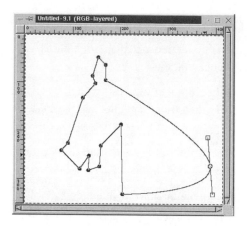

Click on each point in turn and practice making curves so that you really get the hang of it. Try pulling your handles out longer and notice the difference the change makes in respect to your curves. Now try shortening the handles, and you'll notice your curve gets sharper. To make an angle, you will need to press the Shift key while clicking your point. This enables the handles to be manipulated separately, giving you the control necessary to form very sharp corners and turns.

> If you're not happy with the placement of your points, you can easily move them by pressing the Ctrl key while dragging a point to a better position.

Setting as a Selection

You will probably notice that you are not seeing the marquee while you are creating outlines with either the Bézier or the Intelligent Scissors tool. When using these tools, you will wait until you are ready for your outline to become a selection. By clicking anywhere inside the outlined area, the area will be converted to a selection, and you will be able to see your marquee, as in Figure 5.11.

> When clicking on your points to either manipulate or move them, you must be careful not to accidentally click inside the selection area and set it prematurely.

FIGURE 5.11

The first Bézier selection upon completion. What a difference a few curves can make.

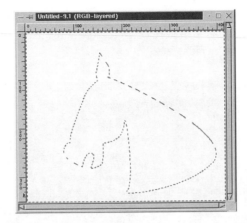

Putting the Bézier to Work

Now that you've experienced the possibilities for using the Bézier to create *new* selections, you have probably already come to the realization that the ability to form anomalous shapes also provides the Bézier tool with an excellent capability to select complex objects from images you already have.

1. Find a picture that contains a complex shape you'd like to isolate, as in Figure 5.12.

2. Begin by clicking around the desired area to form your points. Stay fairly close to the edges you want to form your selection, but at this time, don't worry if the straight lines seem to be covering parts of your selection. Remember that you can always move points if you need to. All you are trying to achieve with this is a sort of rough draft of the desired selection area.

5

FIGURE 5.12

Click the points around the desired area.

3. Now you can begin clicking on your points and maneuvering your Bézier curves until you have the desired area selected to your satisfaction (see Figure 5.13). Pretty amazing, don't you agree?

FIGURE 5.13

Practicing your curves on an interesting shape can quickly enhance your abilities.

After you've mastered the technique of working with curves, try this for an even quicker way to select an area with the Bézier tool:

Place your first point in the desired location, but this time, instead of just clicking in the next points, try dragging and clicking. When you do it this way, each successive point you click will have the handles ready to manipulate as your go, selecting on-the-fly, so to speak.

Intelligent Scissors

This tool has a mind of it's own (hence the name *intelligent*). It works by analyzing the colors of the pixels along the line formed as you select, and then snapping to an edge around the pixels that do not fall into the same color values. It is mostly used for outlining areas of color that contain an edge which has enough difference in color value from the surrounding areas that the tool can differentiate between the two.

1. Find a picture that has a nice large area of contrast.

2. Begin your selection with this tool by dragging your cursor around the area you want to select, just as you would the Lasso tool. Try to get as close as you can to the desired selection area.

3. When you release the mouse button, you'll see the Intelligent Scissors leap into action and try to find the edges that differ greatly in color value.

Intelligent Scissors Options

In addition to Antialias and Feather tools, the Intelligent Scissors tool has a few extra options that are not included with the other tools.

Edge-Detect Threshold

This is basically a tolerance control in which you can set the amount of tolerance you want the Scissors tool to have as far as including other color values while it tries to find an edge. Setting a high tolerance will allow more similar colors to be included along the line of the selection area while the tool tries to detect a good edge with enough difference to isolate.

Elasticity

Elasticity controls how elastic or flexible the tool will be when it does detect an edge. If you have the elasticity set too low, the tool cannot snap into place as it needs to, because you haven't allowed it enough room. If the elasticity is set too high and there are several different areas of color in your image, the tool might snap to a nearby color area that isn't the one you had in mind.

Curve Resolution

If you have a very curvy selection, the Curve Selection allows you to have some control in the way the tool forms the shape of the curves. A low curve resolution setting tends to produce a jagged edge, while a higher setting results in a much smoother, even curve.

Convert to Bézier Curve

This one is self-explanatory. If you have made a selection with the Intelligent Scissors and feel that it requires further modification to the edges, you can convert to a Bézier selection, and your line will form points all around. You can then move and manipulate those points to your satisfaction before making your selection active.

5

> Although the Intelligent Scissors tool is suited to perform certain selection tasks, it is generally faster and easier to use one of the other selection tools, due to the amount of variables that have to be set to work properly together in the Intelligent Scissors options. Stable Intelligent Scissors were a late addition to GIMP version 1.0, and as such, they might not behave predictably and usefully.

The Selection Menu Options

In addition to the options included with each individual tool, there are a number of available menu options for selections. Right-click on an open image to pull up a menu. Click Select, and you'll see the following options:

Toggle

This tool is discussed earlier in this hour; it toggles the marquee on and off, allowing you to view the selection area without the flashing if necessary.

Invert

You will definitely want to remember where this option is. It has the capability to make some selection tasks much easier. In certain instances, it can be less troublesome to select the area that you *don't* want, and then reverse that selection to include only the area that you *do* want. For instance, if you have a complex image surrounded by a one-color background, you could use the Fuzzy Select tool to choose the background color as the selection, go to Select, Invert, and your complex image is now selected instead.

All

By combining Select All with a layer option called Keep Transparent, you can isolate all image areas in a layer while leaving the transparent areas non-selected.

None

Earlier you learned how to deactivate a selection by clicking outside the selection area. The Select None option will perform the same action; your marquee will be removed and the selection area deselected.

Float

There are two basic types of selections, *standard* and *floating*. Standard means your selected area is still a part of your image or layer. If you modify a standard selection, you modify the selection area within your image. A floating selection *floats* or hovers over the image or layer, and you can move or modify it without affecting the original image. There are two ways you can defloat a selection, or cause it to merge with your image. One is by deactivating the selection, and the other is by using the Anchor function in the Layers dialog box.

Feather

This performs the same as the Feather in the tool options, the only difference being that it does not use a slider to control the feather radius, but rather the input of a numerical value.

Sharpen

The Sharpen function gets rid of some of the outermost pixels along the edge of a feathered or antialiased selection, leaving a slightly smaller and sharper-edged selection in it's place—kind of like the opposite of feathering.

Border

By choosing this option, you can surround the selected area with a chosen number of pixels that then becomes the selected area—subject to all modifications such as color fill, and so on. This can be a convenient option to use if you want to transform a selection area into a frame or an outline.

Grow and Shrink

These options allow you to expand or contract the selected area by a chosen number of pixels.

Save to Channel

By saving your selection in a channel, you are storing the selection's shape in a grayscale form that you can reopen and use again in the form of a mask.

5

Select by Color

This is similar to Fuzzy Select, but with more control. When this option is chosen, you'll see another pop-up menu containing five choices. First is *Replace*, which you will use when, like the Fuzzy Select tool, you want to click on a color to have it become the selection. The next three choices, *Add, Subtract*, and *Intersect* also work by letting you click the color to which you would like the option applied. Last, the *Fuzziness Threshold*, controlled by a numerical slider, lets you determine just how much tolerance toward other colors will be allowed when applying any of the previous options.

The Stroke

Talk about useful features, and the Stroke has to be right up there in the top ten. This ingenious little option can transform the outline of your selection (the part that's showing as the marquee) into a line drawing in one easy stroke, therefore, your selection tools also become Drawing tools. By changing the brush settings, you can use it not only to make line drawings and outlines, but also to come up with some very interesting effects. Let me show you how it works.

1. Open a new blank image and create a selection area using a selection tool of your choice.

2. The Stroke function will use the settings from the Brush dialog box, so you'll need to bring up the dialog box (File, Dialogs, Brushes), and choose the options you'd like to see in the Stroke, such as brush size, blend mode, and so on.

3. The color of the stroke will be the foreground color showing in your toolbox.

4. Right-click your image to bring up the menu, and click Edit, Stroke. You've turned your selection into an outline, as shown in Figure 5.14.

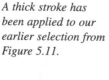

FIGURE 5.14

A thick stroke has been applied to our earlier selection from Figure 5.11.

Using Guides with Selections

When you have an image open, you'll see that there are two rulers in your image window—one just over the image and one to the left. Place the cursor on the top ruler, click, and drag down. You'll notice a colored, dotted line pulling down over your image as you drag; this is a horizontal guide. Now click on the left ruler and drag to see your vertical guide. Guides are helpful when you need to place a selection in a precise location. You can use them in a couple of different ways:

• Use guidelines as markers by placing them in the desired location and then manually moving your selections in line with them.

• There is a *Snap to Guides* option in the View menu that pops up when you right-click your image. When the Snap to Guides option is on, any selection that is moved close to a guideline will then automatically snap into place alongside the line.

Editing Selections

This hour has been devoted entirely to creating selections, but I'd like to just briefly introduce two of the editing functions that you will be using when working with selections.

Moving a Selection

The Move tool, along with the other transformation tools, will be covered in depth in the next hour, but I will touch on it here because it applies so directly to selections. As soon as a selection is made, you'll notice that when you hold the cursor over the selected area, the Move symbol shows up even though you haven't activated the Move tool. This allows you to move your selection *one* time, thereby changing it to a Floating selection. As you move it, you'll see that the area that held the selection is replaced by an area of solid color—the same as the background color in the toolbox. After it is a Floating selection, you *must* switch over to the Move mode if you want to move it again. Now your selection can be dragged anywhere in the image. However, until you switch to the Move mode, it will not move, but rather it will allow you to make *subsections* that can become active selections upon the deactivation of the original selection.

You can move the outline of a selection (the marquee) without moving the contents by holding down the Alt key while dragging to the desired area.

Copying and Pasting Selections

To open the Copy option, right-click on your image and select File, Copy. This places a copy of your selection in the Clipboard, while leaving the original image intact. You can then paste the selection into another area of the same image, or into a different image or layer by selecting File, Paste.

5

If you are working on an image and have to stop, but do not want to lose your selection, be sure to save your image as an XCF extension. This will keep your selection area intact—marquee and all—for the next time you open the image, and it will preserve your layer information.

Summary

Proper selections are an essential element for effectual image editing.

The mere act of being able to zero in on a targeted area of a larger image, whether to extract or manipulate it, can provide unlimited possibilities to your artistic endeavors. The ability to acquire the kind of selection necessary to achieve a desired result is truly a talent worth developing.

At this time, you might be wondering just what you are going to do with the selections after you have them, but because I will be referring to selections throughout the book, I wanted you to gain a complete understanding of the varied selection processes offered in the GIMP.

Q&A

Q When should I set my options, before or after making a selection?

A The Tool options that you pull up with each individual selection tool must be set up before you begin your selection, but the Select options (the ones you see by right-clicking your image and choosing Select) can be applied after your selection is in place.

Q If I have an image with more than one selection, can I move the selections one at a time?

A No. Multiple selections within a single image will act in unison as if they were a single selection when applying any kind of transformation.

Exercise

Find a picture of yourself or a friend. Practice using the various selection tools to isolate different parts of the picture, such as the hair only, and then both eyes, and then the lips. When trying to isolate small areas, you might want to use the Zoom tool. Just for fun, when you have a selection made, right-click the image, select Image, Colors, Hue-Saturation, and play around with the sliders. You might be surprised at what you'll come up with!

HOUR 6

Transformations

You made a good deal of progress by learning to isolate selected elements of images in Hour 5, "Working with Selections." The next logical step is to delve into specifics about some of the great tools for editing images and selections—the transformation tools.

To transform an image means to change or alter it in some way to give it a different appearance. Of course, you can alter your image in any number of ways, such as changing the color or applying a filter, as you will study in later hours. This hour, however, you will focus on transformations of a different sort, using the following tools and applications:

- Move
- Magnify
- Crop
- Transform
- Flip

Transformation Tools

I'll begin with the basic transformation tools that appear in the toolbox window, as shown in Figure 6.1.

FIGURE 6.1

These tools have more versatility than you might imagine.

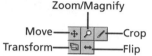

Move

After your brief introduction to the Move tool in Hour 5, you have probably accurately guessed that you should get to know it better.

The first capability I will discuss is the capability of moving an entire image. When the Move tool is activated, think of it as a little grabber, which you can use to grab on to your image and drag it to another location by pressing and holding the mouse button. See Figure 6.2.

FIGURE 6.2

When no selection is made, the Move tool moves the entire image.

> To move an image or layer that has been created within a transparent background, you must either grab the visible portion of the image or use the Shift key while clicking the mouse button and moving the image.

When moving selections within an image, the Move tool works a little differently here than it does in most other graphics programs. It might seem confusing until you get used to the way it functions. When the mouse cursor is held over a completed selection with the selection tool still active, the Move tool symbol appears over it as if you had switched to the move mode. This enables you to move the selection, but only once. If you want to move the selection further, you *must* remember to activate the Move tool by clicking on the Move icon in the toolbox. Otherwise, the selection tool assumes that you want to make another selection inside your original. You should notice that this inner selection area is surrounded by a gray nonflashing marquee (indicating that it is not active), yet it becomes active by clicking in the original selection area. By doing so, the original selection is deactivated. See Figure 6.3.

FIGURE 6.3

If you forget to activate the Move tool, your efforts to move might end up forming inner selections by accident. No reason to despair; simply undo them and turn on the Move tool.

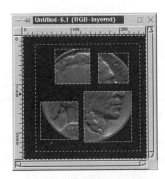

Magnify

Although the Magnify (Zoom) tool does not actually alter an image in a permanent way, I want to cover it in this hour because it can alter the way you view an image while you work on it.

The premise is simple. You can magnify or zoom in on an area to get a closer look at it. This is very handy for work such as repairing old photos where you need to make pixel-by-pixel changes. With the Zoom tool activated, you merely click the image to zoom in and Shift-click to zoom out. You can also zoom in and out by using the plus (+) and minus (-) keys on the keyboard. To zoom in on a particular area of an image, click and drag across that area.

If you pull up the Zoom tool dialog box, you can see that it has only one option, Allow Window Resizing. If this option is unchecked, your image window keeps its original size, no matter how much you zoom. Checking the option enables the window to reduce or enlarge to fit the amount of zoom applied.

A few other zoom features are located in the menu. Right-click an image and go to View. Most of the features here are pretty self-explanatory. You can zoom in, zoom out, or zoom to a certain scale amount among nine choices. You can look at the window information to see window size, scale ratio, and so on and toggle certain window functions on and off. Applying the shrink wrap function resizes your canvas to fit your image. One

6

very cool function you can find in the menu is called New View. This works by opening one or more duplicate windows of your image to show any changes you apply to the original. For instance, if you are working on an image where you need to zoom in a great deal, the duplicate window can show the effects of the changes on a non-zoomed duplicate so that you don't have to constantly zoom in and out to see whether the changes you make are achieving the desired results.

Crop

The Crop tool works by enabling you to choose an image area and eliminate any unwanted edges by cutting them off, much like trimming a photograph with scissors.

Open an image and click the Crop tool to activate it. Move the cursor over your image to the place that you want to begin the crop.

By clicking and dragging diagonally across the image area, you should notice rectangular lines forming an outline to show the selected crop area, as shown in Figure 6.4. As you release the mouse button, a crop window pops up on the screen with information about the crop area, including the size of the crop width and height, which can come in handy if you need an image to be a specific size. The crop window also shows the X and Y origin of the upper left point of the crop. Watch the rulers in the image window as you drag the crop area. The X (horizontal) origin is the amount in pixels from the left side of the image window to the left side of the crop area, whereas the Y (vertical) origin is the pixel amount from the top of the image window to the top of the crop area.

By pressing the Crop button located at the bottom of the crop window, you automatically trim off the extraneous edges from your image and crop it down to the chosen size. There is also a Selection button. This works by snapping the crop lines to the edges of an active selection area; it comes as close as it can to the actual selection, yet still maintains the rectangular crop shape. You can then click the Crop button to perform the crop.

Two extra crop functions are in the menu. With an image open, right-click and go to Image, Transforms, and you can see autocrop, which automatically removes any solid colored borders from an image. The other is zealous crop, which cuts off areas of highly contrasting color surrounding an image area, such as a border.

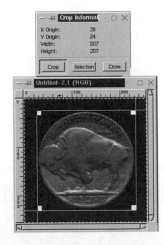

Transform

The Transform tool works its magic by moving image information around to your specifications, thus creating transformed versions of the original. It can be used to rotate, scale, skew, and distort images, selections, or layers. Double-click the Transform tool to bring up the options, which you can see in Figure 6.5.

FIGURE **6.5**

The Transform tool can perform some pretty interesting effects.

Rotation

The first option you will look at is Rotation. This works pretty much as you would expect from the name, enabling you to rotate the image or selection by clicking and pulling it in the direction you want to rotate. As you move, you should notice a small window pop up showing the angle of the rotation. The Rotation tool is especially useful when working with scanned images that might not have been scanned perfectly straight. Look at Figure 6.6 to see a before-and-after version of an image that needed to be straightened with the Rotation option.

6

There are extra Rotation options in the menu. Right-click your image and go to Image, Transforms and you should find options that enable the rotation to be performed by degrees of 90, 180, and 270.

> By holding down the Ctrl key while rotating, you can turn your image in 15-degree increments.

FIGURE 6.6

The original image is at an unattractive slant, but the rotation has corrected it.

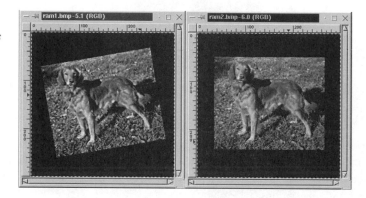

> The Smoothing option of the Transform tool works somewhat like antialiasing as you perform the different transformations, blending the image as it changes. If you perform many rotations in a row, it can sometimes result in a blurry image because it is blending each one in turn. After you know the degree of rotation you want the image to end up with, you can get a sharper look if you go back to the original and rotate only once to the desired angle.

Scaling

This effect sounds interesting, but I promise you won't find any snakeskin here. The Scaling function works by scaling your image or selection to a specific size. With scaling activated, the Scale options, as shown in Figure 6.7, show up as soon as you click your cursor on any corner of the image to begin the operation. The information includes the original image width and height, the current width and height which changes as you scale the image, and the X and Y scale ratios. If you want to merely scale the size of the image without stretching it out of shape one way or another, you must make sure the X and Y ratios match.

FIGURE 6.7

*Scaling an image
down to size is a
quick and easy task
in the GIMP.*

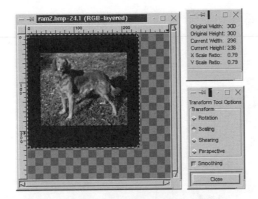

While you're on the subject of scaling, look at the scaling and resizing options in the menu. First, right-click an image and go to Image, Scale. An dialog box appears, as shown in Figure 6.8, which works in the same way as the Tool options for scaling, but this one does the work for you. You simply enter the dimensions you want your image to scale to. By having the Constrain Ratio option checked, which keeps your X and Y ratios the same, the image scales to a smaller or larger version with no shape distortion.

FIGURE 6.8

*You can enter the
desired scale
specifics in the menu
dialog box.*

Now right-click your image and take a look at Image, Resize. This performs a little differently than scaling. Look at the Image Resize dialog box, as shown in Figure 6.9. This enables you to enter the desired dimensions; but rather than scaling the entire image down, it deletes everything except the portion in the dimensions you have requested, much the same as cropping. The dialog box defaults to the center portion of the image, but by changing the X and Y offset values, you can position the sized area anywhere in the image. This is useful if you need to have several different images with the exact same dimensions.

6

FIGURE 6.9

*The Image Resize
dialog box lets you
reposition the loca-
tion of the desired
area by changing the
offset values.*

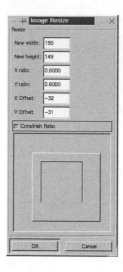

Shearing

Shearing produces a relative X or Y displacement, resulting in a sort of leaning effect, as
seen in Figure 6.10. Clicking and dragging up or down on the corner of an image
changes the Y (vertical) magnitude of the shearing effect, while dragging horizontally
changes the X displacement.

FIGURE 6.10

*The shearing effect
produces a kind of
tilting distort to an
image.*

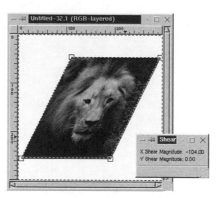

Perspective

The Perspective option enables pulling the corners of an image one by one to any position, altering the image to match the new positions. One nifty effect you can produce
with Perspective is the illusion of receding into a vanishing point (see Figure 6.11).

FIGURE 6.11

*An image with a
different perspective.*

 Performing certain transformations on very large images can be quite memory intensive and thus takes time. Unless you have a pretty good amount of RAM in your computer, you might want to practice with a small image while you are first learning the techniques.

Flip

The Flip tool enables you to flip an image either horizontally or vertically, resulting in a mirror image, as illustrated in Figure 6.12.

FIGURE 6.12

*Vertical flips produce
a mirror image, such
as the one seen here.
Great for making
images in pairs.*

6

Tutorial

Now that you've been through a few hours and have learned some of the basics, put them into practice and create a unique image while you're at it.

In this tutorial, you will make an image that resembles a photo cube.

To begin, you need three images or photos close to the same size range. This might be a good chance to practice your scaling techniques. If you prefer, you can use one photo and put it on all three visible sides of your cube. Using three different but complimentary pictures makes a more interesting effect.

Keeping your three photo images open, create three new blank image windows in a size that looks a little larger than the heads or portions of the photos you plan to use on the cube. Make the width and height the same so they are square. Use the Bucket Fill tool to fill each blank image in turn with a different color by changing the foreground color each time. Because I know the images in this book are in grayscale, I've chosen three very different colors so that you will be able to see the corners and edges clearly when the cube is finished. If you like, you could use different pattern fills in each blank image instead of solid colors.

Using the Rectangle tool, select an area out of the first photo, right-click and go to Edit, Copy. Now click one of the blank images to activate it and choose Edit, Paste. See Figure 6.13. After pasting, unselect by clicking once in the image to get rid of the marquee.

FIGURE 6.13

Create the blank images a little larger than the planned selected photo area in order to create a border effect.

Repeat the copy and paste with the other two photos, placing them in the remaining blank image windows.

At this point, you no longer need the original photos, so you might want to minimize or close them out to make some work space on the desktop.

Open a new blank image as least twice the size of one of the bordered photo images you now have on the screen.

In turn, copy and paste the three smaller images into the large blank image window, and arrange them as shown in Figure 6.14.

FIGURE 6.14

Arrange your photos such as this in the larger image window.

With the last image you placed still selected, activate the Transform tool and the Perspective option.

Pull the corners of the selected image into the beginnings of a cube shape, as in Figure 6.15.

FIGURE 6.15

By using the Perspective option to manipulate the corners of one of the squares, you can see the cube start to take shape.

After you have it positioned in the shape of the cube side, activate the Rectangle tool once again, but this time select the side square and pull it into cube shape using the Perspective option of the Transform tool. You should now have a completed photo cube, as illustrated in Figure 6.16.

6

FIGURE 6.16

Making cubes is a fun way to practice transformations.

Summary

I devoted this hour to studying the powerful-yet-basic transformation tools available in the GIMP.

By knowing how to alter existing images to achieve everything from creating a totally new look to fitting the image into desired dimensions, you can experience a whole new freedom in image manipulation.

Let the metamorphosis begin!

Q&A

Q Can I use the Move tool to move a selection from one image to another?

A No. The Move tool is used to move selections within an image. To move a selected area from one image to another, you have to use the copy and paste functions. Activate the image containing the selection, right-click it to bring up the menu, and go to Edit, Copy. The selection is now in the clipboard. Now activate the image you want to paste the selection into and click Edit, Paste.

Q Is there a way I can enter the amount of rotation I want my image to have?

A No, but you can usually get fairly precise to a desired amount by watching the dialog box containing the angle information while you rotate.

Exercise

Open an image and apply each of the transformation tools to it in turn to really get a feel for each tool and its options. Use an image that you are already very familiar with so that you're able to notice exactly how each change affects it.

Hour 7

Working with Color

Color is perhaps one of the most important aspects of dealing with art and graphics media—because color is richly and deeply embedded into almost everything you do. By merely altering a few colors within a composition, you can completely modify the tone and feel of the entire image, and in turn, how your audience reacts to it. Therefore, put a lot of thought into the color composition of your images before you begin.

Is color really that important? I invite you to take a look at some of your favorite Web sites and pay special attention to the way in which they deal with color scheming. How would they look if they simply altered their entire color scheme one day? They would probably lose that unique feel that makes them distinct, and chances are you would feel a bit thrown off by it. Your images are the same way. You should make sure that whatever colors you use in any graphic have a purpose and are more than random hues without function. People notice and react to color more than they might realize.

In order to work with color effectively in digital form, you first need to touch base on exactly how your computer recognizes color and how using different media can alter the way in which your machine thinks about color.

The GIMP and Color

The GIMP version 1.0 is designed primarily with digital graphics in mind—whether you use them online, embed them in your documents, create animations, or use any other digital media. (The GIMP outshines most other applications when dealing specifically with Web graphics; therefore, the Web is the GIMP's primary focus.) Admittedly, the GIMP is not yet as effective as a professional print tool, although the developmental versions of the GIMP are already showing much promise in that area as well. (That function could very possibly be part of the stable distribution even by the time this book is on shelves.) However, for regular day-to-day printing tasks, the GIMP can perform quite nicely.

Color Models

The Color models define how your computer interprets color and displays it in various media. You should familiarize yourself with these models, because they are essential for understanding some of the language and concepts behind graphics and color in general.

RGB Model

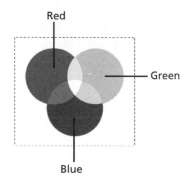

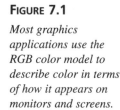

FIGURE 7.1

Most graphics applications use the RGB color model to describe color in terms of how it appears on monitors and screens.

The GIMP deals primarily with the RGB model of color (RGB stands for *Red, Green, and Blue*). This is the model used for representing color on monitors and screens, because it is defined by light instead of by paints and tints. Therefore, any colors represented onscreen are composed of a combination of the colors red, green, and blue.

(Televisions also work in this same way—which you can see if you ever take the time to look at a television really closely. You will see lots of little red, green, and blue dots with varying degrees of brightness.)

For creating Web sites, colors in HTML are also represented in RGB as sets of base-16 (hexadecimal) numbers. One handy function of the Color Picker tool is to automatically show you the HTML code for your color. I have grown to love this feature.

HSV Model

The HSV Model is a way to describe hue, saturation, and value. The GIMP uses this color model in combination with the RGB model. It is the model used by the Color Selection dialog box, shown in Figure 7.2, and in many other filters and dialog boxes.

FIGURE 7.2

The HSV color model is used by the Color Selection dialog box along with the RGB model. You can adjust the hue, saturation, and value by using the sliders.

- *Hue* refers to the color itself—any color in the rainbow, whether red, green, blue, yellow, and so on.
- *Saturation* represents intensity of color. The lack of color intensity results in grayscale, and full saturation results in 100% full color. So if you were to slide the Saturation slider in the color dialog box down, your color would become more and more washed out until you were left with pure gray.
- *Value* is the amount or intensity of light within the color. A color is true at 50% value. By contrast, 100% value is white, and 0% value is black.

You can attain a wide range of colors by using the HSV model, although you should experiment a little in order to get the hang of it. For example, turn up the value, and perhaps tone down the saturation a bit, to see pastel colors. By contrast, you can find deep rich Earth tones by turning down the brightness and, to a lesser degree, the saturation.

7

Indexed Model

The Indexed model refers to images that have a fixed number of colors, usually 256 (8-bit). Each pixel in an indexed image is assigned a specific color index, and therefore indexed color does not use RGB in the strictest sense.

Indexed images are used mostly on the Web (in GIF format) in order to save space and, subsequently, download time. Because indexed images have limited colors, they are usually much smaller in size, although many times this sacrifices image quality.

To reduce the active color depth, right-click and go to Image, Indexed. This will pull up the dialog box pictured in Figure 7.3. (The option Enable Floyd-Steinberg Dithering simply tries to improve the image quality by dithering, or effectively emulating a color by using dots of available color—much like a printed comic strip looks on close examination.)

FIGURE 7.3

The Indexed model is used by graphics formats that use a limited number of colors—traditionally no more than 256 of them. The GIF format is an example of a popular indexed format.

These images can also use any number of *palettes*, which are indexed color maps, to assign specific colors to limited color graphics. This could be a palette of nothing but shades of blue, primary colors, the Windows and Netscape 8-bit palettes, and so forth. These will be discussed at length when you get into Hour 15, "Web Graphics."

Using Custom Indexed Palettes

The GIMP enables you to load and apply any number of custom palettes into your indexed image. *Palettes*, like their real-life counterparts, are predefined tables of specific colors for your image to use. They do limit the amount of colors and the specific colors your image can use, but they can help you get a more specialized Indexed image. For example, they can more exactly match the original colors of a higher quality image or more closely match a system palette, such as Netscape's Web palette, in order to create an image that looks the same across platforms, even on low-end 256 color displays. I will talk more about this in Hour 15.

In order to do this, go to the toolbox menu File, Dialogs, Palettes, and you will see a dialog box, as shown in Figure 7.4, with a drop-down menu from which you can select many default palettes. These palettes are available from the Use Custom Palette option in the Indexed Color Conversion dialog box. With the Color Palette dialog box, you can also create new palettes and edit existing palettes to your liking and apply them to your image.

Any GIMP palettes you make or find online should go in your ~/.gimp/palettes directory. They will then be accessible from the Color Palette dialog box drop-down menu.

FIGURE 7.4

Palettes enable you to customize the exact color values of your indexed images.

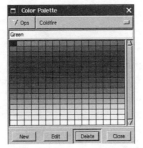

Grayscale

The concept of grayscale is easy. A grayscale image is one that has no color, only 256 shades of black, white, and gray. To grayscale an image, simply right-click and go to Image, Grayscale. Note when you save that not all image formats support grayscale, but most do.

CMYK Model

Print does not use light to display color, but ink instead (or toner, if you like). As you know, lights add value to each other when mixed together, but inks and paints are *subtractive* in nature, as shown in Figure 7.5. (I know it's a black-and-white book…you'll have to use your imagination.) This means that mixing the three RGB colors using light gives you white, but mixing paint using the CMYK colors gives black. (Well, in practice it's more like a dark brown.)

Print deals with color using the CMYK model. (*CMYK* stands for cyan, magenta, yellow, and black; the *K* is for black, because using the letter *B* might cause people to confuse black and blue.) It works by splitting the image into four color channels, each corresponding to the appropriate ink cartridge or toner of matching color.

7

Magenta

FIGURE 7.5

The CMYK model of color is used for high-quality printing. Unlike RGB, it uses four main color channels instead of three. Black is, of course, needed for a good-looking printout.

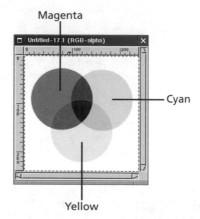

Cyan

Yellow

If you are primarily concerned with your images coming out properly in professional-quality print, it is best to work on them in CMYK mode. The conversion from RGB to CMYK is less than perfect. (Although you will never have a perfect representation of print colors on your monitor, you can still get pretty close.) CMYK support is not yet fully implemented in the current stable release of the GIMP, but as far as I know the next version of GIMP currently in development, will have much better support for CMYK. I assume then that your primary concern right now is creating graphics for onscreen display or for casual printing. I have covered CMYK simply for the purpose of understanding.

Color Channels

Channels describe the colors to your output source, whether it is a digital screen or a printer. They do this by simply being in charge of one color per channel, at which point the device combines them into a multicolored image that is human readable. Therefore, whenever I speak of RGB channels, I speak distinctively of the red, green, and blue portions of an image. The GIMP enables you to manipulate the separate color channels individually and create new channels if you want.

In order to view the working image's channels, go to the Layers and Channels dialog box from a right-click, Layers, Layers & Channels (see Figure 7.6). The first tab of this dialog box shows your image's layering information. Because you are now working with only one layer, you can go ahead and click the tab labeled Channels. Here, you will see your image as represented by the three RGB channels. You can now click any one of the eye icons to make a channel momentarily invisible and edit one channel individually. There are a few situations in which you might want to do this, and I will cover these later. For now, experiment to gain a basic understanding of how channels work.

FIGURE 7.6

Color channels enable you to work on any color element of an RGB image individually. This can be handy for creating effects with color.

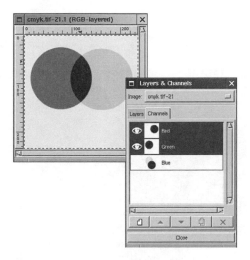

Working with Transparencies

In any working image, you can have in any area a transparency, which is an area of an image with no color. Of course, not every image file format supports image transparencies, but for those that do it is a fantastic feature.

You can create a new image from scratch using transparencies. Simply go to File, New and select transparent as your Fill Type. When the image pops up, you will see that it is covered with a light and dark gray checkerboard pattern, as in Figure 7.7. This is to let you know that what you are looking at is indeed considered invisible by the GIMP.

FIGURE 7.7

A transparent image lets you insert any element without having a background of any kind.

7

You can specify the size and color of the checkerboard pattern for transparencies by going to File, Preferences and clicking on the Display tab, as pictured in Figure 7.8. From there, you can specify the checks to be lighter or darker and larger or smaller using the Transparency Type and Check Size options.

FIGURE 7.8

The checkerboard preferences.

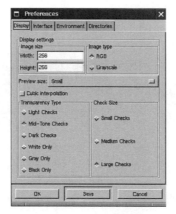

Now that you have a transparent image, you will probably want to put something on it. For this example, I will use a selection copied from another image.

- First, you will need a source image with something you would like to set against a transparent background.

- Then, after you have successfully tweaked the selection to your liking (using any selection tools necessary—sometimes the Bézier is needed for those tricky shapes), you can copy it with a right-click, Edit, Copy (see Figure 7.9).

- Going back to the transparent image, you can paste it (right-click, Edit, Paste) and position or transform it as you see fit (see Figure 7.10).

- After you have an image with a transparency exactly the way you like it, you should save it in a format that supports image transparencies. GIF comes to mind. (Remember that before you can save a file as GIF, it must be reduced to an indexed color format, because no GIF can have more that 256 colors.) To reduce the color depth, right-click, go to Image, Indexed, and select the 256 colors option in this dialog box.

FIGURE 7.9

Copying your source selection.

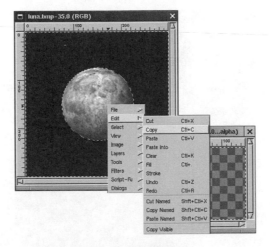

FIGURE 7.10

Now your selection rests comfortably on a transparent background.

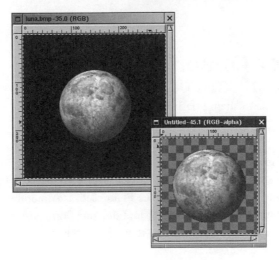

- Now you can save the image as a GIF. Go to File, Save and name the image whatever you like with the GIF extension, and select GIF in the Determine File Type drop-down menu.

- The Save as GIF dialog box will appear, as in Figure 7.11. Here you have two options: You can specify internal comments (in case you want a copyright notice or your name in there) or you can choose Interlaced (which refers to the way in which GIF renders over the Web—see the section "GIF" in Hour 15). Click OK here after you're finished.

7

FIGURE 7.11

Saving the image as a transparent GIF.

Other Color Options

Many color options are available by right-clicking the image and going to Image, Color. I'll introduce some of them briefly here.

Equalize

The Equalize function tries to adjust and correct images that are too washed out or too dark. It does this by setting the darkest pixels to black and the lightest ones to white and adjusting everything else in between (see Figure 7.12). Sometimes this actually works. Of course, if you're like me, you might find this function more useful as a graphic filter than as a photo repair tool. Sometimes, it can give your image that certain look that's right…even if it is a bit odd.

FIGURE 7.12

Equalize can correct photos or simply add a strange effect to your images.

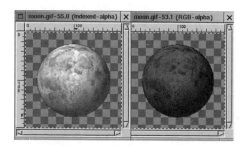

Posterize

Posterize reduces the color depth of your image—but in a different way than normal indexing does. It does it by using a number called the Posterize level. This level determines the number of colors used—the lower the level, the lower the number of colors used. It's a fun function to play with (see Figure 7.13).

FIGURE 7.13

The posterize function reduces the quality of your image; used sparingly, it can be a cool effect in and of itself.

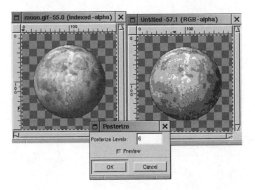

Threshold

This dialog box, shown in Figure 7.14, shows a graphical representation of the amount of brightness within an image. Each line from left to right represents a certain brightness value. The higher the value, the more pixels there are with that particular level of brightness. You can then select a range of lines within the dialog box and watch what happens. Only the pixels with a brightness value within the selected range will show through. Pixels within the range of selected values are turned completely white, whereas values outside the range are turned black. Used within a reasonable range encompassing a relatively large selection area, this can increase the contrast, intensity, and, subsequently, the quality of those slightly faded images.

Color Balance

By using Color Balance, you can alter the colors of your entire image by affecting your pixels towards the values represented at the end of the sliders (see Figure 7.15). The Preserve Luminosity option keeps your image from changing its brightness, which otherwise tends to happen with this tool.

7

FIGURE **7.14**

Threshold lets you display portions of your image according to brightness.

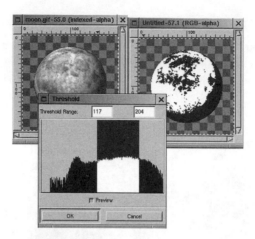

FIGURE **7.15**

The Color Balance dialog box is where you can quickly adjust color in your image in subtle ways.

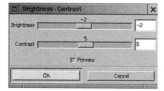

Brightness/Contrast

You can adjust the relative brightness and contrast of any image with this tool in the same way that you would adjust the brightness and contrast on your monitor (see Figure 7.16).

FIGURE **7.16**

This tool is self-explanatory.

Hue/Saturation

The tool shown in Figure 7.17 enables you to adjust the relative color of your image quickly and drastically. The Master option enables you to alter all pixels in the entire image at once, whereas clicking on any color option will enable you to change only those pixels within that certain color range.

FIGURE 7.17

The lightness option in this dialog box is synonymous with value in the HSV color model.

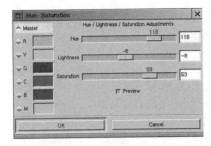

Curves

This tool lets you change the colors and values of your image by manipulating a graphical representation of your image's colors (see Figure 7.18). It is quite a complicated tool, but when you play with it enough, chances are you will find it quite useful. It lets you change the brightness and hue at any point by dragging the curve around freely. The curve itself represents your image's RGB values.

FIGURE 7.18

The Curve tool is both very handy and complex at the same time.

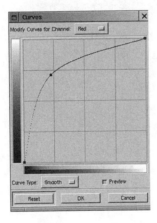

The Value option in the drop-down menu refers to altering all three RGB colors at the same time. (Not *value* meaning brightness, as in HSV. This tool deals strictly in RGB.) You can also deal individually with red, green, and blue.

Why would you use this tool instead of the Hue–Saturation dialog box? Well, this tool gives you much more control. By changing the Curve Type to Free instead of Smooth, you can now move your curve every which way to achieve all sorts of funky color effects. By inverting a curve, for example, you can invert the image. Likewise, by creating a parabola out of the curve, you can create a cool solarized effect that might be useful somewhere. In any case, the best way to figure out this tool is simply to play with it.

7

By the way, always make sure that the Preview option is checked, so you can observe what this tool is doing to your image while it does it.

Levels

Unlike the Threshold tool, the tool shown in Figure 7.19 lets you alter the amount of brightness and saturation your RGB values have by adjusting the *range* of values. By moving the arrows at the bottom, you can adjust the brightness and contrast output of your pixels. This way, you can enhance or subdue the brightness and shadow properties in any part of an image you choose. By moving the black arrow to the point where your lines begin to group together, and doing the same thing for the white arrow, you equalize your image's values to the point where your image is not quite so muddy. It's a good clean-up tool, as well as an effect tool.

FIGURE 7.19

The Levels tool lets you alter your image's brightness and contrast properties by manipulating a histogram.

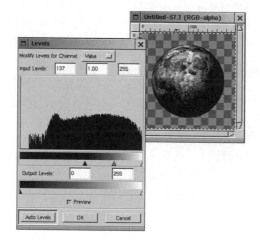

A Few Others

Desaturate—Converts your image to grayscale, without actually reducing the color depth, so you can still apply color to the image.

Auto-Stretch Contrast—This tool enhances the contrast and brightness of the RGB values of an image by stretching the lowest and highest values to their fullest range, adjusting everything in between. This is noticeable only with washed-out images and can be a good fix-it tool for bad photographs.

Auto-Stretch HSV—The same as the previous tool, except that it adjusts the HSV values to their fullest extent. Used for the same purposes, too.

Normalize—Does the same thing as the Auto-Stretch tools, but not so drastically. It does this by only stretching the values as a whole, and therefore keeping the relative color balance intact. This is perhaps the most useful "washout fixer" tool, because it will not disturb the colors otherwise.

Gradients

Gradients are a concept presently found in other graphics applications, but *no other program* I have ever come in contact with can even begin to compare to the intensive and extremely powerful use of gradients that the GIMP gives you access to. This is really one area that distinguishes the GIMP and makes it a killer app. With it, you can add realism to your graphics that will never cease to amaze.

A *gradient*, defined in the simplest of terms, is the transition from one color to another. So a basic gradient is a transition from black to white. Pretty elementary stuff. But the GIMP takes it way, way beyond that. Not only does it enable you to place gradients in a variety of positions and shapes, but it also enables you to create custom gradients, using more than two colors (any number you can handle), *including transparencies*. Now this is too cool, as I will later demonstrate. But for now, start with something simple.

In this first tutorial, you will create a simple beveled button with a metallic look.

1. Create a new image. This can have any color background you want, although transparent is preferred if you're going to save it as a GIF. After you have a blank canvas, you can start by selecting a rectangular area with the rectangular Select tool.

2. Now that your selection is made, as in Figure 7.20, fill it in with a simple gradient. To do this, you first need to get the colors how you like them. For this example, I used the default black and white, although you are perfectly free to use any colors you want. Then double-click the Gradient tool icon to bring up the Tool Options dialog box. (You can also do this by going to File, Dialogs, Tool Options on the toolbox.) In the Tool Options dialog box, make sure the Gradient drop-down menu is set on Linear, as shown in Figure 7.21.

7

FIGURE 7.20

Making the first selection.

FIGURE 7.21

The Tool Options dialog box gives you access to a few gradient options. In this example, you use the Linear option.

3. You can now make your gradient. Click the lower-right part of the selection, and drag the selection tool line to the upper-left corner of the selection. This makes a gradient from black to white, going left to right, in a diagonal fashion, as shown in Figure 7.22.

FIGURE 7.22

The gradient is made neatly within the confines of the selection.

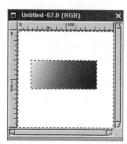

4. Now activate the rectangular Select tool again, and click the selection to deactivate it (which you can also do via right-click, Selection, Anchor). Now you will want to make a new selection to reflect an inner raised portion of the button. Make the selection inside the range of the old one, equidistant from the edges of the previous selection.

5. Click the upper-left corner this time, and drag to the lower right. This will create an opposite style gradient, and give your button a bold, metallic sheen, as shown in Figure 7.23. You can now put text in it, reduce it to indexed color depth, and save it as a GIF.

FIGURE 7.23

By making your selection only a few pixels from the edge of the previous selection and inverting your gradient, you have managed to create a solid metallic look.

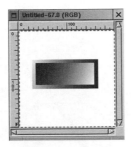

This tutorial showed an example of using the simplest kind of gradient. Now you will want to get a bit more complex with it. You can start by changing the shape of the gradient.

1. Create a new image and make a selection of some kind. Then in the Tool Options dialog box, you will see many gradient shapes under the Gradient option. Select Bi-Linear and apply it to your selection. As you can see in Figure 7.24, this creates a gradient that starts from where you began to draw with the Gradient tool.

FIGURE 7.24

Creating a bilinear gradient.

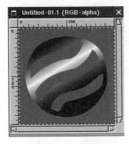

-   Now click the Radial option and apply it to your image. Now you can see, as in Figure 7.25, how it applies the gradient beginning from your initial cursor position.

Of course, one of the coolest features of the Gradient tool is its capability to go from one color to a transparency by selecting FG to Transparent from the Blend menu in the Tool Options dialog box, as in Figure 7.26.

7

FIGURE 7.25

Radial gradients are great for creating lighting effects.

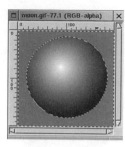

FIGURE 7.26

Gradients can also fade into transparency. This is a great feature for enabling parts of your selections to come through unaffected by the gradient.

FG to Transparent is also really handy for adding a light or shadowy feel to an object or environment. And you can reduce the opacity in the Tool Options dialog box to create enough effect without disturbing the composition of your image.

In the Gradient drop-down list, there are also three Shapeburst options, which do nearly the same thing. They make gradients from the middle of a selection to the outer edge, regardless of shape or size. This is pretty evident on text. Here's how to do a quick 'n' nifty text effect:

1. Make a text selection using the Text tool and leave it unanchored.
2. After selecting your two colors, drag the tool inside the selection from the inside to the edge, and watch the magic happen, as shown in Figure 7.27.

FIGURE 7.27

Adding more texture to any shape is easy with this gradient effect.

Gradient Editor

Now you've come to the good stuff—the Gradient Editor (see Figure 7.28). This tool makes it all worthwhile. It enables you to move beyond one color and make custom gradient using any combination of colors you choose. Using these gradients makes it possible to generate photo-realistic lighting and shadow effects, landscape effects, and a plethora of other things.

To get to the Gradient Editor, go to File, Dialogs, Gradient Editor in the toolbox menus.

FIGURE 7.28

The Gradient Editor gives you access to all kinds of advanced gradient functions.

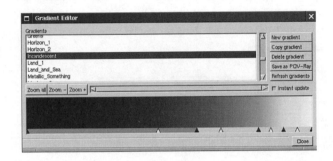

After you have the Gradient Editor open, as shown in Figure 7.28, you can scroll through a list of predefined gradients and they will be previewed in the box at the bottom. After you have selected a gradient, you can apply it to your image by going to the Tool Options dialog box and selecting Use Custom Gradient from the Blend pull-down menu.

After you have selected a custom gradient, there are all kinds of nifty options to play with. You can alter any of the colors in the gradient simply by right-clicking on an active segment and selecting Left Endpoint's Color or Right Endpoint's Color. This brings up the Color dialog box so that you can alter the color. An active segment is any segment between black arrows that is a darker shade of gray. You can activate any segment you want and move the segments around with the black arrows to change the shape and feel of your gradient. The white arrows represent segment midpoints, and changing their position won't move the segments but will alter the segment color balance.

You can create a new gradient by clicking New Gradient. Learning this powerful editor and all its options can be tricky, but it is very useful and is one of those things that is best learned by experimentation.

But wait...there's more!

7

That's right. Now scroll down the list of gradients until you come across one named Burning Transparency. Now you can see that one of the active gradient colors is transparent. You can use these gradients for nifty lighting effects.

1. Start a new blank image or use an already existing one if you like. Now make sure that your favorite gradient is selected in the gradient editor.

2. Now that you've got that, you should select the option Custom (From Editor) in the Blend drop-down menu in the Tool Options dialog box for the Gradient tool.

3. Now draw your gradient. To make it more like a lighting effect and not overpower your image, you should set the opacity of the gradient at no more than 50% in the Tool Options dialog box. This fades the gradient into your image with varying degrees of opacity.

FIGURE 7.29

One of many custom gradients in action.

4. You can now try it with different gradient schemes. For example, using the radial gradient from within a source of light will give you a cool lens flare effect. Using the bilinear gradient gives an object more depth, and using the Shapeburst sometimes looks cool.

Summary

Gradients can help you do a lot of really cool things. Now that you've had an introduction to them, I invite you to play around with them as much as you can. You will visit gradients yet again, especially in combination with the GIMP's powerful layering capabilities, in later hours.

As far as the color models go, the GIMP mainly uses RGB, HSV, Indexed, and Grayscale. However, if you do need along the way to do a little prepress, it is a good idea to understand CMYK so you'll know the differences between print and digital media. Doing professional quality print and prepress with the GIMP is not terribly difficult with a little knowledge and preparation, and it's covered in depth in Hour 24, "Using Peripherals with Linux."

Q&A

Q **If I reduce my color depth to grayscale, can I still use colors in certain parts of my image?**

A No. By reducing to grayscale, you have changed the color model of your image. Attempting to add color will simply add shades of gray. If you want to work with a black-and-white image and add hits of color to it, the thing to do is to use the Desaturate option. That way, your image appears black and white, but it is still an RGB image, so you can continue to use color in it.

Q **When I reduce my images to a straight indexed 256-color palette, some of them look good whereas others don't look good at all. What's up with that?**

A It depends on how many different colors your image has to begin with. If your image consists of many shades of blue, for example, an indexed image will create a palette consisting of 256 different shades of blue, which should look pretty good. It saves space without losing image quality. If, on the other hand, your image has every color in the rainbow, reducing to 256 colors might not be your best option. If you absolutely must save space, using the JPEG format might be a better bet. However, if you have to save in an indexed format, but the quality is still poor, dithering is one option that might help alleviate the problem. Also, by playing around with custom palettes, you might stumble on one that more closely matches the image's colors.

Exercise

Gradients are a very powerful feature and a topic that I've only begun to cover here. To get used to dealing with gradients, you should think of them as doing more than one thing. They add texture, create lighting and shadow effects, create the illusion of certain types of material, and accomplish other such nifty things. A neat thing to do with gradients is to experiment with them in various selections using different gradient shapes. You will be surprised how different your gradients can look with only a few alterations.

To familiarize yourself with gradients, one really good thing to do is to experiment with them as lighting resources. Grab an image, preferably a well-lit one, and try out some of the gradients with transparencies to create effects of light and shadow. Again, a radial gradient that ranges from a subtle light color to transparency makes a great lens flare effect. Likewise, a dark-to-transparent gradient can add enough shadow to give an object texture and mood.

7

To learn more about the color models, the best way is to open up the Color Selection dialog box, check the various options, such as R, G, B, H, S, and V, and watch how this affects your color window as you move the sliders around. Then come up with a specific color (such as candy apple red) and try to create that exact color using the different color options. Trying to come up with exactly the same color by eye can be a bit of a challenge because they do behave in their own way, but it will get you used to working with all of them.

Hour 8

Introduction to Layers

Layering is one of the most powerful and versatile features a graphics program can possess, yet it can be confusing until you understand exactly how it works. After you grasp the basic concept and learn to put this feature to work for you in practical applications, you will realize what a fantastic tool it can be for manipulating images, and will undoubtedly find yourself using layers on practically every image from this point on!

In this hour, you are going to learn the fundamental steps of layering—what layers are, how they work together, and how you can use them to create some very unique art effects.

The first portion of the hour is focused on an introduction to basic layering tools and concepts, and during the second part of the hour you will proceed to layering some simple images, progressing toward more advanced hands-on layering techniques in the next hour.

What Are Layers?

Because layers are unique to graphic arts, there is really not a *perfect* analogy to describe them. Try to visualize each layer as a transparent sheet containing one portion of an image, which can then be stacked with other sheets, each having the capability to be moved, edited, rearranged, and manipulated independently. After the desired result is achieved, all layers can then be merged into a single image.

To understand this, let's look at it from a slightly different perspective. Let's say you are an artist working on an oil painting. For the first part of your painting, you've painted in a glorious blue sky and an awe-inspiring mountain range. You've spent hours upon hours getting those mountains to look just *right*. Your painting is far from finished, but now you're getting nervous about adding anything to it because you don't want to risk spoiling your beautiful background. You think to yourself, "If *only* I could paint the rest of the picture on another canvas until I have *it* just the way I want it, and then place it over my mountain range and magically blend the two together!" Well, as we all know, oil paintings don't work that way, but that is precisely what you *can* achieve with digital art when you're using a graphics program with layering capability such as the GIMP.

Sounds pretty cool, doesn't it? Let's get started.

The Layer Dialog Box

Each time you open a new image, it automatically consists of one layer, the background layer. Think of the background layer as your canvas. Open a new blank image and right-click on it to bring up the menu. Go to Layers. As you will notice, several layering functions are listed in the menu. Click Layers and Channels to bring up the Layer & Channels dialog box, as in Figure 8.1.

FIGURE 8.1

Every image has at least one layer.

Begin by looking at the dialog box under the Layers tab and work your way down to understand the functions.

- *Mode*—This refers to *blend modes*, and leads to a drop-down menu listing the many blend modes available. Blend modes enable blending of the pixels of different layers in various ways. The blend modes will be covered in more detail when you get to the advanced layering techniques.

- *Keep Transparent*—When you have placed an image of any kind into a transparent layer, the Keep Transparent function will restrict any editing of the transparent portion of the layer. Changes or alterations will only affect the nontransparent portion.

- *Opacity*—This enables you to set the opacity for each individual layer. By lowering opacity, you can *see through* to the layers underneath. With the slider set to 0, the layer becomes totally transparent. At 100, it is totally opaque.

Adding and Deleting Layers

Notice the row of buttons with icons along the bottom of the dialog box.

The far-left option is the Add Layer option. Clicking this will bring up the new layer options, as in Figure 8.2. You can add a new blank layer in your choice of transparent, white, or background color. The size automatically defaults to match the size of the existing image. Here you can also give your new layer a name. When you are working with many layers in one image, it's helpful to give them identifying names to easily recognize them. If you choose not to name them, they will default to layer numbers, such as Layer 1, Layer 2, and so forth.

FIGURE 8.2

Name your layers to help identify them at a glance.

If you forget to name a layer or decide to change the name, double-click on the name to bring up a naming dialog box.

The next two buttons are used for moving an active layer either up (placing on top of the other layers) or down (under other layers). To activate a layer to move, click on the layer name or thumbnail image of the layer you want to move and apply the Up or Down button.

The fourth button, with the icon that resembles two sheets of paper, can be used to make a duplicate of the active layer. If you have a layer that you don't want to risk messing up by making unalterable changes, click this button and make a duplicate copy to work with.

> Each individual layer is like an individual image. Most changes to a layer can be undone either by right-clicking on the image and selecting Edit, Undo, or by pressing Ctrl+Z, just as if you were working on a non-layered image.

The next button, appearing as an X, is the Delete function. By pressing this button, the active layer will be removed from the image.

The last button, resembling an anchor is (you guessed it!) used to anchor (or permanently set) a floating selection within the layer. Anytime you place a text string or other active selection in a layer, it acts as a floating selection—complete with flashing marquee—until you anchor it to the layer.

Selecting and Moving Layers

On the left of the Layers and Channels dialog box, you will see an eye symbol. This indicates that the particular layer is visible. By clicking on the eye, thereby removing it from view and disabling it, the layer can no longer be seen. Click again to bring back the eye and your layer will be visible again.

Click just to the right of the eye and you will find an icon resembling the Move tool (see Figure 8.3). Normally, each layer can be moved or edited independently of the others. By activating this symbol on two or more layers at a time, these layers can be moved or edited as a unit.

Next is the thumbnail image and name of each individual layer. The layer highlighted in blue is the active layer.

> You can change the size of the dialog window thumbnail images by selecting File, Preferences, Preview, in the toolbox. There you can set the thumbnail sizes to small, medium, or large. You can also turn the thumbnails off completely if you prefer.

FIGURE 8.3

When the Eye icon is activated, you can see the layer. The four-pointed arrow resembling the Move tool can lock layers together to be moved as one.

The Layer Dialog Menu

In the Layers & Channels dialog window, right-click on the thumbnail image or name of the layer to bring up the Layer dialog menu, as in Figure 8.4.

FIGURE 8.4

The Layer dialog menu has a few more options to consider.

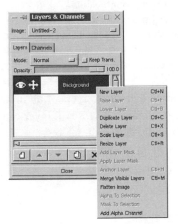

The *New, Raise, Lower, Duplicate, Delete,* and *Anchor Layer* buttons just described perform the same if activated from the menu or if activated using the dialog box icon symbols for these functions.

Scale and Resize function in the same capacity as the Scaling and Resizing options you learned about in Chapter 6, "Transformations." The only difference is that here, the scaling or resizing is applied to one or more chosen layers.

Merge Visible works by allowing you to merge only the layers with the eye activated, indicating their visibility. When you are working with a very large image or one that contains many layers, it can be extremely memory-intensive because your computer is coping with the image information contained in each separate layer. The merge visible function enables merging of the layers that you have already completed work on, freeing up some of that precious memory. When you choose to merge visible layers, an options box will appear where you will see the following choices:

- *Expanded as Necessary*—This option is used in a situation where some layers are smaller than others, usually due to resizing or scaling down after adding the layer. This will adjust the resulting merged layer to include all image areas.
- *Clipped to Image*—This option works by clipping out any extraneous areas surrounding the merging image area, such as a case where layers have been resized to be larger than the original image.
- *Clipped to Bottom Layer*—This option clips the merging layers to the same dimensions as the bottom layer.

For the most part, you will probably create all the layers in an image to match the dimensions of the background layer. If you try to copy and paste an image or selection that is larger than the layer being pasted to, it will be automatically cropped to the size of the layer you're pasting into.

Flatten Image is the command used to merge all layers of an image. By flattening the layers, you will have just one merged image and lose all layer capability and information. You are required to flatten an image before it can be saved in any image format other than XCF, which is the native GIMP format that allows saving with layer capability intact. Make sure that you are completely finished editing your layers before flattening and saving in another format.

If you are working on an image that might require further editing, but need a copy to save in a format other than XCF, right-click on the layered image, and select Edit, Copy Visible. This copies all visible layers into the Clipboard, and then they can be pasted as one into a new blank image and saved in your choice of format. Save the original as XCF, and the layers will be intact for making changes later.

The remainder of the options found in the layer dialog menu are used when working with masks and alpha channels, which will be discussed in Hour 10, "Using Masks."

Aligning Layers

There is one more option that I would like to briefly touch on before the tutorials begin.

Align Visible Layers can be found by right-clicking the image and viewing the layers menu. This option is used for positioning layers in an extremely precise manner. By activating the Align Visible Layers option in the menu, a dialog box will appear containing many alignment settings to choose from, as in Figure 8.5.

FIGURE 8.5

Layers can be aligned in a variety of ways.

Each alignment option also has a drop-down menu containing even more detailed alignment settings. For example, you can choose not only to align all visible layers horizontally, but you can also specify where the alignment should be in relation to the image, such as left, right, or center.

For most image editing, you will not need the precision alignment offered here, but you will find it to be a valuable addition to layering especially when creating and editing animations.

Tutorials

I've heard it said many times that experience is the best teacher, and I believe that wise old saying is the absolute truth. By working your way through the following tutorials, you will be able to see layering in action and understand just how easy and incredible it really is.

For these lessons, you will need images located in the tutorials folder on the CD-ROM that comes with this book, or you can use similar ones of your own if you have them.

Lesson 1—Basic Layering

To begin, open the images lion.jpg and moon.jpg, as shown in Figure 8.6.

FIGURE 8.6

The first layering technique will require only two images.

Open a new blank image. Set the size to 256 × 256. Right-click on this image and select Layers, Layers and Channels to bring up the Layers & Channels dialog box. You will see that you have one layer, known as *background*. Click on the Add Layer button in the lower-left corner of the Layers & Channels dialog box and add a new transparent layer. Name the new layer *moon*. You now have a blank image with two layers, as in Figure 8.7. The layer known as moon is highlighted in blue in the dialog window, showing that it is active.

FIGURE 8.7

Begin with a blank canvas, and add layers as you go.

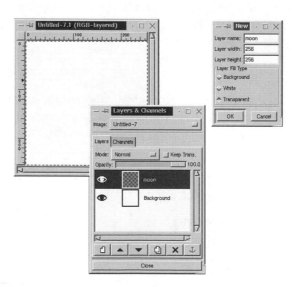

Now go back and right-click the moon.jpg image and select Edit, Copy, so that it is in the Clipboard ready to paste.

Check to make sure the moon layer is active in the new image then right-click, Edit, Paste. You have pasted the entire moon image into the moon layer you created. After you copy and paste an image or selection into a layer, you must anchor it to the layer either by clicking once in the floating selected area or clicking on the Anchor button.

Repeat the same steps to add another new layer, but name it *lion*. Copy and paste the lion image into the lion layer.

Now comes the interesting part. With the lion layer active, adjust the opacity slider to around 50 or so, and you will see your moon layer showing through the lion, as in Figure 8.8.

FIGURE 8.8

By reducing the layer opacity, the moon appears to be shining through the upper layer.

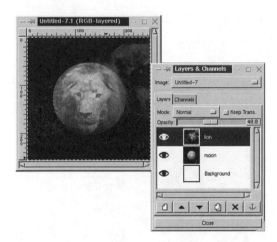

Okay, you can see where this is headed, but the outer portion of the lion image is still visible, which detracts from the moon image, so let's get rid of that part.

Open the Brush dialog box by selecting File, Dialogs, Brushes. Choose a large soft brush. Now activate the Eraser tool and erase the area of the lion layer that is surrounding the moon area. Because the lion is the only layer that is *active* at this time, the Eraser will not affect the other layers. Adjust the opacity of the lion layer to around 30 or so to let the moon texture come through. Abracadabra—your image is complete, as in Figure 8.9. You've just begun to experience what layering is all about.

FIGURE **8.9**

The "man in the moon" might look a little different through the eyes of a lion!

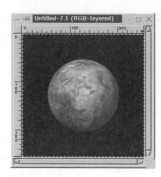

Lesson 2—Layering Multiple Images

In this lesson, you will combine the use of layers and transformation tools to create a reflection.

You will need the moon image again for this tutorial, so open moon.jpg. You will also need water.jpg, and stars.jpg. See Figure 8.10.

FIGURE **8.10**

Here you have all the components of a good picture. You just need to perform a little magic known as layering on them.

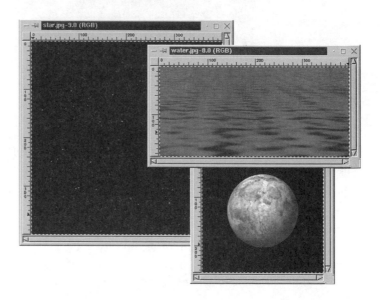

Begin by opening a new image, size 400 × 400. Open the Layers and Channels dialog box and add a new layer; name it *sky*.

You will want the image of the stars as the first layer, so copy and paste it into the *sky* layer. Always remember to anchor after copying and pasting.

8

Next, create another new layer, name it *water*, and copy and paste the water image there. Activate the Move tool to drag the water to the lower half of the layered image, as in Figure 8.11.

FIGURE 8.11

With the Move tool, you can position a layer anywhere in the image.

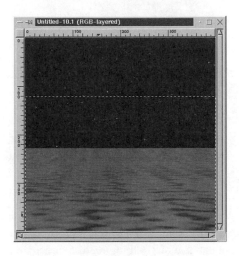

 As you move or scale a layer, you will notice that the black and yellow dashed line that usually marks the borders of an image is now surrounding the active layer only. This shows you where the layer boundary is for the particular layer you're working on. It will not be visible after you save the image.

Now you are going to create one more layer, name it *moon*, and copy and paste the moon image there, but you will not want to include the black background surrounding the original moon image. To easily get the moon out, activate the Fuzzy Select tool and click on the black portion of the moon image, which turns that portion into a selection. Right-click on the image and choose Select, Invert, and you will have a selection of the moon only. Copy, paste, and anchor this selection to the empty moon layer.

The moon image is slightly too large for this scene, so you will need to scale it down to size. Activate the Transform tool in the toolbox and set it to Scale. Right-click on the name moon in the Layer & Channels dialog window to bring up the menu, and choose Scale.

By either clicking and dragging on the corners of the moon layer, or setting the desired size in the Scale options box, you can scale it to the right size to fit in with the rest of the image (see Figure 8.12).

FIGURE 8.12

Scaling is applied to
the active layer, but
does not affect the
other layers.

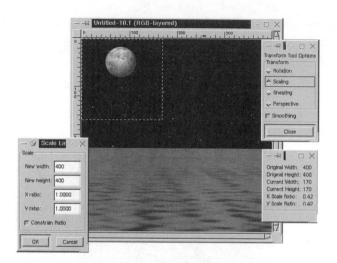

Okay, now the moon is the right size, but is not in the right position. Activate the Move
tool to drag the moon over and center it in the sky. Don't forget that, unless you hold
Shift, the Move tool is not capable of grabbing on to a transparent area. You must grab
the actual image portion, which is the moon itself in this case, to be able to move the
layer.

At this point, your image is only lacking one very important thing. On such a clear and
star-filled night as the one depicted here, the sky would surely be reflecting in that tranquil water!

To form the reflection, first activate the Rectangle Select tool and select the top portion
of the image, all the way down to where the water line begins. Right-click on the selection and choose Edit, Copy Visible. This will copy the selected portion of all visible layers. Click in the selection to unselect as it is now saved in the Clipboard and ready to
paste. Add a new layer and name it *reflection*. Paste the selection you just copied into
this layer.

What you will have to do now is flip the layer containing the copy of the moon and
stars and move the resulting reflection to its rightful place in the water. Do this by
double-clicking the Flip tool, selecting Vertical in the options box, and clicking anywhere
on the layer to flip it. To be able to see through this reflection layer, lower the opacity
to around 20.

Activate the Move tool and move the reflection layer into position, lining up the skylines
just along the edge of the water. Adjust the opacity so that the moon is slightly visible
and the stars have just the slightest glimmer in the water. Figure 8.13 illustrates the completed image and the layers used to form it.

FIGURE 8.13

Thanks to layers, a full moon reflecting in the water sets the scene for a peaceful night at sea.

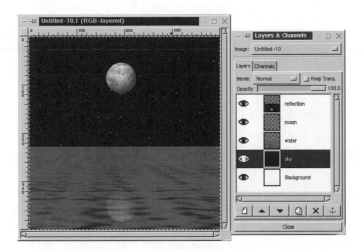

8

Summary

By learning the basics of layering during this last hour, you have discovered the key to unlock one of the most important powers an image-editing program can possess.

The capability to combine and yet independently edit portions of images will unquestionably ensure that you gain a new and distinct form of mastery over your creations.

Q&A

Q How many layers can I have in a single image?

A Unlimited. The GIMP will allow you to add as many layers as you want. However, layering *does* require a good amount of memory from your computer, and the bigger the images, the more memory it takes. As long as you are fortunate enough to have a nice large amount of RAM, the sky is the limit!

Q Can I view just one layer at a time?

A Yes. The eye symbol in the Layers & Channels dialog window enables quick-and-easy viewing of one or any number of layers at a time. Just click on the Eye icon to add or remove a layer from view. By Shift-clicking on the eye, you can hide all but that layer.

Exercise

Practice your newly discovered layering techniques on the images you have been working with in the tutorials for this hour. Add a new layer to each image and apply changes of your own, such as using the Airbrush tool and a large brush to paint in some clouds over the full moon. Don't forget to place a reflection of the clouds in the water!

HOUR 9

Hands-on Layering

Now that you've had a little glimpse at the power of layering, you probably have about a million or so great ideas popping into your head concerning ways you can use the techniques you just learned.

Hold on though, because there's even more to this layering business! This hour you are going to look at combining the versatility of layering with the usefulness of blend modes.

After you've gone over the blend modes in detail, you'll spend some time doing step-by-step tutorials, and put a couple of the blend modes to practical use so that you will be able to see their functionality first hand.

Blend Modes

Layer blend modes can basically be described as methods or various ways of combining pixels in an image or layer with the pixels in the images or layers underneath.

The GIMP contains 15 blend mode options. Although blend modes are usually applied during layering operations, they are also available in the Brush Selection dialog box and can be applied directly to an image with any of the painting tools.

To view the blend modes, open either the Brush or Layers & Channels dialog box and click on the blend mode drop-down menu, as seen here in Figure 9.1. You must have an open layered image for the menu to function in the layer dialog box.

FIGURE 9.1

The 15 blend modes are located in the drop-down menu.

The drop-down menu in the Layer dialog box actually contains only 14 blend modes. The drop-down menu in the Brush dialog contains an extra mode called *Behind*, bringing the total number to 15.

Blend Modes Quick Reference Guide

Let's begin by examining the different modes with a brief description of each.

1. *Normal*—All pixels on the selected layer completely cover the lower layers, and can only be blended by varying the opacity setting.

2. *Dissolve*—This mode also requires a reduction in the opacity setting to see results. As the opacity is decreased, so is the number of visible pixels in the current layer, which results in a speckled appearance.

3. *Multiply*—This works by multiplying color values in the selected layer with the colors in the lower layers to produce darker colors. To multiply means to increase, so think of it as increasing the depth of color. When working with blend modes, each color channel is treated as a value from 0–1. In the case of Multiply, for example, if you had two channels at .5 and .5, multiplying them would result in .25, a darker value, which is why Multiply makes images look darker.

4. *Screen*—This option produces lighter colors because they are combined by multiplying the inverse of blended colors. Think of it as multiply in reverse.

5. *Overlay*—This will combine the multiply and screen modes, depending on the color of the underlying layers. Lower color values get darker, whereas higher values get lightened.

6. *Difference*—This compares the color values of all layers and subtracts any lighter values in the selected layer, showing the difference.

7. *Addition*—This blends together the color values of all layers involved.

8. *Subtraction*—Subtracts the selected layer's color from the combined color of the underlying layers.

9. *Darken Only*—Makes a comparison of color values in all layers and picks the darkest pixels of each.

10. *Lighten Only*—Works much the same as Darken Only, except this one chooses the lightest pixels of each layer.

11. *Hue*—Applies the hue of the selected layer to all layers.

12. *Saturation*—Applies the saturation (color intensity) of the selected layer to all layers.

13. *Color*—Works by applying the combined hue and saturation of the selected layer to all layers, yet will not affect the luminance, or brightness of the underlying layers.

14. *Value*—Known as luminance or luminosity in other programs, this will blend the brightness of the selected layer with the hue and saturation of the underlying layers.

15. *Behind*—This mode is only available in the Brush dialog box. It works by enabling you to paint on transparent areas while not affecting other image areas, seemingly painting *behind* these other areas.

Examples

I will attempt to illustrate some of the modes here, but I have left out a few that would not illustrate well in the grayscale constraints of this book.

You can get a much better idea of how the modes function by actually applying them in turn to an image so you can see the color changes, so let's approach it from that angle.

Open the cameo.jpg image from the tutorial section of the CD-ROM.

Add a new transparent layer, and use the rectangle Select tool to select half of the picture from the middle out—as in Figure 9.2—and anchor the selection. By doing it this way, you will be able to compare the original image with the results of the different blend modes.

FIGURE 9.2

By testing the blend modes on just part of an image, you will really see the effects.

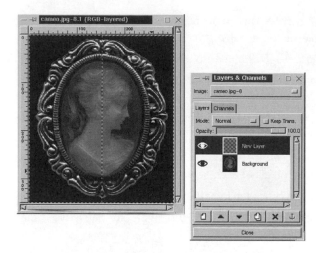

Pick a foreground color that you would like to see blended with the image in the varied modes. I used a medium purple (R=128,G=0,B=128) for my illustrations. Use the Bucket Fill tool to fill the selected half of the image with your chosen color.

Because you are in the default Normal blend mode, the color will fill the selected area, covering the lower layer area, as in Figure 9.3.

FIGURE 9.3

In the Normal mode, the only way to blend layers is through the opacity setting.

Now click on the drop-down menu for blend modes and switch over to Dissolve. You'll have to adjust the opacity to see the changes brought about by this mode (see Figure 9.4).

FIGURE 9.4

The Dissolve mode gives the appearance of the selected layer dissolving into the lower layer.

Turn the opacity setting to 100 and apply the Multiply mode to see the *dark side* of an image, as in Figure 9.5.

FIGURE 9.5

The Multiply mode produces a dark look.

Next, try setting the mode to Screen for a lightened up look (see Figure 9.6).

Now set the mode to Difference for another look, as shown in Figure 9.7.

Now change to the Addition mode, as in Figure 9.8

9

FIGURE 9.6

Screen mode delivers a much lighter appearance

FIGURE 9.7

This mode really does make quite a difference.

FIGURE 9.8

By adding the upper layer's single color to the lower layer, a look is produced that is somewhat similar to looking at the lower layer through a colored transparent sheet.

Take a few minutes and apply each of the rest of the blend modes to your image and note the effects. You'll want to take advantage of the versatility of these powerful color manipulators.

Tutorials

As you just found out for yourself, blend modes can be applied to entire images or just portions. In this first tutorial, you will use that knowledge to achieve a specific look.

Working with Color

Open the car.jpg image from the tutorial section of the CD-ROM (see Figure 9.9).

FIGURE 9.9

I'm thinking of getting a paint job. I wonder how my black car would look in a lighter color?

Use the selection tools to select only the painted portions of the car, as in Figure 9.10.

FIGURE 9.10

Use the Lasso or Bézier selection tool to select the part you want to change.

Add a new transparent layer; name it paintjob.

Set the foreground color to a color you would like to see on the car. I've chosen a pale blue here.

With the paintjob layer active, use the Bucket Fill tool to fill the selected area with the chosen color (see Figure 9.11).

FIGURE 9.11

The selected area becomes filled with color.

Now you can get somewhat of an idea of what the car will look like with the lighter color, but you can't really see the details. This is a situation where you can use a blend mode to help out.

Most of the blend modes will still let the dark original color of the car come through. Because you want the car to be lighter, apply the Screen mode from the blend mode menu. Voilà! Check out the results in Figure 9.12.

FIGURE 9.12

A virtual paint job can happen in a matter of moments by choosing the right blend mode.

Working with Black and White

Because the blend modes work by blending colors in such a large variety of ways, let's take a look at unleashing the power of color in an image.

A very popular technique used in everything from movies to photos is the use of just a drop of color to bring the focus to a certain item in a black and white image. One reason the technique is so popular is because it is very effective. An image can end up with a completely different feel by using this method.

In this tutorial, we will use a combination of layering and blend modes to achieve this color (or should I say *lack* of color) effect.

Open the puppy.jpg image from the tutorial section of the CD-ROM (see Figure 9.13).

When you look at this image, what do you see? More than likely, you'll probably say it's a very happy little pup running through the green grass.

FIGURE 9.13

The bright contrasting colors in this image draw your eyes to the grass and the dog.

Take a look at the lone flower in the lower-left corner of the picture. Sure, you probably saw the flower before, but your eye was still naturally drawn to the larger areas of color in the image. Let's make the flower, rather than the puppy, the focal point of the picture.

Make a copy of the image to work on.

Add a new transparent layer and set the blend mode to *Saturation*.

Set the foreground color in the toolbox to either black or white.

Activate the Paintbrush tool. Open the Brush dialog box and choose a medium sized soft brush.

Now by sweeping the brush over the image, you will in essence remove all color, leaving just a grayscale look to the picture. While you are painting, leave *only* the flower unpainted, preserving the color.

Take a look at both the original and the edited copy side by side. It's the same image, but notice how your eye is now drawn to the flower in the second image.

> Although you can apply blend modes either by selecting the mode in the Brush box dialog or Layer dialog box, you might find it more helpful to use layering at first, until you learn what the modes do and know just what effect you want to achieve. When you choose from the Brush dialog box, the chosen mode is applied to the brushed area, but to test a different mode, you would have to undo and start over with the brush. By using the Layer dialog box, the chosen mode is applied, but you can change modes to view the different effects.

Blending Images

You've seen how a single color in a layer can affect an image by applying the various blend modes. Now try something a little different and use one of the modes to blend two images together.

Open the 2men.jpg and sunset.jpg images from the CD-ROM (see Figure 9.14).

FIGURE 9.14

These two images will blend into one more interesting images.

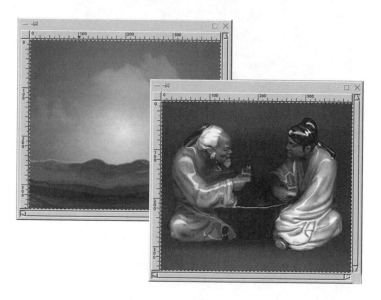

Add a layer to the 2men.jpg image, and then copy and paste the sunset.jpg image into that new layer.

Go to the Blend Mode options and choose Difference. Notice how you've given a whole new look to the original image of the men with just the click of a button. Figure 9.15 illustrates the difference a blend mode can make.

FIGURE 9.15

A much more captivating image is extremely easy to achieve with the magic of blend modes.

9

Summary

In this hour, you got a taste of what can be achieved by learning about the blend modes and how you can combine them with layering techniques for some interesting results.

The time you have put in to understand layering will be invaluable to you in the following hours and, as you will soon discover, you will put this knowledge to use time and time again.

Q&A

Q **Some of my layer options are grayed out. What gives?**

A An option that is grayed out in the Layer menu means that for one reason or another, the option is not accessible. Usually it is for an obvious reason, such as the Raise or Lower Layer options will not be accessible unless there is another layer to raise or lower it from.

Q **After adding a new transparent layer to my image, I tried to use the Bucket Fill tool to add a color to the layer, but nothing happened.**

A In or out of layers, the Bucket Fill tool will not fill a totally transparent area that is not selected. Just use a selection tool to select the entire area of the layer, or right-click and select Image, Select All, and the tool can then be used to fill the selected layer with a color or pattern of your choice.

Exercise

Use the blend modes on a variety of different images to see the changes you can bring about. Try this: Fill the first layer with a pattern from the Pattern dialog box and put a layer of color over it and experiment by trying each mode and noting the effects. Then try mixing two patterns together and blending them. The more you dabble, the more you will remember just how they work!

HOUR 10

Using Masks

Wow! You're not even halfway through the book yet, and you're applying layers like an old pro.

By now you are probably really getting hooked on the total versatility that layering offers for editing your images.

This hour will teach you a few final tricks involving layering, namely layer masks and channels. Yeah, you heard me right, there are even more cool things you can do using layers! You will learn how those mysterious layer masks work and follow through with some tutorials to apply what you've learned, including:

- Gradient masks
- Photo edge masks
- Text masks

What Are Masks?

Think of a party or Halloween mask. They're used to cover or conceal parts of your face, but can be removed at any time, thus revealing your identity by uncovering the parts of your face that were hidden. A *layer mask* is much the same. It is used to cover certain parts of your layer. It can enable you to hide or reveal specific portions of your image and apply special effects just to those portions.

In a way, a selection is somewhat like a mask. You can select a specific area and the rest of the image will in essence be *masked off* or protected from any applied changes. Masks take this capability a step further by allowing you to apply changes to a layer based on the alpha values of the layer.

I like to think of a mask as a custom stencil. They are basically grayscale alpha channels that you can attach to a layer. When changes are applied to a layer using a mask, the black parts of the mask are viewed by the layer as totally open to visibility, white portions are totally immune, and various shades of gray allow various degrees of the change to be visible.

Creating Masks

Masks can be created from images, selections, gradients, or entirely from scratch. Here I will use a simple image to illustrate basic masking.

Open an image, (see Figure 10.1), and right-click on it to bring up the Layer dialog box and add a new layer in white.

FIGURE 10.1

The original image before the masking process begins.

Next, I right click the thumbnail image of my new layer to bring up the Layer Dialog menu and click Add Layer Mask. This brings up the Add Mask Options box (see Figure 10.2).

FIGURE 10.2

Three options are available for the initial mask.

The mask options box contains three choices to start the mask with:

- *White (Full Opacity)*—By choosing white , you get a totally opaque mask. It completely covers your layer in white until it is edited.
- *Black (Full Transparency)*—This option creates the mask in black, which appears as totally transparent; you will be able to see your layer through it.
- *Layer's Alpha Channel*—This means that the mask will be created out of the grayscaled version of alpha values in the layer.

For this example, I have chosen to create a white mask, which is also the default option. As you will see in Figure 10.3, a new thumbnail image indicating the mask appears in the Layer dialog window to the right of the layer thumbnail. Because I haven't begun to edit the mask, it appears as solid white.

10

New layer

FIGURE 10.3

A thumbnail image of the mask appears next to the layer thumbnail.

Layer mask

To begin editing the mask, click on the thumbnail to activate the mask. A white border will appear around the thumbnail to indicate that it is active. If you want to switch and work on the layer, click the layer thumbnail and the white active indicator border will appear there instead.

Because black is the totally *open* or transparent color as far as masks are concerned, I chose black as the foreground color in the toolbox and used the Paintbrush to paint in an area of black. Notice in Figure 10.4 how the area that has the black applied to it allows the image to show through the white layer.

FIGURE 10.4

Like magic, the black areas of the mask become totally transparent.

You see how the white area of the mask is totally opaque and the black transparent. Now, as I switch my foreground color to a shade of gray and paint in the mask, you'll notice that area becomes partially transparent, as in Figure 10.5. Look also at the mask thumbnail in the Layer dialog window and see how it shows the mask I just created.

FIGURE 10.5

Compare the masked image with the mask thumbnail to see how the mask works.

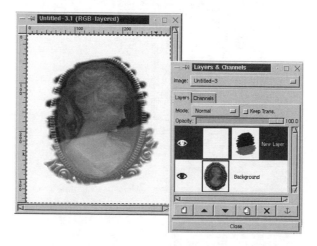

Viewing the Mask

If you want to view only the mask in the image window, hold down the Alt key while clicking the mask thumbnail image. A green border will appear around the thumbnail to indicate mask visibility. Alt+click again to view as normal. To view your layer with no mask, Ctrl+click on the mask thumbnail, and you will see a red border around the thumbnail indicating the mask is hidden. Ctrl+click again to return.

Applying the Mask

After you have a mask the way you want it, right-click on the mask thumbnail to bring up the menu and select Apply Layer mask. This brings up an options box, as seen in Figure 10.6, which gives you a choice of whether to apply or discard the mask.

FIGURE 10.6

With these options, you can apply the mask, thus merging it with the layer, or discard it, meaning it will be totally removed.

Most filters and effects can be applied to masks, giving you great creative freedom when making them. However, some filters and effects cannot be utilized until the mask has been applied to the layer.

Masks with Selections and Channels

If you have made a complex selection and would like to make it into a mask, add a new layer mask and click on the Layer Mask icon to activate it. The selection will still be active (as shown by the flashing marquee) and you can manipulate it within the mask.

If you have already made a mask, but would like to turn it into a selection, you can do that also. Look in the Layers menu and you will see an option called Mask to Selection. This automatically turns the mask into a selection, which can be useful if you want to edit the mask further by utilizing the selection options, such as grow, shrink, feather, and such.

By using the Copy and Paste functions, you can paste a selection or an entire image directly into a layer mask, where it then becomes the grayscale mask. This is a neat effect to use if you want to merge two images into one.

To add a mask to an image containing only one layer, you must first add an alpha channel by going to the Layer menu and clicking Add Alpha Channel. You can then add the layer mask as usual. When editing the mask, the black areas will appear as the checkered transparency. You can add another layer and lower it under the original layer, and the mask will allow the lowered layer to show through the transparent areas.

Mask Tutorials

Now you've seen the beginnings of how this masking business works, but it can be kind of confusing until you actually do a few. By completing each of the following tutorials, you should gain a good basic understanding of the way masks work. Once again, you will prove correct the old adage about experience being the best teacher.

Gradient Masks

Gradients are one of the easiest ways to make masks, and you can really get some cool effects by using the two together.

For this lesson, open the image named elephants.jpg from the CD-ROM (see Figure 10.7), or feel free to use one of your own.

FIGURE 10.7

Let's see how a gradient mask will affect this image!

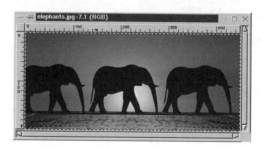

1. First of all, right-click the image and select Layers, Layers and Channels, to bring up the Layer dialog box, and then add a new layer in white.

2. Right-click the new layer name to bring up the menu and add a layer mask in white. You will now see only a blank white area in your image window.

3. Set the foreground color to black and the background color to white in the toolbox. (This is the default, so they are probably already set as such.)

4. Double-click on the Gradient tool to bring up the gradient options. Choose Linear. Leave everything else at the default settings.

5. In the image window, place the gradient in the mask beginning not quite all the way over to the right and dragging all the way to the left.

You've just created your first gradient mask. It should look something like Figure 10.8.

FIGURE 10.8

The gradient mask has the elephants walking out of a mist.

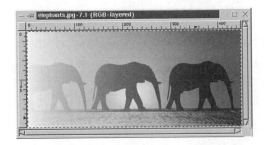

10

Photo Edge Masks

For these tutorials, you will use the image tiger.jpg (see Figure 10.9) from the CD-ROM.

FIGURE 10.9

Through masking, you can give this image several different looks.

For the first tutorial, another gradient mask will be used.

1. Begin by opening the image and follow the preceding steps 1 through 3 from the previous lesson to get the mask started.

2. Double-click the Gradient tool to bring up the options, but this time, choose Shapeburst Angular.

3. Place your cursor right in the center of the image and drag to the edge in any direction. A unique photo edge effect, as shown in Figure 10.10, can be created in just a matter of moments!

FIGURE 10.10

This technique comes in handy for "softening" the look of an image.

For even more editing control on gradient masks, right-click on the image to bring up the menu, and select Image, Colors, Brightness-Contrast. Notice the different effects you can achieve by increasing the contrast (see Figure 10.11).

FIGURE 10.11

This is the same mask as before, but with the contrast adjusted to around 85 or so.

You've seen what you can do with a gradient mask. Now let's do something a little different with another mask.

1. Open your image and add a new white layer.

2. Add a layer mask, but this time in black so you can see through it to the image.

3. Activate the Bézier selection tool and select an area in a unique shape surrounding the head in the image, as in Figure 10.11.

4. Right-click in the image window to bring up the menu, and choose Select, Invert.

5. Set the foreground color in the toolbox to a very light gray. Activate the Paintbrush tool, choose a large brush, and paint the gray in the now selected area around the tiger's head. Deactivate the selection. As illustrated in Figure 10.12, there's another kind of photo edge easily mastered with the use of masks.

FIGURE 10.12

Your photo edge creation capabilities are unlimited after you learn to apply masks.

10

Just for fun, let's apply one final step to this last mask to really make it special.

1. To bring back the selection, you can either select Edit, Undo or right-click on the mask thumbnail in the Layer dialog window and click Mask to Selection. You will see the marquee reappear around the tiger's head.

2. Right-click on the thumbnail again and choose Apply Layer Mask. When the options box pops up, choose Apply there also. This will attach the mask to the layer, but you will still see the selection. Once again, right-click the image and choose Select, Invert.

3. Right-click again on the image and select Script-Fu, Shadows, Drop Shadow. When the options window pops up, set the blur radius to 30, opacity to 100, and make sure the Allow Resizing option is unchecked. Deactivate the selection, and see what a difference the drop shadow has made to your photo edge—check out Figure 10.13.

FIGURE 10.13

A drop shadow applied after masking really makes this image stand out!

Text Mask

For this last tutorial on masking, let's attempt something a little more intricate. First of all, you will need to open two images from the CD-ROM, lion1.jpg and clouds.jpg (see Figure 10.14).

FIGURE 10.14

For this technique, use two images together.

1. Go to clouds.jpg and right-click, Edit, Copy.
2. Now, go to lion1.jpg and add a new layer. Paste the cloud image into the layer and anchor it.
3. Right-click on the cloud layer and select Add Layer Mask. Choose white in the Mask Options box.

4. Set the foreground color in the toolbox to black, and activate the Text tool.

5. Click on the image to bring up the text options and choose a nice chunky font and set the size fairly large. Type in whatever text you desire and click OK. Wow, look at what has just happened to your image! Because the text was inserted in black (transparent) into the mask, it has allowed portions of the lion image to show through the clouds, as illustrated in Figure 10.15. Now, don't you love masking?

FIGURE 10.15

Masking has enabled an interesting merging of two images with text.

10

Summary

In this hour, you learned about the magic of masks and a few of the techniques involved in creating and using them. By learning how to work with masks effectively, you have gained a valuable new skill in the world of image manipulation.

Q&A

Q If I use the Mask to Selection option, which part of the mask becomes the selection?

A The opaque (white) portion of the mask is the part that will become your selected area. If you want the transparent (black) area to be selected, you can perform the Mask to Selection function, and then use the Select menu to choose Select, Invert.

Q I made a pretty cool mask. Can I save it to use in another image?

A You sure can, but it's a little tricky. First, add a new layer in black and place it directly below the masked layer. Turn off layer visibility in all layers except the black and the masked layer so that you see only the mask in the image window and select Edit, Copy Visible. Now create a new image window with the same dimensions and select Edit, Paste. Save it in your choice of format and when you want to use it again, copy and paste it into the new image's layer mask. If your new image is a different size, you might want to rescale the mask image to match before you move it.

Exercise

Practice your mask making abilities on simple images and get to where you feel comfortable creating and using them. Try applying masks to images of your own using the same lessons you learned in the tutorials with the CD-ROM images.

HOUR 11

Special Effects

The first part of this book has been devoted to the intrinsic nature of the GIMP, how it works, and how you can find your way around to recognize and use the basic tools and functions required to get the job done.

Because you've studied so hard and accomplished so much in such a short time, I think you deserve a break, so for now, and essentially for the next few hours, consider that the bell has rung and recess has begun—have some fun with graphics!

This hour, you will look at an assortment of special effects that can be easily performed with the aid of the basic GIMP tools and a little imagination.

Tips and Tricks

What I mean by *special effects* is the art of creating or adding some distinguishing characteristic to an image, whether to give the appearance of a real-life object or just to achieve something that looks cool. The following is a list of a few things to keep in mind when you are thinking about special effects.

- Many times through experimentation or just plain playing around, you can stumble across an astonishing effect. When experimenting, try to keep a mental note of the steps you perform as you go so that you'll be able to duplicate the look if you find a good one.

- Of the available tools, one of the handiest for producing awesome looks is the Gradient tool, which was introduced in Hour 7, "Working with Color." If you haven't yet toyed around much with this, I encourage you to do so now. Open the Gradient dialog box and check out the various built-in gradients.

- So many factors must be taken into consideration when trying to achieve a certain look. Take a close look at the objects around you in the room. Notice the way the light shines on them and the shadows they make. Try to visualize what steps it would involve to create a realistic looking graphic of a particular object.

Creating Sharp Images from Scratch

Sometimes you can get a really good graphic idea in your head, but you need to know the right techniques to make it happen onscreen. Your goal this hour is to cover some of the more common tricks to help you learn to create the look you want.

Begin by looking at a couple of ways to create *something* from *nothing*.

Simple and Complex Shapes

Forming shapes with the selection tools can be a quick-and-easy way to create images. In just a few steps, you can make a fairly complex object out of a simple beginning shape.

To illustrate this point, I'm going to start out here by opening a new blank image window, adding a transparent layer, and using the Lasso tool to form a single odd-shaped selection, as in Figure 11.1. Open a new window and follow along for practice.

FIGURE 11.1

This little selection stands a pretty good chance of actually becoming an interesting piece of work.

Now you can add some color; I've chosen purple and black as the foreground and background colors in the toolbox. Bring up the gradient options by double-clicking the Gradient tool. Leave most of the default settings in place, but change the gradient option to Bilinear. This will enable the color to gradate from black to purple and back to black again.

Apply the gradient starting from the middle portion and dragging to one end of the selection. You should have something similar to Figure 11.2.

FIGURE 11.2

The bilinear gradient adds color and depth.

Okay, now you have the basic start you need to form your shape. With the selection still active (as indicated by the flashing marquee), right-click on the image and select Edit, Copy, and then select Edit, Paste. This will give you an identical selection placed over the first one. For this new selection, use the Transform tool to rotate it. Double-click the Transform tool to bring up the options, and then choose Rotate. You'll see the rotation box appear around the selection. Grab one of the corner handles and rotate it to the right (around 20 degrees). Now activate the Move tool and move the rotated selection to where you can line up the tip of it with the tip of the first selection, as in Figure 11.3. You undoubtedly see where I'm headed with this, don't you?

FIGURE 11.3

The raw beginnings of an object taking shape.

11

Repeat the previous steps of copying, pasting, rotating, and moving, but add another 20 degrees to each rotation. Keep repeating as often as needed to bring the shape to the stage of desired completion, as shown in Figure 11.4.

By using the previous technique of copying, pasting, and rotating with basic geometric shapes, you can form some pretty interesting objects, as illustrated in Figure 11.5. (If you enjoy working with geometric shapes, you're going to love the GIMP plug-in known as Gfig. You'll learn more about it in Hour 20, Using Plug-ins and Extensions.")

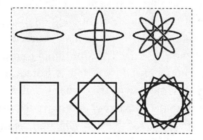

Drop Shadows and Glows

The technique of applying drop shadows and underglows can really make an image stand out and be noticed, and is easily accomplished in the GIMP by using layers.

There are a couple of ways to add a drop shadow, one of them being in the shadow options of Script-fu. This one is simple; right-click on the image, select Script-fu, Shadows. You have your choice of drop shadow or perspective shadow, each having various options.

Another way to get a drop shadow is to actually make one out of the image shape itself, which is the method explained here.

Add a drop shadow to the previous homemade image and you'll see what a difference it can make.

First, select the image that you want to place a shadow behind. For the image you're using here, choose the Fuzzy Select tool (with Sample Merge activated) on the background, and then choose Select, Invert. If the selection you are working on is part of the background layer, you will need to select Edit, Copy, and then select Edit, Paste to paste it into a new transparent layer before adding the shadow.

To make the shadow, right-click on the image and bring up the Layer dialog box. Add another new transparent layer. Name it *Shadow*. Use the Bucket Fill tool to fill the selected area in the new layer with solid black. Deactivate the selection.

Right-click and select Filters, Blur, Gaussian Blur (either one), and apply a blur strength of about 15 or so. In the Layer dialog window, use the Lower Layer button to place the shadow layer under the image layer. Because the shadow is in its own layer, you can use the layer's opacity slider to make the shadow appear paler if you like.

What you will want to do now is offset the shadow so that it appears that the light source making it is over to one side. To do this, right-click and go to Image, Channel Ops, Offset. This brings up an options box where you can choose the amount of offset (in pixels) for both the X and Y values of the shadow layer. (Remember, X is horizontal and Y is vertical.) Positive numbers will offset the shadow to the right for X and down for Y. If you want the shadow up or to the left, enter negative numbers (for example, -8). In Figure 11.6, the drop shadow layer offset is X8, Y8. You can also offset the shadow by moving the layer, but the channel ops gives you more control if you want to offset it in an exact amount.

11

FIGURE 11.6

Use the offset to place the shadow in either direction. Here it is shown down and to the right from the image itself.

Now you'll work on giving a glow to a selection.

For this, you'll want to begin by following the same first steps as you used to create the drop shadow. Place the selection in a transparent layer. Add another transparent layer and name it *Glow*. This time, however, instead of filling the selected area of the new layer with black, use a lighter color. White is good for achieving a halo effect, whereas bright green gives a radioactive appearance. (I am somewhat partial to red and purple glows myself.)

Deactivate the selection and apply a Gaussian Blur, this time making it a slightly higher blur strength. Try 20 to begin with. You can play around with the blur strength to get the desired effect. Lower the glow layer under the image layer.

Because my image began on a white background, the glow doesn't show up too well, so I've used the Bucket Fill tool here to fill in the background layer under the image and shadow with a darker color (see Figure 11.7).

FIGURE 11.7

A glow is made by using a brighter color than a drop shadow and leaving out the offset.

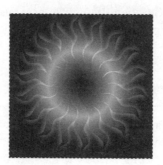

Imitating Real Objects in 3D

One thing the Gradient tool is extremely useful for is to give a sense of depth to an object so that it has more of a 3D appearance rather than just a flat two-dimensional look. In the next tutorial, you will start with a simple shape and take it through several changes to make it seem more *real*.

Open a new blank image window with a white background. Bring up the Layer dialog box and add a new transparent layer to work on. (The reason I like to add a transparent layer before beginning is so that later on, if I choose to do so, I can easily change background colors without affecting the object I'm making.)

Use the Ellipse/Circle tool and make a perfect circular selection in the image window. (Reminder: Holding Shift as you select will create perfect circles.) Open the Pattern dialog box, choose a pattern, and use the Pattern Fill option of the Bucket tool to fill the circle. Then deactivate the selection. In Figure 11.8, I've begun by filling my circular selection with a built-in GIMP pattern called *Marble #1*.

FIGURE 11.8

A plain circular selection gets a pattern fill to start it on its way to becoming an object.

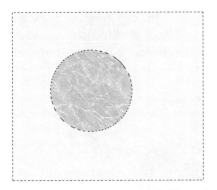

Now you will attempt to give it some depth. Imagine there is a light source just above and to the left of the circle. It would shine on the area of the circle it was closest to and the other side of the circle would appear darker because it wasn't in the path of the light.

To achieve this look, you will rely on the Gradient tool. Because you don't want to change the color or cover the pattern, but do want to add depth, you need a gradient that goes from transparent (letting the complete pattern show through where the light is hitting the object) to black (forming the shadowy darker side). This is a good opportunity to make a custom gradient. Bring up the gradient editor by selecting File, Dialogs, Gradient Editor, and clicking the New Gradient button in the upper-right corner. This brings up a box where you can give the gradient a name. (I've named mine trans-to-black.)

Now, going back to the gradient dialog box, right-click in the area where the gradient colors appear and another options box will pop up. This is where you set the colors you want in the gradient. In the top of the options box, you'll see where it says *Left End Points Color*. This means the color that will begin at the left side of the gradient. Because you can place gradients in any direction you want by merely dragging the cursor in the different directions, it doesn't really matter which color you choose to go on the left or right. Directly under Left End Points Color is the option called *Load From*. Clicking that will bring up a window where you can choose a color to insert into the left end point. Because you are making transparent to black, choose transparent, which is RGBA (0.000, 0.000, 0.000, 0.000) and appears as the checkerboard. Now right-click again to bring up the same options, but this time go to *Right End Points Color* and choose black. Your custom gradient is now set in the gradient editor. You can leave it in the editor for future projects.

Activate the Gradient tool by double-clicking it to bring up the options, and then choose Radial for the gradient option and Custom (from editor) for the blend option. The radial option gives a sunburst effect if it is applied from the center out. But because you want

11

the effect of the light source to be in the upper-left, place the cursor in the selection where the light source would be shining on to the object, and drag it to the lower-right outer portion of the selection. Now the circle you began with will take the shape of a sphere, as in Figure 11.9.

FIGURE 11.9

It's amazing what a little gradient shadowing can do to a plain, flat circle!

Take the light effect even one step further and apply an extra little sheen to your sphere to give it more of a glossy appearance. Activate the Airbrush tool, set the foreground color to white, and open the Brush dialog box to choose a medium-sized, soft-edged brush. By spraying in a little spotlighted area right at the point where the imaginary light is shining, the sphere will have gained a much shinier look, as in Figure 11.10. (This is called a *specular*. Specular highlights appear as bright white reflections of the light source on the surface of the object.)

FIGURE 11.10

With the addition of a specular, the sphere takes on the look of a well-polished bowling ball.

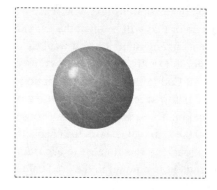

Now try another little trick and cut off the top of the sphere and hollow it out to make a bowl.

Activate the Ellipse Select tool and make an elliptical selection in the upper half of the sphere, starting at a point on one outer edge and ending on the opposite edge, as in Figure 11.11.

FIGURE 11.11

The elliptical selection is the first step to cutting the sphere.

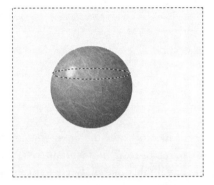

Now, right-click on the image and choose Select, Invert. Use the Eraser tool to erase the portion of the sphere that's now just above the elliptical part. Once again, right-click, choose Select, Invert, and your image should look like the one in Figure 11.12.

11

FIGURE 11.12

Now it's starting to resemble a bowl.

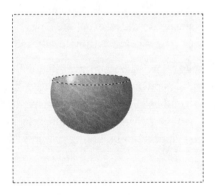

All you need to do now is shade the inner portion of the bowl. Because your imaginary light source is coming in from the upper-left, it is shining into the bowl at an angle, lighting the right inner portion, with the left side of the bowl shadowing in. To get this to look right, use the transparent to black custom gradient that you made previously, but this time you will apply it in the opposite direction.

Open the Gradient dialog box and click on the trans-to-black gradient to select it. Activate the Gradient tool and, with Radial as the gradient option, and Custom as the blend option, begin the gradient to the far right side of the elliptical selection and drag it to the left. Deactivate the selection, and your bowl is complete (see Figure 11.13).

FIGURE **11.13**

The Gradient tool plays a major part in achieving a realistic look.

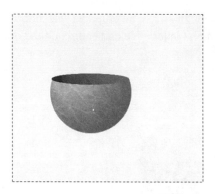

Okay, that was pretty easy, wasn't it? Now take the bowl you created and add a perspective shadow to give it one more touch of realism. While there is a perspective shadow filter in the Script-fu options, you can do this one by hand so that you will get a better understanding of how a perspective shadow works.

By noticing where the light source is coming from, you can judge where the shadow will fall. An easy way to understand this is to think of how the shadows around your house fall at different times of the day. At high noon, there are no shadows because the sun is directly above you, and as it slowly moves west to set, the shadows get longer and longer on the east side. Thinking realistically in those terms then, because the light source was on the left of the bowl, the perspective shadow will naturally fall to the right.

The first step is to select the bowl. Now open the Layer dialog box and add a new transparent layer named *Shadow*. In this new layer, fill the selected area with black (gray if you want a lighter shadow). To get the shadow to fall to the right, activate the Transform tool and choose Perspective. Grab the upper corners of the selection one at a time and drag to the right until the shadow appears to be falling correctly according to the light source, as in Figure 11.14.

FIGURE **11.14**

The shadow layer can be manipulated into shape using the Transform tool.

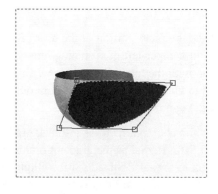

Deactivate the selection and apply a Gaussian Blur, just as you did for the drop shadow. Move the shadow layer underneath the bowl layer, and there you have it. You can lower the opacity in the layer if the shadow is too dark (see Figure 11.15).

FIGURE 11.15

The effect is accomplished by blurring and moving the shadow layer under the bowl layer.

Stained Glass Effect

There are many different ways to get a stained glass look. After you start experimenting, you might find that it's easier than you imagined. To get you started, you'll create a simple stained glass image.

Open a new image window (white) in a size large enough to be comfortable to work with. The first thing you'll do here is make the basic outline of the *lead* that will hold the *glass* panes together. Open the Layer dialog box and add a new transparent layer. Name it *Lead*. (You're going to be using the original plain background layer later on, so don't delete it.) Set the foreground color in the toolbox to a medium gray.

To make the outline design, use the Paintbrush tool to draw in the lines. Or do as I've done in Figure 11.16 and draw a combination of straight paintbrush lines and form simple shapes with the different selection tools using the Stroke function. Because the stroke size is controlled by the chosen brush size, the lines will all match. (Here I am using a brush called Circle Fuzzy 05).

Now to give the lead some depth and thickness. Right-click and select Filters, Map, Bump map. When the options box appears, leave the default settings, but do make sure you have the correct layer (lead) selected under the Bump option. Apply the filter.

Add a new transparent layer (name it *Color*) and lower it under the Lead layer.

With the Color layer active, use the Fuzzy Select tool to select an area within the lead lines. (To do this, make sure that Sample Merged option is checked in the Fuzzy Select options.) To ensure that the selected area goes right in to the lead lines, you might want

11

to right-click, and choose Select, Grow (by about 2 pixels or so). Use the Bucket Fill tool to fill the selection with a color of your choice. Repeat the Select, Grow, and Bucket Fill steps for each of the other areas between the lines, using a different color for each until the image is completely colored in, as in Figure 11.17.

FIGURE 11.16

Straight lines and stroked selections are good for drawing a simple design.

FIGURE 11.17

You can make the stained glass as colorful as you like, or use one color for all the panes if you'd want a more monochromatic look.

It's getting there, but let's add a little texture to the glass panes. Add another new transparent layer and call it *Texture*. Lower it to just under the Color layer. Right-click on the image and choose Select, All. (The reason to select the entire layer is because you are going to use the Bucket Fill tool. Remember that the Bucket Fill must have either a selection or an area of color to fill. Because the layer is transparent, it must be selected.) Now open the Pattern dialog box and choose a pattern that has a good rough texture to it. (Here I've chosen one called Green 3D.) Use the Bucket Fill tool (set to Pattern fill) to fill the new layer with the pattern. Because you want to use the texture from this pattern, but not the green color, right-click and select Image, Colors, Desaturate.

Now you need to blend the layers so that the texture can be seen through the colored panes of glass. Go to the Layer dialog box and set the Blend mode to Overlay in the texture layer. Activate the color layer and do the same for it. Your stained glass should look similar to Figure 11.18.

FIGURE 11.18

The addition of the texture gives it a more realistic appearance.

You could leave it at this, but don't you want to see some light shining through your window?

Activate the original white background layer. Set the foreground color in the toolbox to white and the background color to black. Open the Gradient tool and choose either Shapeburst Angular or Radial for the Gradient option.

Place the cursor in the center of the image and drag to any edge. The light now brightens up the stained glass (see Figure 11.19).

FIGURE 11.19

A light shining in is a must for a stained glass image.

11

Summary

There are usually several different ways to achieve a particular look. In this hour, you learned some of the techniques that are used to create certain effects. You'll find in the world of graphics, the more techniques you know, the better off you'll be. Even if you think you'll never use a specific effect, it can't hurt to practice the techniques and learn how each step works, so you can apply that knowledge in various combinations to come up with tricks and techniques of your own.

Q&A

Q I've seen special effect tutorials for other graphics programs. Can I use these same lessons in the GIMP?

A Definitely! Most graphics tutorials can be easily translated to work in the GIMP. Of course, because all program interfaces are different, you might have to experiment a little to find the corresponding tools, filters, and so on. In fact, translating other tutorials can be a great learning tool for finding your way around the GIMP.

Exercise

For this hour's assignment, look around the Web and find a graphic that appeals to you— try and find something simple yet challenging. Study it and see if you can use the tools available in the GIMP to duplicate it (or even improve upon it).

HOUR 12

Using Filters to Improve or Distort Images

Filters are one of the best features in the GIMP. With them, you can enhance any image and create all kinds of special effects to shock and amaze. Filters are perhaps one of the most fun things to use with GIMP, as well as one of the most useful.

By using filters, you will be able to do things to your images that would take quite a while to duplicate by hand. So filters are not only neat to play with, but they can also be a tremendous time saver when creating images that you use frequently.

What Exactly Are Filters?

Basically, filters belong to a group of functions in the GIMP known as *plug-ins*. A plug-in is an extension to GIMP that lends it added functionality and extends its capabilities. A filter, then, is a specific kind of plug-in that is involved in manipulating graphics directly to achieve any number of alterations and special effects. For the most part, most plug-ins are filters.

NEW TERM *Plug-in*—A piece of code written to interface directly with the GIMP. This allows for third parties to augment the GIMP's already impressive list of features and capabilities.

Filter—Any plug-in that specifically alters an image in various ways to create new and unique effects.

For those of you who have used graphics programs before, plug-in filters in the GIMP work similarly to plug-ins in Photoshop and the like. Additionally, there are more and more filters being written for the GIMP all the time. (And the best part is that, to my knowledge, they are all free and open).

Most of the plug-in filters are not written by the original authors of GIMP, they are written by many people from all over the Internet in order to fill a specific need. However, this can theoretically mean that some filters are bound to be a little less useful or well written than others. For the record, I've installed every GIMP plug-in known, and 99 percent of them work like a champ.

Many filters have their own dialog interface, although they tend to follow the defacto interface conventions and for the most part fit in with the GIMP quite seamlessly.

Using Filters

You use filters just like you would any other GIMP function—right-click, and go to the Filters submenu. From there, you will have access to a whole plethora of special effects filters that you will no doubt spend countless hours playing with over and over. The selected filter will then either directly apply the effect or pull up a dialog box from which you can select options.

Filters that Come with the GIMP

If you installed the GIMP from the CD-ROM that comes with this book, chances are you already have access to most of the plug-ins available at this time. However, I will begin with the simplest of plug-in filters that come with the GIMP.

The graphics filters in the GIMP are all accessible by right-clicking the Filters menu. From there, you will see all the filters sub-categorized into different menus.

You are going to begin using filters that are most commonly used to improve photos and images.

Blur and Sharpen Filters

The simplest and most often used of all filter functions is the Blur function. This function has three available filters that work in slightly different ways. (If one thing can be said about UNIX people, it's that we strive to be thorough.)

Blur 2.0

The first blur filter, accessible from the Blur submenu of the Filters menu, is named Blur (see Figure 12.1).

FIGURE 12.1

Blurring can add a soft touch to your pictures and cover up some flaws in the process.

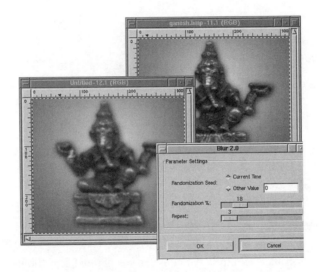

The Blur dialog box has a few options to choose from, as shown in Figure 12.1.

- **Randomization Seed**—A value that the plug-in uses in order to create a random blur value—this can be anything. But unlike most blur filters, this one lets you choose the value you want to use for a randomization seed, instead of just picking one for you. (I fail to see where this could be useful, but it is kind of empowering). In any case, the seed can be based on the current time or on a value you supply.

- **Randomization %**—The amount that the randomized Blur function is applied to your image. This, more or less, alters the amount of blur.

- **Repeat**—The number of passes the filter uses to blur your image. As with anything, the more times it is blurred, the deeper the blur effect.

12

Gaussian Blur

Below the Blur option on the Filters menu you will see two Gaussian Blur filters: IIR and RLE. They do essentially the same thing, they let you blur an image by varying degrees.

Supposedly, IIR is somewhat faster for photographic quality images whereas RLE is better for line art and such. (I personally have never really seen any difference between the two.) In any case, to use a Gaussian blur, select it from the menu, and a dialog box will appear as in figure 12.2 (in this case the RLE dialog box).

FIGURE 12.2

These blur filters are a little more straightforward—if not as feature-laden.

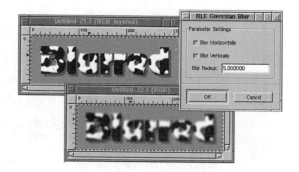

The Gaussian Blur options include the following:

- **Blur Horizontally and Blur Vertically**—Defines how the blur is applied—by selecting both of them your blur is applied evenly on both planes.
- **Blur Radius**—Controls the radius of the applied blur (how many neighboring pixels are affected). The higher the number, the more intense the blur.

Pixelize

Another handy blur filter is called *Pixelize*. Stated simply, it distorts your image by enlarging the pixels, creating an image much like the masking of anonymous faces on the six o'clock evening news (see Figure 12.3). You can set how large you want your pixels to be, as well.

FIGURE 12.3

Well... maybe not a true improvement in this case. Pixelization is a neat effect. Sometimes it can add that "digitized" feel to an image.

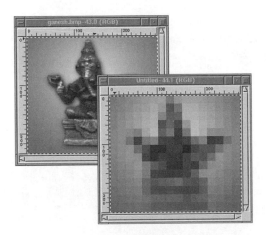

Motion Blur

Motion blur—now here's a cool effect (if used in the right place). It emulates an object in motion by applying a custom directional blur. This adds the effect of motion trails that are universally recognizable.

Of course, slow shutter-speed, or really bad photography, causes this effect in real life. In some cases, however, it does capture the effect of a fast moving object. (Or just really shaky hands!) Whatever effect you're going for, this filter works quite nicely (see Figure 12.4).

FIGURE 12.4

As you can see, this effect can be valuable with many graphics and photos. Notice how the effect makes the truck appear to be traveling at high speed, while the same effect makes the second picture seem to have had a shaky-handed photographer.

12

In the Motion blur dialog box, the Length option refers to the length of the trail effect.

The Blur type options enable you to choose from three blur effects, one of which (Linear) is shown in Figure 12.4, and the other two are shown in Figure 12.5. These effects are great for experimentation.

FIGURE 12.5

Changing the blur type can make quite a difference.

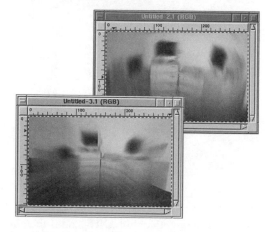

Angle sets the direction of the blur trail in degrees of a circle.

Enhancing Your Images

The next filters are those that do the opposite of blur; they attempt to sharpen and enhance graphics. It's been my experience that applications are usually better at blurring images than at sharpening them. There are, however, certain situations where using these filters sparingly can vastly improve the quality of your image, as shown in Figure 12.6. By covering flaws, cleaning out anomalies, and adding just a touch of desired effect, it is possible to rescue those photos that might have been unusable before. This means making them appear better without any visible signs of digital alteration.

FIGURE 12.6

Making a fuzzy image look much cleaner and sharper.

Sharpen

As you can see from Figure 12.6, the Sharpen filter can help to add detail and tweak a photo to a better state. Of course, this filter is no substitute for a good scan or photography. It can't fix everything; too much of this effect will result in an effect that's easily detected as *fake*, but it can add just enough sharpness to make the difference between a photo that's slightly fuzzy and one that's clear and focused.

It works by finding the areas in an image with high contrast and drastic color changes (such as edges of things) and increasing the brightness and contrast in those areas between the neighboring pixels.

In the Sharpen dialog box, you will see a thumbnail preview of your image, and a slider control for adjusting sharpness. This effect is best used sparingly and subtly. It works best when no one can tell that any alterations have been made, and it's a great filter for the heavily detail-oriented individual.

Despeckle

Despeckle attempts to remove noise from flawed images. This is especially effective on scanned images, graphics scanned from print media, or any picture containing scratches, odd pixels scattered here and there, and other anomalies (see Figure 12.7).

FIGURE 12.7

This filter is used to clean up spotty images. It is applied very thickly here to illustrate that this can also be used as an effects filter, giving the image a painted look.

Radius adjusts the size of the areas in which the filter smoothes out the colors between neighboring pixels. A value of 1 is an area of 3 × 3 pixels, a value of 2 is 5 × 5, a value of 3 is 7 × 7, and so on.

The Despeckle dialog box, (shown in Figure 12.7), shows that you can use this filter with or without the Adaptive and Recursive options. Adaptive will try and determine the best radius value for you. (Sometimes this works well, and sometimes it doesn't). Recursive, in effect, increases the intensity of the effect—sometimes a little too much. (Recursive applies more effect in a smaller radius size.) By using these options together, you get an effect that's recursively applied in an adaptively sized radius (the same as adaptive, but a little stronger).

Black Level and White Level options are also available. Use Black Level to repair damage on darker pixels, and use White Level for lighter pixels.

NL Filter

The NL filter tries to combine the best of the Sharpen and Despeckle filters. In fact, this plug-in is actually a combination of filters (see Figure 12.8).

FIGURE 12.8

Attempting to clean this spotty image up a bit.

The Alpha Trimmed Mean filter is a lot like the Despeckle filter—it tries to remove image noise. It also works in much the same way as the Despeckle filter. You can adjust the radius as you would in Despeckle, and the Alpha variable in this case changes the behavior of the filter. A lower value will smooth pixels, as in a blur filter, and a higher alpha will try to despot the image.

Optimal Estimation is another smoothing filter that is similar in effect to Alpha Trimmed Mean. It works by determining the optimal range of color values within an area of surrounding pixels.

Edge Enhancement is similar to the Enhance filter—it tries to *unblur* an image by brightening and sharpening the edges (areas of contrasting color) in an image.

Destripe

The Destripe filter tries to fix images with muddy stripes (or snail trails) on them—usually a result of a poor scan job.

Noise Filters

Noise filters are useful for a number of things. They can improve images that have too much contrast between color boundaries or are too sharp. Also, they can be used to add a different texture to an image.

Noisify

This filter, shown in Figure 12.9, lets you add and adjust random *noisy* pixels in an image.

FIGURE 12.9

Adding texture with the noise filter.

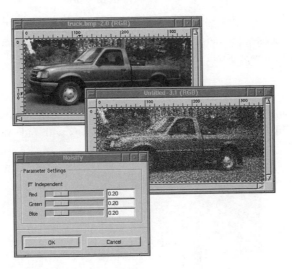

12

Each RGB channel is individually adjustable. A value of 0 is no noise, and a value of 1 is total garbage. Obviously, this filter should be used with subtlety.

Randomize

This filter is similar to Noisify, but with many more options and effects (see Figure 12.10). It shifts the colors of the pixels in the graphic. The Randomization types determine how this filter accomplishes this.

FIGURE 12.10

Randomize is a good effect for adding many different tones and textures to your photo. (Who picked the names Hurl, Pick, and Slur, anyway?)

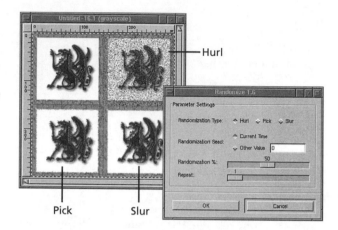

Hurl

Pick   Slur

- **Hurl**—Changes a pixel's color to a random value.
- **Pick**—Picks a color value to apply to a pixel from a randomly chosen neighbor.
- **Slur**—Chooses the neighbors above a pixel for a color value. This results in a slightly different effect than Pick.

Spread

Spread does what it sounds like—it spreads pixels around in any direction and amount you choose. This can be useful for creating animations with fade-outs and so forth (see Figure 12.11).

FIGURE 12.11

Spreading an image can create a unique and very cool effect.

The Spread filter, if used *sparingly*, is great for reducing the effect in gradients commonly known as *banding*. Banding is where the gradient shift is so pronounced that the individual colors are visible in banded lines, especially on video hardware that renders at less than 24-bit color. This is not a good effect; however, a little spreading can fix this (see Figure 12.12).

By setting your levels subtly, you can effectively add just enough randomization to rid your image of that annoying banding. By the way, this effect is great for use on HTML documents with gradient background images. You'll achieve a much smoother effect this way.

FIGURE 12.12

This effect might be difficult to spot in a black-and-white book, so you may want to try it out yourself. Also, sometimes the Randomize filter works better on gradients than the Spread filter does. It just takes tweaking.

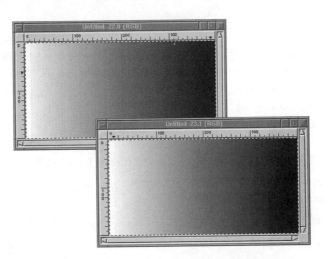

12

Obtaining Filters

To obtain new plug-in filters, you need look no further than www.gimp.org. There you will find a site called The GIMP Plug-in Registry. It has a database of all registered plug-ins for you to scroll through and choose from. Most of these are filters, although other functions are available here as well. Download and compile those you like. Of course, for now you are concerned only with the effects filters specifically, and luckily those are generally the easiest to install.

To install a graphics filter, you need to untar/ungzip the file, read the README document, and run the plug-in installation tool called gimptool, like this

```
tar -zxvf plugin.tar.gz
cat README ¦ more
gimptool —install-bin plugin
```

This will compile the source code and install the binary plug-in for you. Pretty simple, actually. Restart GIMP for changes to take effect.

Summary

This hour gave you some insight into how filters and plug-ins work, and how images can be improved by using filters (and not just distorted with a lot of weird effects that are cool but never used). Of course, you're not done messing with filters and plug-ins just yet—in fact, you're just getting started. Obviously, this book can't cover all the plug-ins there are, but going over the ones most commonly used will give you enough impetus to move into the various tutorials and techniques.

In order to use these filters effectively, the best advice is *less is more*. The filters covered in this hour are designed to help images move from okay to high quality. Using them too much can make your images look like they've been tampered with. You'll most likely use these filters when you want to avoid making your images look altered.

Q&A

Q What if I change my mind about a filter? Can I still undo it?

A Fortunately, yes. Undo functions with plug-ins just as it does with any of the standard tools. Just remember Ctrl+Z when you get into trouble with an image.

Q Are there any filters that are not plug-ins?

A Not to my knowledge. Filters are either plug-ins written by a third party, or something the GIMP deals with internally. (Assuming that anything working outside of the GIMP is considered a separate application.)

Exercise

The best thing to do with these particular filters is to tweak images; that is your assignment. Find some good scanned photos, perhaps of friends and family, and find the visible flaws in the images—few pictures are perfect. Then try to improve those photos with the filters, looking closely for any serious imperfections you can find, either technical or aesthetic. (The Zoom tool can be handy for this). As you work, you might find out that sometimes it is easy to *over-correct* an image, leaving it worse than before. The skill to acquire from this exercise is the ability to know when to stop. It takes some practice to get the hang of determining when you've tweaked enough. I've ruined many images by going one step to far. Thank goodness for multiple undo's!

Hour 13

Artistic Filters

You've seen a little of what filters can do. In this hour, you will expand on what you've learned in Hour 12, "Using Filters to Improve or Distort Images," and get into some of the more eccentric and exciting effects you can create with some filters and a little experimentation. These are the kinds of things that make the unhardened graphics newbie *ooh* and *ahh* with delight and amazement.

Using Filters Artistically

These filters (and most filters you encounter in GIMP) are designed to add some abstraction to your image—sometimes in order to approximate a certain real life effect (such as painting and brush techniques, murals, and so forth), and sometimes to create something new and unique. All filters are subcategorized into different menus such as Artistic, Color, Combine, Distort, and so forth, depending on what they do specifically, but ultimately they are made with the same goal in mind—to abstract your images.

You will use these filters in the same way you activated the enhancing filters in the previous hour—only the desired effects of using filters has changed somewhat. Now you should concentrate *not* on making your image more life-like, but just the opposite. Of course, there is no way to cover all the GIMP filters here because there are so many, but the most common and useful ones will be touched, giving you a basic understanding and the knowledge to apply them in given situations, such as the tutorials in upcoming hours. Many filters work in much the same way so it should be relatively easy to figure out what any new filters you encounter do and how they work.

Now then, perhaps the neatest filter available in GIMP is the GIMPressionist. This filter (or better yet, plug-in encompassing a whole suite of filters) does not come with the base distribution of GIMP at this time. However, if you installed the GIMP from the CD-ROM, chances are you do have it on your system. If not, it is available from the GIMP Plug-in Registry at http://registry.gimp.org/.

GIMPressionist

It's things like GIMPressionist that make running Linux and working with free software all worthwhile. It does many intensive and fantastic effects and textures, and it can make any ordinary image look really cool. The GIMPressionist will quickly become one of your most used and well-liked utilities in GIMP. It's great for creating a set of graphics with a matching look and feel (Web graphics come to mind), adding just enough texture to a photograph to transform it from ordinary to unique, with minimal effort, and doing some weird things with pictures.

The term GIMPressionist, as if you haven't already figured it out, is a play on words with impressionist, which is, of course, the famous school of art that uses different brushes, paints, and stroke methods to paint everyday subjects with that fuzzy, *just glanced-at* appearance. GIMPressionist expands on this concept by giving you access to many different brushes, styles, and patterns for you to distort your images just enough to give them an *impressionist tone*. And, as with anything in the GIMP, everything in GIMPressionist is expandable—you can add your own brushes and patterns later on if you choose. It really is a marvelous plug-in. It is also a pretty complex and sophisticated one, as you will soon see.

To use GIMPressionist, you obviously need an image to start with that you want to manipulate. In this example, as shown in Figure 13.1, start with an image and open the GIMPressionist dialog box by choosing Filters, Artistic. Before you begin, you should make sure that a local copy of the GIMPressionist data files are located in your .gimp directory (You can do this by copying the contents of /usr/share/gimp/gimpressionist to ~/.gimp). This will enable you to make customizations easily.

Remember that GIMPressionist, as with most plug-ins, needs a full-color RGB image on which to work. Indexed and grayscale images will have most filter options ghosted out.

FIGURE 13.1

The GIMPressionist dialog box. Papers are textures that you apply to the image using the brushes.

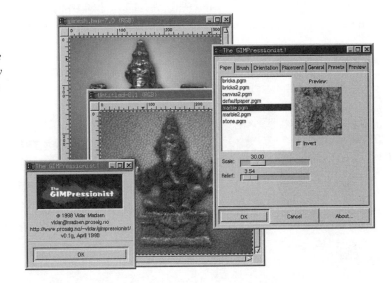

In the Paper area, GIMPressionist gives you options for a paper texture to apply to your image—this will be a kind of backdrop or canvas that your image will be *painted* on. The Scale lets you set the size of the pattern, and the relief changes the depth of the embossed effect. (A relief of 0 equals no textured canvas, which is sometimes more desirable.) Select any paper texture you like, and then click the Brush tab, as shown in Figure 13.2 (You can add more paper patterns by copying the pattern in grayscale PGM format to .gimp/gimpressionist/Papers.

13

FIGURE 13.2

GIMPressionist brushes. Installing more of these is as easy as copying a grayscale PGM file to the .gimp/gimpressionist/Brushes directory.

Here you will have many brushes to choose from. Which brush you use will alter the appearance of the entire effect, because the brush is the element that determines the texture of the painting effect. You can alter the size of the brush, Relief, and Stroke Density, which reflects how many times the brush is applied to the image. (A Stroke Density that's set too high can distort your image beyond all recognition— but sometimes you want that.). The slider below the brush preview sets the brightness/contrast of the brush in view. Figure 13.3 demonstrates the effect applied with different brushes.

FIGURE 13.3

As you can see, the wide range of brushes to choose from (and create) gives the GIMPressionist nearly infinite capabilities.

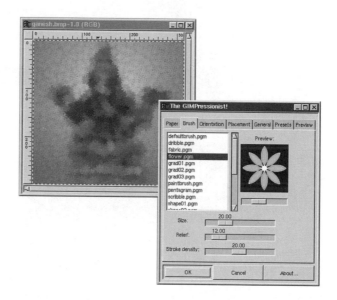

In the Orientation tab (see Figure 13.4), you will see options for altering the brush stroke pattern. These are fun to play with, but a little complex at first. The Directions option lets you choose how many different stroke positions your brush will create (the angles at which the brush is applied). The higher the number of stroke positions, the more complex and random the effect will appear (see Figure 13.4). The Start Angle option is the angle in degrees that your stroke position will start out with (an angle of 0 is the original brush angle as shown in the Brush preview). Angle Span is the amount of derivation from its original angle your brush will rotate.

The Orientation options let you change what type of directional application your brush will form. These are different patterns that determine the way in which the brush is applied to the picture. A Radial orientation applies the brush in a circular fashion around the image, each stroke painted from center outward. Random orientation paints them in any direction. These options are pretty self-explanatory. Sometimes the difference ensued by using these options is visible, and sometimes it's not—experiment.

FIGURE 13.4

Many ways in which a brush can be applied. Changing the direction and orientation values can drastically alter the feel of the image.

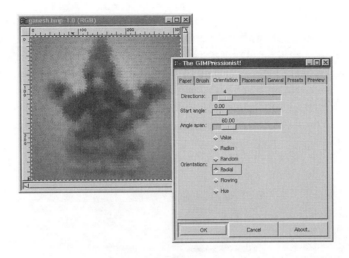

The Placement tab has two options: Random or Evenly Distributed. A randomly painted image (randomly applied brush) has a more organic feel, whereas an evenly distributed one has a much cleaner, more sterile feel.

By clicking the General tab, you will see options that will affect the texture of the painting itself. Edge Darken lets you create an effect similar to a photo edge mask by painting a border around your image. Edge Darken changes the width of your border; the border can be either a simple matching paper pattern or painted as a solid color. Paint Edges applies the effect all the way to the edge of the image, regardless of the presence border (see Figure 13.5).

FIGURE 13.5

General options for GIMPressionist and the difference between a solid and patterned border.

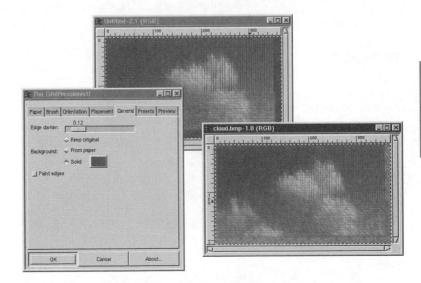

13

After tweaking and tinkering with the many GIMPressionist settings and spending a lot of time coming up with that perfect effect, you might want to save it in order to apply it to future images (or in order to create a matched set of graphics). The options in the Presets tab (see Figure 13.6) lets you do just that! In order to save all your brush, pattern, and stroke settings, click on Save Current, and you will be prompted to name your setting presets. After doing so, it should appear in the list (you might need to click the Refresh button in order to see your entry in the list for the first time). From now on, in order to apply your preset to an image, click Apply. All your settings are now in place, and clicking OK will apply your settings to the picture exactly as before.

FIGURE 13.6

Saving your settings is a must if you come up with anything extraordinarily cool. Additionally, the GIMPressionist comes with a few custom presets that are pretty good.

Now that you've been playing around with these settings, you will probably want to preview the effect before applying it, as it might need more tweaking. The Preview option (see Figure 13.7) enables you to do that. Just click the Update button to view your changes.

FIGURE 13.7

Previewing the changes before applying them or saving the preset can save a lot of time and energy.

One of my favorite things to do with the GIMPressionist is to use this effect in combination with layering to achieve a composite effect. This is actually pretty easy to do. By altering the background of an image differently than the focus of your composition, you can draw attention to the main subject.

- The first thing to do is to create a layered image. I will first copy the selected subject (with the Bézier tool), paste it into a new layer (see Figure 13.8), and then apply the GIMPressionist filter to the background layer, which is separated from the subject, in a way that will give it a surreal feel. For this example, I chose an effect that is pretty heavy to subdue the background (see Figure 13.9).

FIGURE 13.8

Copying the subject into a new layer.

FIGURE 13.9

The background layer gets a new look. Now the subject matter appears to be floating above the rest of the image.

13

As you can see, there are simply a million possibilities with the GIMPressionist plug-in.

IWarp

Have you ever seen Kai's Power Goo? Well, this is essentially the same thing under GIMP (with the benefit of being free and running in UNIX). With it, you can manipulate many intense warp effects by hand. You can pull up its dialog box by selecting the Distorts menu.

In the IWarp dialog box (see Figure 13.10), you can interact and apply the effect manually by dragging the mouse (and keeping the mouse button clicked) directly over the preview window. You will see six options for what kind of distort you want to apply.

- **Move**—Smudges the *paint* around your image.
- **Grow**—Enlarges the affected area.
- **Swirl CCW**—Swirls the area in a counter-clockwise fashion.
- **Remove**—Removes any applied effect in the given area. (This is a really neat effect to watch in action.)
- **Shrink**—Shrinks the area in a *pinching* fashion.
- **Swirl CW**—Swirls in a clockwise motion.

FIGURE 13.10

An IWarp effect in action—from different to just plain nuts. (I've always thought that lions would look cooler with big German Shepherd ears.)

At the top of the dialog box you will see two slider controls. Deform Radius adjusts the size of the area your mouse will affect, and Deform Amount adjusts the depth of the applied effect.

If ever you go too far with your effect and want to start over, click the Reset button. The bilinear next to it will create a smoother effect, but might take longer to render. I find it best to just leave it checked.

Adaptive Supersample is useful for creating a higher quality image. It is like an antialiasing method for smoothing out the image by adding intermediary pixels between colors, thereby increasing color depth and detail. This option takes longer to render, but sometimes the slight increase in quality is worth it.

This filter also has animation capabilities, for a *morphing* effect, switching from the original image to the distorted one. In order to use this, click the Animate tab (see Figure 13.11), and activate the Animate option. You can choose the number of frames the animation will have (the higher the number, the smoother the animation, but this also increases the file size). The other two options choose the animation style: Reverse plays the animation backward from distortion to original, Ping-Pong goes from the original image to the distorted one and back to the original again. Using both these options creates a reverse Ping-Pong. And finally, using neither of these options animates from the original to the distortion.

> Remember: If you want to save your animation, you will need to save it in a format that supports animations, such as MPEG or GIF89a. You will learn more about animations in Hour 23, "Animation—The Basics."

FIGURE 13.11

Creating an IWarp animation. Unfortunately, this is an unanimated book, so it's something you will need to experience first hand.

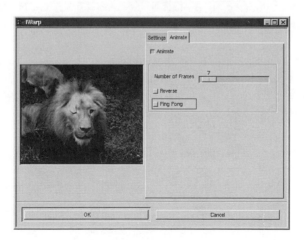

13

Cubism

Cubism is another interesting painting effect, similar to GIMPressionist, but much less complex. It creates a painted effect using gradient cubes applied at different angles (see Figure 13.12).

FIGURE **13.12**

*Cubism tries to emu-
late a different style of
painting.*

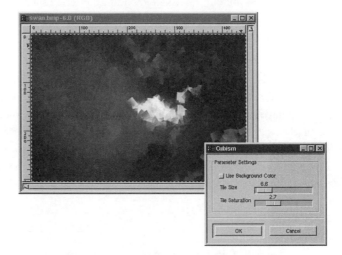

Mosaic

Mosaic, from the Artistic menu, creates the illusion of an image painted onto a stained glass type of texture (see Figure 13.13). It creates a pattern of bordered polygons of variable size and texture, and approximates the fill pattern of your original image.

FIGURE **13.13**

*Mosaics can make
good backdrops for
various compositions.
There are a lot of
options here, but they
are pretty easy to fig-
ure out.*

Whirl and Pinch

This is a fun filter. It is accessible by selecting Filters, Distorts. It whirls and pinches your picture by means of variable slider controls (see Figure 13.14).

FIGURE 13.14

Whirling and pinching.

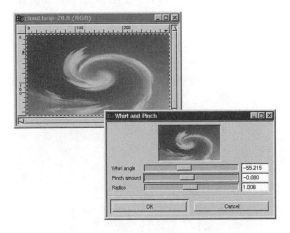

Waves

This is a pretty simple and effective filter. It distorts your image with the illusion of waves and ripples (see Figure 13.15). It has a preview window, and with the sliders you can alter wave intensity and size.

FIGURE 13.15

Adding a rippling water effect can be great for some backgrounds and textures (not to mention emulating the look of water).

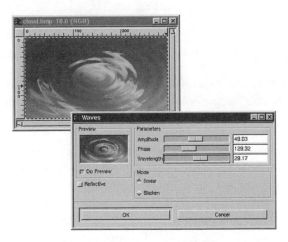

13

Apply Canvas and Apply Carpet

These two are so similar so I will cover them at the same time. The Apply Canvas plug-in creates a texture map for your image, much like the Paper function in GIMPressionist, and gives the image the appearance of being painted on a certain texture (see Figure 13.16). The dialog box gives you many options and can be previewed from within the plug-in.

Apply Carpet does essentially the same thing, except that it adds a carpet texture to the picture. This can make the composition look like one of those latch hook rugs (found at the local arts and crafts store).

FIGURE **13.16**

You can never have too many textures.

Light Effects

The plug-ins that add the illusion of lighting are particularly interesting—especially the Lighting Effects plug-in. They can add a measure of depth and realism to your image.

Lighting Effects

This filter is pretty complex. If you are familiar with raytracers and modelers, this plug-in works in much the same way they handle light. The Lighting Effects filter enables you to create a *light source* and place it in the composition using an XYZ coordinate system (although, it must be *in front* of the image respectively, as this is not a true modeler by any means). This and the capability to alter the type, intensity, and reflective qualities of the light give you an amazing amount of control over the lighting in your composition (see Figure 13.17).

FIGURE **13.17**

A simple composition with the added element of spot lighting. What a difference a little light can make!

The interface of this plug-in takes a little getting used to, but the utility of this plug-in outweighs it complexity. The first thing you need to do in order to add some light is to choose a type of light source for your image. You have four choices: Point Light, Direct Light, Spot Light, and No Light. You can preview the effect by clicking the Preview button (see Figure 13.18). (This can take a second or two, depending on the size and complexity of the image).

FIGURE **13.18**

Editing the type of light source and setting the position.

By clicking the Light tab (as in Figure 13.18), you will see options for changing the position of your light source (This option is not available on Spot Light). This is done with the XYZ coordinate system. Essentially you move the source along a 3D grid: X for left and right, Y for up and down, and Z for forward and backward. Most of the time you'll adjust the sliders by eyeballing the image and finding what looks best.

The Material tab, as shown in Figure 13.19, enables you to set the reflective quality of the object in your image. This changes how the *light* interacts with your object, which can change the feel and texture of your object to be more dull, glassy, metallic, diffused, and so on.

13

FIGURE 13.19

*Setting the reflective
qualities.*

Miscellaneous Effects

Here are a couple of commonly used filters that might be of interest, not to say that the filters in these two hours are the only plug-ins worth messing with in GIMP. I tried to take a random sampling of the filters that *I* find most useful, and leave discovering the rest of them up to you. I don't want to take all the fun out of it for you.

Alien Map

Alien Map, as illustrated by the name, is a pretty weird one. It alters the color map in your image in a randomized way, leaving you with something that looks like it was taken from the point of view of an alien life form with infrared and ultraviolet capabilities (ever see *Predator*?). In any case, this filter is pretty easy to use, and can be handy if you want to create something with that certain sci-fi or psychedelic look.

To use it, go to the Alien Map dialog box and manipulate the *alpha* slider bar left or right until you achieve the desired effect, as shown in Figure 13.20 (Alpha refers to how much effect is applied).

User Filters

Yes, you read it correctly. The GIMP, with the aid of the User Filters plug-in, can handle Photoshop Filter Factory Filters. And because there are literally hundreds of these available, this capability is fantastic.

FIGURE 13.20

Playing with color, but definitely not for making images look more realistic.

To clarify, these filters are a certain type of filter used in Photoshop, so this does not mean that the GIMP can handle *all* Photoshop plug-ins, such as the many commercially available offerings from Kai, Alien Skin, Ulead, and the like. But it can run User Filters, which do come in .8bf format.

In order to install these filters, you must first install the GIMP User Filter plug-in (available on the CD-ROM under Plug-ins), and then acquire the Filter Factory filters. Due to licensing restrictions, I cannot include those filters on the CD-ROM, but you can download them from `http://www.netins.net/showcase/wolf359/plugins.htm`.

Note that many of these filters are stored in PiCo format. PiCo is a file converter that archives and converts different Photoshop filters. Unfortunately, many Filter Factory filters are stored in FFL archives, which need to be converted to .8bf format before GIMP can use them. I know of no PiCo-compatible application for UNIX, so in order to use these filters from within GIMP you will need to first decompress them using your friend's Windows box. You can then copy them to your machine. You can get PiCo at `http://pico.i-us.com/`.

After you get these the User Filter .8bf's uncompressed and copied over to UNIX, you can put them in /usr/local/share/gimp/userfilter. Now you can start using these filters. (If you have Windows machines on your network, this is even easier for you. Save hard drive space by creating a symlink to the directory on the PC containing the filters.)

Using these filters is easy. Open an image, find User Filters in the Filters menu and click the Filter Manager tab (see Figure 13.21). Here, you will see a list of all User Filters installed on your system. Scroll through the list until you come to a name that interests you. Then click the Preview tab and watch the action.

13

FIGURE 13.21

*Choosing from many
different User Filters.*

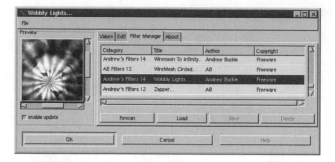

On the Values tab, you will see a bunch of slider controls that might be enabled (see
Figure 13.22). In the GIMP, unfortunately, these sliders are never labeled, so it is your
guess as to what values they control for each filter. But not to fret, just play with the sliders with preview enabled to see what the sliders do for each filter. This is one plug-in filter that requires a lot of tinkering and experimentation. (How many times have I said
that?)

FIGURE 13.22

*Altering some option
for this particular fil-
ter, and the result.*

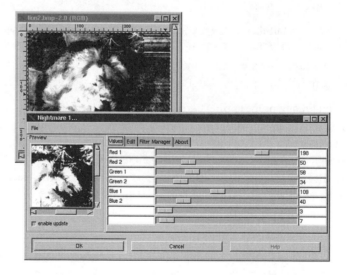

Summary

Now that you have played with filters, you should be at least familiar enough with them
to be able to confront any new plug-in filter with the confidence that you are able to figure out what it does. Although I would have liked to, it is simply beyond the scope of
this book to illustrate and describe every plug-in. Instead, learning some of the simplest

and most complex ones should be sufficient for assisting you in the tutorials ahead, which will purposely utilize some filters you have not yet encountered.

Filters are truly a blessing. They make short work of otherwise tedious tasks, and they're fun. The only thing you need to be leery of is the overuse of any cool new techniques. Truly, in practice, less is more, and an effect used sparingly usually has more impact. There have been too many times that I have been guilty of wearing out new tricks, and it is even easier to observe in other people's work. A Web site that would be slick, if only it weren't for the fact that there are five lens flares on every page would be a prime example.

Q&A

Q I try to apply a certain plug-in, but it's ghosted out in the menu.

A Well, if you've made sure that your image is in RGB color depth, you might want to check for layering. Some plug-ins won't work with layers, while others require them. The presence of another open image, or a selection, can also be an issue. It just depends on the filter itself.

Q How do I know which .8bfs I can use with the User Filters plug-in?

A To my knowledge, only Filter Factory filters work. Any Photoshop filters that require the presence of dynamic libraries such as msvcrt.dll and the like will not work under GIMP, which is to say any filter that behaves more like a separate application will not work. That's what GIMP plug-ins are for.

Exercise

Tinker with all the filters I did not get to in this hour and see if you can find uses for them (and there are, many of them). Traditional logic would compel you to use the filters you know for purposes you need, but sometimes playing with filters just to see what they do can be an enlightening experience. You may come up with effects that you never thought of.

Try the Lighting Effects plug-in on some of those old photos lying around. A simple photo cube and light source is enough to impress the heck out of your friends and family, and it's really not all that difficult to do. (But don't tell them that.)

13

Hour 14

Cool Text Effects

The creation of cool text effects is something that has been around just about as long as text itself. The earliest efforts began as an art called *calligraphy* (the art of writing beautifully) and have been traced as far back as circa 2500 B.C.

Why turn simple text into works of art? The answer to that is straightforward and totally logical—to attract and focus attention on a particular word or group of words. For instance, when you design a logo or Web page header that is the first thing you want people to look at. Any other information comes secondary to that. It's a way of making a good first impression and having something that sticks in people's minds.

Think of some of the ways that text effects have unconsciously impacted your way of thinking. I know the bold white cursive Coca-Cola text on the red background is so ingrained into my brain that just glancing at it can make me thirsty. I associate that particular text effect with the product itself. Or how about the simple and conservative IBM logo? It makes me think of business and computers. My point? Text effects are a powerful way to get noticed and be remembered.

With GIMP, creating cool text effects is a snap. This hour checks out some of the steps involved in producing some striking text looks.

Working with the Text Tool

As you remember from Hour 3, "Basic GIMP Tools," when the Text tool is activated, a click anywhere in your image window will bring up the text options box. From there you choose a style from a list of installed fonts and can also control such things as font size, antialiasing, slant, and so on.

When you place a text string in an image, it becomes a text *selection*, complete with flashing marquee, enabling changes to be made only to the selected area. However, text is automatically considered a *floating* selection. This means that you can move it freely around without affecting the other areas of the image, but it also means that while it is floating, the regular Selection menu items (accessed by right-click, Select) are non-functional on it. You anchor the floating selection in the same way as a regular selection, either by clicking once in the selected area or using the Anchor option in the Layer dialog box.

> If you want to use the Selection menu options on a floating text selection, you must first change it to a regular selection. Place and anchor the text selection in its own layer, and then right-click, Layers, Alpha to Selection. This brings back the selection marquee around the text, but this time, it will not be considered a floating selection, but just a normal selected area. To change it back to floating, right-click, and select Select, Float.

Dazzling Text Effects from Scratch

While there are usually any number of ways to produce a given look, I've chosen several popular text effects here and will illustrate direct and simple methods for achieving each one.

Beveled Text

Beveling is one of the easiest and most attractive ways to add a touch of depth to your letters. By beveling, you add a sort of incline or slope to the outer edges, resulting in more of a 3D look.

Soft Rounded Bevel

Adding a soft bevel to text can be performed with little effort, thanks to the GIMP Gradient tool.

To appear beveled, the text just needs a little shading around the edges. Try the following steps on a text string of your own to see just how easy it is to add a little depth to your words.

Open a new image window. Right-click to bring up the Layer dialog box, and then select Layers, Layers and Channels. Add a new transparent layer to place the text in. Choose the foreground color as the color you want the text to be, and set the background color to black. Insert the text.

With the text still selected, double-click the Gradient tool to activate it and bring up the gradient options.

For the settings, choose FG to BG (foreground to background) for the blend option, and Shapeburst Spherical for the gradient option. Use the cursor to drag the gradient across your text and unselect it.

Figure 14.1 illustrates how a text string would look before and after the addition of a soft bevel.

FIGURE 14.1

A slight bevel can really give your text some shape.

Shiny Bevel

To dress up the bevel a little more, you can give it sort of a smooth shiny plastic appearance. A few well-placed airbrush strokes can take care of this.

Add another new transparent layer. Make the foreground color in white, and choose a small soft brush size using the Brush dialog box.

Use the Airbrush tool to spray on some highlights in strategically placed spots as if a light were shining on the text. (Remember the definition of speculars in Hour 11, "Special Effects"?) To soften the look of the speculars even more, you can use one of the blur filters if you'd like (right-click, and select Filters, Blur). In Figure 14.2, you can see how the addition of the highlights has added some gloss to the text.

14

FIGURE 14.2

A shiny plastic look has emerged with the aid of a few highlights.

Plastic text is nice, but just for practice, take this text one step further and give it more of a glassy look.

First, give this text a background pattern by activating the background layer and using the Bucket Fill tool to fill with a pattern from the GIMP Pattern dialog box. That way, when you make the text into see-through glass, there will be something there to show through. Another alternative would be to place an image into the background layer.

Okay, now to turn that plastic text into see-through glass, activate the original text layer and change the blend mode to Multiply for a result similar to the one shown in Figure 14.3.

FIGURE 14.3

Plastic becomes see-through glass with a change of a blend mode.

Now that you have the text looking like glass, you might as well take it all the way and assume the sun could be shining directly on it. How about putting a few sparkles here and there?

Add one more transparent layer.

Using the Paintbrush, place just a few small white dots of paint in the new layer at points on the text where you think a sparkle would look good.

Right-click, and select Filters, Light Effects, Sparkle. You can play around with the sparkle options here. If you don't get the look you want right away, undo and start the sparkle over with different settings. In Figure 14.4, you can see the settings I used to achieve some nice big sparkles.

FIGURE **14.4**

This text is getting flashier by the minute!

Sharp Bevel

Another sort of beveled look is a bevel with a sharp incline and, like the soft bevel, it can also be fashioned using nothing but the GIMP basics.

To begin, open a new image window, add a new transparent layer (name it *original*), insert some text and create a soft bevel using the technique you just learned with the Gradient tool.

Now, add another new transparent layer (name it *bump*) and insert the same text again directly above the original text. Anchor the selection.

The next step involves using the Bump Map filter to map the second layer over the first. To bring up the bump map options, right-click, and select Filters, Map, Bump Map.

In the Bump Options box, (see Figure 14.5) there is an option called *Active Layer*. (This can get a little tricky.) Although the layer that is showing in the Layer dialog box as active should be the layer called *bump*, you want to map this bump layer to the layer called *original*, so choose original in the bump options active layer setting.

> The bump map is a versatile filter. Try applying it on a plain one-layered text selection for a very small bevel along the edge.

14

FIGURE 14.5

There are a lot of bump map options.

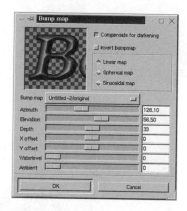

By doing this, you will not only gain a sharp bevel, but can also change the look of it using the bump map options. The *Azimuth* can be used somewhat like a light source that can be moved all around, creating different shading effects, while you also have control over options such as Depth and Elevation. See Figure 14.6 for an example of text that has had a bump map applied over a soft bevel, resulting in a very sharp bevel.

FIGURE 14.6

Attaining a sharp bevel is another GIMP talent.

Metallic Text

Metallic text is an extremely popular look and is also easy to produce by using the Gradient tool with your own chosen colors or GIMP's wide array of built-in metallic gradients.

Smooth Metal

For a smooth and shiny metallic look, begin by opening a new image window and adding a new transparent layer. Insert a text string.

Set the foreground color to white and the background to black.

Double-click the Gradient tool and, in the options box, set the blend option at FG to BG. Set the Gradient option to Bi-Linear.

Start in the center of the text (any letter) and drag either up or down to the edge for a smooth silvery metal, as in Figure 14.7. I've also applied a drop shadow here to make the text stand out against the white background.

> When adding text to an image, always place it in its own transparent layer. If you decide to add a drop shadow using the Script-Fu shadow option while the text is floating, the shadow layer will form its own layer *above* the text layer and have to be moved underneath using the lower layer option in the Layer dialog box. If the text is applied in the background layer, the shadow will not be able to be moved beneath it.

You can change the metal color to gold, copper, and so on, by right-clicking, and selecting Image, Colors, Color Balance and adjusting the sliders there.

FIGURE 14.7

A shimmering metallic forms from a black-and-white gradient.

Brushed Metal

What if you want a brushed effect instead of a smooth metal effect? No problem. Use the Custom (from editor) as the blend option, Linear for the gradient option, and choose Brushed Aluminum in the gradient editor (select File, Dialogs, Gradient editor). Figure 14.8 shows the brushed aluminum gradient applied.

FIGURE 14.8

Brushed metal is ready-made in the gradient editor.

14

To achieve even more of a brushed metal appearance, try adding a small amount of noise (right-click, Filters, Noisify), and then applying a motion blur.

Golden

You'll definitely want to play around with the built-in Golden gradient. Add it to text as a linear gradient for a smooth gold, or try applying it using one of the Shapeburst blends for a look similar to the one in Figure 14.9.

FIGURE 14.9

Golden text will add a touch of class to any image.

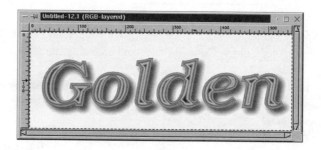

Here you've looked at a couple of the metallic gradients, but there are still more in the editor. Be sure to check out Metallic Something and Cold Steel if you like metallic looks.

Cutout Text

To give text the appearance of having been *cut out* of an image (sort of like a stencil sheet that you can spray paint through), you can utilize the Drop Shadow function, but using a slightly different technique with it. Basically, you get the effect with an inverted drop shadow. This technique works best with text that is light to medium colored or filled with a pattern. The shadow would not show up in black or very dark text unless you used a lighter shadow color.

Open a new image window. Bring up the Layer dialog box and add a new transparent layer. Activate the Text tool, insert your text, and anchor it in the transparent layer. Now, right-click, and select Layers, Alpha to Selection. Right-click again, and choose Select, Invert. Now that your selection is inverted, you're ready to apply the drop shadow. Right-click, and go to Script-Fu, shadows, drop shadow to bring up the shadow options. Keep the default options, but make sure that Allow window resizing is unchecked. Apply the shadow, unselect it, and you have a cutout, as in Figure 14.10.

FIGURE **14.10**

*No scissors are
required for this type
of cutout!*

Easy Emboss

If you want your text to look embossed, but that old gray Emboss filter just doesn't cut it, try this technique for a quick and easy emboss that leaves your colors intact:

First, open a new image window. Choose a pattern and use the pattern fill option of the Bucket tool to fill the blank image. Add a new transparent layer over that, choose your text and insert it. Use the Bucket tool to also fill the text with the same pattern. Anchor the text selection. (At this point, the text seems to have disappeared, but it hasn't really!). Right-click, and go to Layers, Alpha to Selection. Ah, there it is. Now, right-click, Select, Invert. You're right if you're thinking all this seems awfully familiar to the last tutorial! The steps are basically the same up to a point.

Okay, now that you have the inverted selection, you're ready to emboss. Right-click and bring up the Script-Fu drop shadow options. Reduce the X and Y values around 2 this time and the blur radius to 5. (Once again, Allow window resizing needs to be unchecked). Apply the shadow.

So far, it looks pretty much like the cutout, hmmm? Just one more step to the embossed look. Right-click and bring up the Script-Fu shadow options one more time. This time, change the X and Y values both to -1 (minus 1), blur radius to 5, and set the shadow color to white instead of the default black. Apply the shadow, unselect it, and there you have it (see Figure 14.11).

FIGURE **14.11**

*A subtle and elegant
look can be achieved
with embossing tech-
niques.*

14

For a reversed emboss (a raised look as opposed to pressed), you can follow the same steps, only apply the white shadow with the positive X and Y values and the black shadow with the negative X and Y values, for a result similar to the one in Figure 14.12.

FIGURE 14.12

Try a raised emboss for a slightly different appearance.

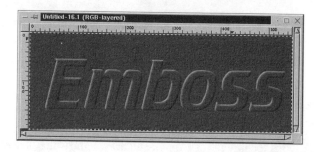

 At this point in the development of GIMP, the Text tool does not allow the input of more than one line of text at a time. A simple workaround for this is to open a text editor and enter multiple lines of text as you want them to appear. Highlight these multiple lines of text, and then place them in the text box by either clicking the middle button or clicking the right and left mouse button simultaneously.

Summary

This hour you examine just a few of the millions of different ways to spruce up text. By learning to perform some of the fundamental techniques step by step, you will be able to understand how easily certain effects are made and begin dabbling with the steps to create your own custom looks. And if you love cool text effects, you're going to be blown away when you get to the hours on Script-Fu (Hours 21, "What the Heck Is Script-Fu?" and 22, "More with Script-Fu"). The things you learned this hour will later serve to give you a greater insight into the way Script-Fu works.

Q&A

Q The Gradient tool affects all the letters in my text string. Is there a way to apply a gradient to just one letter at a time?

A The Gradient tool sees the text string as a single selection. If you want to apply a gradient to each letter separately, you will need to insert each letter one at a time and apply the gradient before inserting the next letter, or put each letter in a separate layer. You could also use the Fuzzy Select tool to select one individual letter at a time.

Q After placing some text, I changed my mind about the color, but when I used the Bucket Fill tool to change to a different color, it didn't fill completely to the edges. Why not?

A More than likely, the Bucket Fill tool had a low fill threshold setting. Bring up the bucket fill options to raise the threshold.

Exercise

For the assignment this hour, work on training your eye to spot the different text effects in your surrounding, which you might not have noticed before. Look at your bookshelf and check out all the cover text. Open the fridge and see what text the pickle jar artist used. You might come up with some great ideas this way!

14

Hour 15

Web Graphics

The World Wide Web (WWW) and the Internet, have seen a phenomenal growth in popularity in the last couple of years, and for good reason. It is the fastest and most versatile form of communication there is. After you have Internet access, you have access to resources all over the world in the form of Web sites. A Web site can consist of nothing but text, or be chock full of images, pictures, animations, sounds, music, and even streaming videos.

On the Web, sometimes the presentation of information is as important as the information itself, hence the prevalence of Web graphics. This hour, you are going to look at some of the fundamental aspects of creating graphics suitable for the Web, including:

- Web-friendly file formats
- Web-safe color palettes
- Basic Web site elements

File Size

When you make graphics to use on the Web, you must take into account that the larger the files are, the longer they will take to load when someone accesses your site. The idea is to keep all graphics with as small a file size as possible without losing quality. You might be able to create fantastic images for a site, but keeping them small enough for Web surfers on slower modems can be a major challenge. In Linux, you can check the size of a saved file either by using a graphical file manager or by going to your shell and typing *ls -l <filename>*.

File Formats

At this time, there are primarily two file formats used for Web graphics, each having different properties and uses. One is *JPEG* (Joint Photographic Experts Group) and the other *GIF* (Graphics Interchange Format). Take a closer look at each of these in the following sections.

JPEG

JPEG is the format to use for photographs that you want to display on the Web. It allows the use of millions of colors, also making it ideal for images with lots of gradients and color complexities. JPEGs use what is known as a *lossy* compression scheme, meaning that you can control the file size by means of compression, but the more you compress, the more image quality will be lost.

When you save an image as a JPEG in GIMP, an options box will appear where you can choose the compression percentage from 0–100 (0 being totally compressed and 100 being uncompressed). A good starting point is to set the slider to around 85 or so for minimal loss of quality with reduced file size. Because it really depends on the particular image, you might want to save several copies of your image in order to play with the compression ratio and get the smallest file size you can while retaining decent quality. To get the lowest possible file size, it's often recommended to save at an unacceptably low quality (say, 50), and then work slowly upward until the image is acceptable.

After you save an image in JPEG format, it will lose quality each time you edit and resave it. It's best to save a copy of images in another format, such as GIMP's native XCF format if you think they will need further editing. Saving the image in a JPEG format should be performed only on completion.

GIF

GIF is probably the most widely used format on the Web. GIFs enable you to save images with transparent backgrounds. You create images only in rectangular or square windows, but when you want only a portion of the image to be visible, such as a round button or a non-rectangular shape, transparent backgrounds can be an invaluable asset.

Another reason for the popularity of the GIF format is that you can make animations (moving images). You're going to learn more about creating animations in Hour 23, "Animation—The Basics."

The down side to GIFs is that they do not support millions of colors, but just a mere 256 or less, and therefore any image you create in high color must have the color depth reduced before saving as a GIF. Because of this, the images you are most likely to turn into GIFs are simple items such as logos, navigational buttons, divider bars, and so forth.

To reduce the colors and save an image in GIF format from the GIMP, right-click on the image and choose Image, Indexed. This brings up the Options window where you have several choices of color reduction methods, including 256 color, Web safe, and customized palettes.

In the same Options box, you have the choice to save the GIF as *interlaced*. This means that when your Web page containing the image is accessed, the image will load in levels, first appearing fuzzy and slowly sharpening to its final stage. It's a good idea to interlace your Web images so that people can have something to look at while the page finishes loading.

Unlike JPEGs, GIFs use a *lossless* compression scheme, meaning that no image quality is lost when it is compressed into the GIF format.

There is one more promising file format that is edging its way into Web design. *PNG* (Portable Network Graphics) possesses not only transparency capabilities, but also full color and relatively small file size without loss of quality. At this time, however, PNGs are only supported by the latest browser versions (Netscape and Internet Explorer 4.0 and up) and therefore cannot be viewed by any of the older browsers. As time passes and more and more people upgrade browsers, you will no doubt begin to see PNGs as one of the major Web file formats.

Web-Safe Palettes—Necessary or Outdated?

Until recently, most people had 256-color computer monitors, whereas the new computers and monitors you see now virtually all support millions of colors. What does this mean to Web page design? It is something that will probably be debated until all the old

256-color monitors finally wear out! When an image is created and put on the Web in full color, the results are beautiful on a full-color monitor, but they are sometimes less than satisfying on a 256-color monitor. If there are colors used that are not in the *safe* palette, the 256-color system tries to accommodate by arranging the colors it does possess to appear in the places of those it does not. This is known as *dithering*. Sometimes dithering doesn't cause too much loss of quality and other times it can be disastrous.

You have several choices to make in regards to which color palette to use when designing for the Web. If you feel that most of the people who will be visiting your site will be using high-color monitors, you don't need to worry about the safe palette. If you are designing a site that you expect to be viewed by the masses, you might want to consider the pros and cons of sticking to Web-safe colors so that your site will look good to all viewers.

> When designing graphics for a Web page, you might choose to work in full color because certain filters and functions will not work on indexed images. You can always reduce to indexed color after you're finished. When working with large areas of solid color, however, you should try to use a color from the safe palette to avoid later instances of dithering, which can make solid areas appear spotty. Make copies of your work, save them in two different file formats, and check them out by changing your monitor settings to 256 colors (type *startx — -bpp 8* at the console). Ideally, the goal should be to have images that are wonderful on high-color monitors, yet still presentable on 256-color monitors, rather than settling for mediocre all the way down the line.

You probably noticed in the Indexed Color Conversion window that there are options to reduce to 256 colors or to the Web-optimized palette. These aren't quite the same. When you reduce to 256 colors, the image will use the 256 nearest matching colors it can find. The Web-safe palette actually consists of only 216 specific colors. Even though there are 256 colors built in to a system palette that is used in the operating system, 40 of these colors differ between operating systems and are, therefore, eliminated from the Web-safe palette, leaving 216 colors that are the same on all platforms.

To view the Web-safe palette within GIMP, select File, Dialogs, Palettes, and you will find the Web palette listed among the many built-in GIMP palettes (see Figure 15.1). To choose a color from the safe palette to work with, click it, and it will appear as your foreground color in the toolbox.

FIGURE 15.1

The Web-safe palette is included in the Palette dialog box.

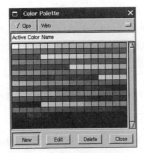

Making Good Looking Web Sites Quickly and Effectively

There are several key elements to keep in mind when designing a Web site, even if it's just a personal one. The best kinds of sites are classy, interesting, organized, easily navigable, and quick to load. The graphics used can play an important part in all these functions. Here you will take a look at a few of the different kinds of graphics that can come together and really make a site flow.

Backgrounds

The type of background used can set the look and style for an entire site. You can, of course, choose to go with a plain solid color background, but a graphic or textured background can add a special flavor and uniqueness. In general, backgrounds should not be overpowering, but should add just enough depth and color to a site to give it its own look.

When creating backgrounds, remember that they should be subtle enough so that the text placed over them can be easily read. If you prefer very dark colored or busy backgrounds, you might want to consider putting your text in a table containing a solid color, having the background show in the areas surrounding the table. Also, if you have information on your site that people might want to print, such as instructions or directions, you will want dark text over a light background so that when printed, the text will show up on white paper.

Textures as Backgrounds

The easiest backgrounds to make are simple textures. These are similar to painting with textured paint in your home, adding color and a decorative touch to plain walls.

Besides being easy to make, textured backgrounds are good to use because you really only need a small piece of texture that can then be *tiled* (repeated over and over with seamless edges) as the background. This helps keep your site's total file size down.

Create a quick and simple texture here to illustrate the effect.

First, open a new canvas in a small size, to around 100 × 100, and fill with a background color.

Now choose a darker shade of the same color, open the Brush dialog box and choose one the texture brushes. Activate the Airbrush tool and spray the texture evenly over the entire image, as in Figure 15.2.

FIGURE 15.2

Because this will be tiled, it doesn't need to be very big.

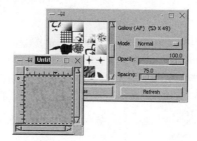

Okay, it doesn't look like much yet, but there are a lot of ways to go with it now. You can get some really good textures with filters such as Canvas and GIMPressionist. In Figure 15.3, the motion blur and bump map were applied to achieve something like a stucco texture. All that is left is to turn it into a seamless tile by selecting Filters, Map, Make Seamless.

FIGURE 15.3

A couple of quick filter applications give the texture some depth.

The seamless patterns supplied in the GIMP Pattern dialog box can be a great resource for ready-made background textures and ideas.

When you've made a seamless background texture you like, you might want to save a copy of it as a pattern. (See the "Saving Patterns" section in Hour 4, "Using Brushes and Patterns in Depth" to refresh your memory). That way, you can use it later with the Bucket Fill tool to make other matching graphics.

As you can see in Figure 15.4, the textured background, when tiled, adds a unique quality to the page that a plain background just doesn't possess.

FIGURE 15.4

Even a simple texture can add a nice touch to a site.

Backgrounds with Sidebars

Another popular background is the sidebar background. This consists of incorporating a sidebar into the tileable background image. This is a good technique to use if you want some decorative contrast on your page without texturing the entire thing, or if you want a specific area on the side in which to place navigational aids, such as the page shown in Figure 15.5.

You can also make a sidebar background that tiles works a little differently. You only want the bar to show up on one side and not repeat horizontally, but yet tile vertically. To do this, you need to make the image as wide as needed to prevent overlap. Although a lot of people browsing the Web still have their monitor resolutions set to 640 × 480, the resolution on some larger monitors can go much higher. If you made a graphic only 640 pixels wide and tiled it, it would repeat horizontally when viewed on large monitors using higher resolutions. Don't worry though. Many times, viewers using the larger 17–21 inch monitors keep the resolution at no more than 1280 × 1024, and if the resolution is set higher than that, they are probably not browsing the Web at full screen, but in a smaller window. At this point, it's a safe bet to make this kind of background graphic with a width of 1280. Because it has to be made so wide, the height needs to be kept low in order to keep the file size down.

To create a sidebar, open a new canvas to around 1280(width) × 50(height).

Decide how wide the sidebar portion should be. You can make it any size you like, but most of the time, sidebars are around 100–150 pixels wide. To select the sidebar area, use the Rectangle selection tool and begin at the upper-left corner of the image. Drag to the right as far as the width you've chosen for the bar and all the way down to select the area, as in Figure 15.6.

FIGURE 15.5

A sidebar can be used as an organizational tool for navigation buttons and links.

FIGURE 15.6

Here, the sidebar area is 130 pixels wide.

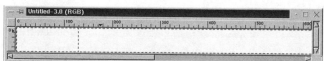

For this sidebar, I chose a pattern from the Pattern dialog box and used the Bucket Fill tool to fill the selected area. To make the sidebar really stand out, select the area just to the right of the bar and use the Gradient tool (with black as the foreground color and the gradient option set to FG to transparent) to make a shadow effect that will still tile nicely. See Figure 15.7 for a zoomed in view.

And finally, Figure 15.8 shows the final background tiled in Netscape Composer (my favorite free HTML editor).

FIGURE 15.7

A shadow effect will give the sidebar a separated look, as if it's hovering over the background.

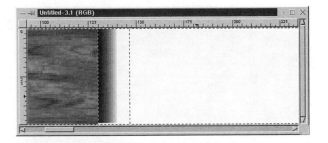

FIGURE 15.8

The sidebar helps to define a style for the page.

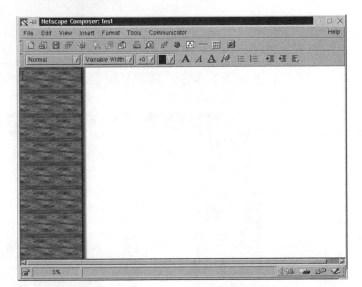

Buttons, Bars, and Bullets

A lot of the graphics you see on Web sites are functional as well as decorative. Buttons and bullets are used as links to other pages and sites, whereas bars are used to divide and organize sections of a page.

Use the selection tools to create the right shapes, and then decorate the shapes to fit in with your look. In Figure 15.9, I've selected several shapes to make some matching accessories for the sidebar background made previously.

These shapes are filled with the same pattern that was used for the sidebar. Depth can be added by inverting the selections and applying a drop shadow with the x and y values set to 0. Then the selection can be inverted back again and have a regular drop shadow added, as in Figure 15.10.

FIGURE 15.9

These selections will be easily transformed into buttons and bars.

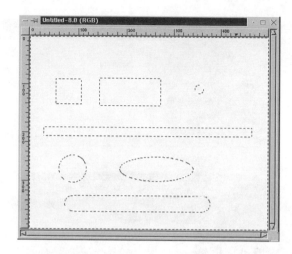

FIGURE 15.10

Matching the accessories to the background gives a nice clean look.

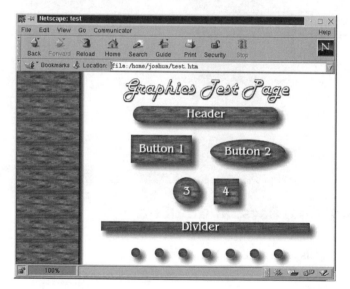

You can also try to make buttons and bars with the beveling technique (see the section, "Beveled Text" in Hour 14, "Cool Text Effects." That is, bump map a layer in the color or pattern of your choice over a layer with a gradient. Depending on the gradient used, you can get some very eye-catching shapes this way, as illustrated in Figure 15.11.

FIGURE 15.11

Interesting beveled shapes can be created using gradients and the bump map filter.

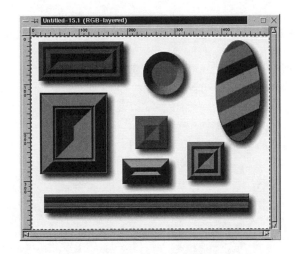

Consoles

A *console* is a good way to go if you have a lot of links that you want to make buttons for. Basically, it is a *container* to hold and organize all your buttons, kind of like a remote control.

Open a new canvas, to around 200 × 400. Add a new transparent layer. Use the Rectangle selection tool to select an area about 20 pixels from each edge. Now give this rectangular selection some rounded corners. Right-click, and choose Select, Grow, and grow 15 pixels. You should have a selection similar to the one in Figure 15.12.

FIGURE 15.12

Growing the rectangular selection a little changes the sharp corners to semi-rounded ones.

A metallic look might be nice for the fill, so use the Golden gradient from the Gradient editor to fill in the selected area in a Bi-Linear slant. To give the appearance of an indentation in the middle portion of the console, repeat the same process, but select a smaller rectangle within the first, as in Figure 15.13. Fill in this selection with the same Golden gradient, but this time in the opposite direction.

FIGURE 15.13

A smaller rectangle, also filled with the Golden gradient, gives the console some form.

To add some definition to the inner selection edges, apply a stroke using a small soft brush setting and one of the darker colors in the gradient.

Now add the buttons. Choose the selection tool of your choice and hold down the Shift key to place your shapes in the console. Apply the Golden gradient to these selections as well, this time dragging straight across. That's all there is to it. Use the Text tool to identify the buttons. See Figure 15.14 for the completed console.

FIGURE 15.14

Button organization can be an art all by itself.

To add links to buttons in a console, it will need to be converted into an *image map*. This is a method of choosing a selected portion of an image and assigning the link URL to that portion only. That way, the buttons, although all part of the same image, can link to different places. Another way to accomplish this would be to *dice* the image into a series of smaller graphics that then fit back together, appearing as one on the completed page.

15

Summary

This hour gives you a brief introduction to some Web-weaving techniques from a graphical point of view. Although there are many other aspects to be considered in building Web sites, graphics are an integral part of Web pages. Learning how to create and manipulate Web-ready images in the GIMP gives you a head start on Web site design.

Q&A

Q I have an image surrounded by a colored background that I'd like to make transparent for a GIF. How can I get the color to be transparent?

A Select the color or portion of the image you want to change and right-click, and choose Edit, Cut. Anything that is included in the selected area will then become transparent.

Q Why make all those navigational buttons? Can't I just put everything on one big page?

A You could, but a large site on one page would require a lot of scrolling to go through the entire page, and people don't like to scroll! As a rule of thumb, anything over two to three *screens* worth on a page is considered bad design. Plus, the link buttons to other pages can help keep everything categorized for people who are looking for a specific thing.

Exercise

Because this hour was spent discussing Web graphics, your assignment is to get on the Net and use a search engine to find sites that have interests similar to what you might like to have on your personal Web site. Check out the ways other people have designed their sites and created graphics. Make a mental note of things you like and things you don't.

HOUR 16

Photo Compositing

Even though GIMP possesses a multifarious array of tools and functions that can be used for such feats as creating cool Web graphics, animations, and so forth, I know there are many of you out there who would like to really focus your graphics skills on photo manipulation. The next two hours were written with you in mind.

In Hours 9, "Hands-on Layering," and 10, "Using Masks," you got a glimpse of what can be done with photos using layering and masks. During this hour, you will concentrate on combining the methods you've learned with some additional tricks to achieve some very popular and surprisingly easy composite effects.

What Is a Composite?

A *composite* is something that is composed or made up of separate parts or elements. When you refer to composites in terms of photographs and graphic images, basically you are talking about combining two or more images into one.

There are multitudes of ways you can go about combining images. By using layering, opacity, and blend mode techniques, you can virtually see *through* one image into another. With the use of masks and gradients, you can make one image appear to *fade* into another. By utilizing the selection tools, you can select portions of one image and place them into another, or you can create a collage effect by placing image selections adjacent to each other in a larger area.

Creating Composites

To plan a composite, the first thing to do is try and visualize the arrangement of the images. After you have the general idea of what you what, it's just a matter of using the right tools to get them there, and believe me, GIMP contains all the right tools to create the various types of composites.

Using Selections in Composites

To illustrate basic compositing, I am going to start with two images, and combine them into one more interesting image. Take a look at Figures 16.1 and 16.2. Open the sunset.jpg and skull.jpg images from the CD-ROM to practice with.

For this type of composite, use one of the many selection tools (the Lasso or Bézier would both work well in this instance) and select the skull in the first image (see Figure 16.3).

Now, right-click, and select Edit, Copy, to copy the selection into the Clipboard. Then right-click, and select Edit, Paste into the other image to get the final picture, as in Figure 16.4.

FIGURE 16.1

This image could use some color in the background.

FIGURE 16.2

This one is all background. Are you thinking what I'm thinking?

16

FIGURE 16.3

Carefully select only the skull so that you will be able to move it out of this dull background.

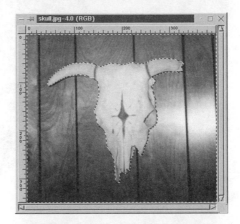

FIGURE 16.4

A very quick and simple composite image.

Using Feathering

By adjusting the feathering control when you make a selection, you can give a soft-edged look to your images and make interesting composites and collages.

To illustrate this technique, I will use three images, as shown in Figure 16.5 (cat.jpg, tiger.jpg, and lion2.jpg). These are also available in the CD-ROM tutorials section.

FIGURE 16.5

When combined, these images will make a unique collage.

The first thing you need to do is rescale the three individual images so that the image areas you want to use are sized to fit together in the correct way. The next step is to open a new blank image window and set the dimensions large enough to accommodate all three. I've filled my new image window with a radial gradient just to give it some extra color.

This time, before making the selections that will be moved into the larger image, activate the feathering options (accessed by double-clicking the selection tool of your choice) and set the feather radius to around 40 or so to give a nice soft blended edge to each.

One by one, you can select the desired areas and Edit, Copy and then Edit, Paste into the larger image area. You should end up with a picture collage something similar to Figure 16.6.

FIGURE 16.6

Feathering can really give a composite a soft touch.

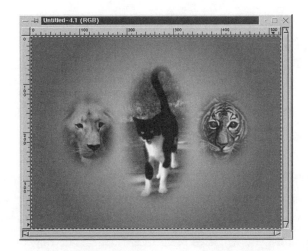

Now let's try taking it even a step further by feathering, copying, and pasting *this* entire image into another background.

Open a new image window and fill it with a pattern of your choice. Make a feathered selection containing the previous image and select Edit, Copy, and then Edit, Paste into this new image. Anchor it. You will have a double-feathered image, as in Figure 16.7.

FIGURE 16.7

Feathering and moving to a leafy background adds an enhancing touch to this collage.

16

You can make some interesting collages by using the feathering approach with family pictures or images with the same theme, such as wedding or vacation photos. Arrange the feathered selections adjacently in an image area large enough to accommodate them all. To make the composite a little more interesting, try making each selection a different shape. Try making a collage theme with your own images, and then decorate the blank spaces with text and designs.

Opacity

You learned about using the opacity slider with layers in earlier hours. Now let's put the opacity function to work to create a composited image.

For this, you will need to open cards.jpg and derringer.jpg from the CD-ROM, (see Figures 16.8 and 16.9).

FIGURE 16.8

You don't need complicated images to make an interesting composite.

FIGURE 16.9

This will fit together nicely with Figure 16.8.

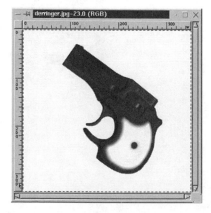

The first thing to do here is bring up the Layer dialog box to add a new transparent layer to the cards image. That is where you will put the derringer.

Go back to the derringer image and use a selection tool to select only the gun. This is an instance where the Fuzzy Select tool will probably be the best one for the job. Activate the tool, click on the white portion of the image to select it, and then right-click, and choose Select, Invert to place the selection marquee around the gun.

Right-click, Edit, Copy, and you are ready to Edit, Paste the gun image into the new layer you created in the card image.

Now you are ready to use the opacity slider. With the derringer layer as the active layer, change the opacity setting to around 50 or so—just enough to let the cards show through, as in Figure 16.10. Now your image is complete.

FIGURE 16.10

This composite gives an eerie but effective reminder that these cards are known as "The Dead Man's Hand."

Blend Modes

The use of blend modes in a composite can create some striking effects, as you learned in Hour 9. You'll use a blend mode here to blend two images in a certain way.

For this exercise, open the bird.jpg and sky.jpg images from the CD-ROM (see Figure 16.11).

To begin, give these two images the same sort of hue before you mix them so they will blend together well. The bird image has a sort of golden hue, so give the sky image a similar hue by right-clicking, and then selecting Image, Colors, Hue-Saturation. Adjusting the hue slider until you see a similar golden tint to the clouds and sky. When you are satisfied, click OK, and then right-click the image, and select Edit, Copy.

Now, go back to the bird image, add a new transparent layer and select Edit, Paste to paste the sky into this new layer. Anchor it.

Now comes the blending magic. Click in the blend mode drop-down menu and choose Multiply Watch as the two images transform into one, as illustrated in Figure 16.12.

FIGURE 16.11

With the help of blend modes, these two images will appear as though they were meant to be together.

FIGURE 16.12

The bird looks much more at home with a few clouds in the sky.

Gradients

You can get some fascinating effects when you use gradients and masks to make composites. I must warn you though, after you learn to use these two functions together, you can spend hours on end coming up with a million different looks to any given image! You might get hooked.

For the technique demonstrated here, you can use the images bird.jpg and bird2.jpg (see Figure 16.13) from the CD-ROM.

FIGURE 16.13

This procedure will use two variations of the bird image, the original and the lithograph copy.

Open the bird.jpg image and right-click it to access the menu and open the Layer dialog box (click Layers, Layers and Channels). Add a new transparent layer.

Open the second image and right-click, Edit, Copy, and then paste it into the new layer of the first image. Remember to anchor it.

Right-click the thumbnail image of this new layer in the Layer dialog box and choose Add Layer Mask. Choose white in the Add Layer options box.

In the toolbox, set the foreground color to black and the background color to white.

Double-click the Gradient tool to activate it and bring up the gradient options. Choose Radial. Apply the gradient to the mask beginning in the center of the image and dragging to any edge.

Your result will be a mixture of the original image and the lithograph copy, giving the illusion of the bird picture fading into a black-and-white drawing around the edges (see Figure 16.14). You can intensify the effect by adjusting the brightness and contrast before you apply the layer mask.

FIGURE 16.14

Astonishing effects can be achieved with the use of gradient masks.

Framing Photos

Now that you're learning all these great photo effects, you will probably want to show off your work. Whether you are going to display your images on your desktop or print them, a good way to give a final finishing touch is to add a frame.

To begin the frame, open any image. I will use the simple composite from the beginning of this hour.

Check the size of the image by right-clicking, and going to View, Window Info.

Now you need to decide just how large the image will need to be with a frame added. Because the image for the example is 400 × 350, it would be good to make the frame 20 pixels wide. Open a new blank window and make it 40 pixels bigger than the original image in width and height, making it 440 × 390. That will give you 20 pixels on each side to form the frame.

Go back to the original image and select Edit, Copy, and then Edit, Paste into the new window. It will automatically be centered on the plain background, giving it a border. Deactivate the selection.

Click on the Fuzzy Select tool to activate it and click once anywhere in the plain border area. This area will now become surrounded by the selection marquee, as shown in Figure 16.15.

FIGURE 16.15

The border area is selected and ready for whatever effect you choose to apply.

For this image, a wood border will look good, so you can use a pattern fill. Open the Pattern dialog box (File, Dialogs, Patterns), and choose one of the wood patterns. The one for this example is called wood#1. Double-click the Bucket tool to activate it and bring up the options box. Choose Pattern Fill and click in the selected area to fill it.

Now you have a nice wood frame around the image, but before you deactivate the selection, there's one more thing you can do to really make it look good.

Right-click the image and go to Script-Fu, Decor, Add Bevel. Use the default setting in the Bevel Options box and click OK. Deactivate the selection and there you have it. A quick-and-easy beveled photo frame, as illustrated in Figure 16.16.

16

FIGURE 16.16

A beveled wood frame sets off the image and takes little effort to make.

Now try a frame with a little more pizzazz.

Once again, open any image, get the dimensions and make a new blank image window 40 or so pixels larger. Select Edit, Copy and Edit, Paste the original image into the new blank window. Use the Fuzzy Select tool to select the border area.

This time, fill the border area with a light-colored pattern. For the illustration, I've chosen *wood*.

This time, you are going to add a shadow to give the impression that your image is underneath the border, just as a real picture would be underneath the mat of a picture frame. With the border area still selected, right-click on the image and go to Script-fu, Decor, Xach-Effect. Leave the default settings and click OK. The image will have a shadow from the top and left sides of the border. Now add a small shadow on the other sides by right-clicking once more and selecting Script-Fu, Decor, Xach-Effect. This time, change the x and y drop shadow offsets in the options box to -2 (minus 2) and apply it. Deactivate the selection. The image now has the appearance of being set behind the mat, as in Figure 16.17.

FIGURE 16.17

A shadow adds depth and realism to the image border.

This is looking pretty good, but let's make it just a little fancier.

Right-click the image and select Script-Fu, Modify, Add Border. For this image, try a nice thick frame. Change the x and y sizes in the Add Border options box to 25 each and choose a color complementary to the image. (This color will end up being lightened by the Xach-Effect, so choose one darker than you want). Click OK and watch as an instant frame surrounds the image.

One final step to really make this look work will be to add shadows to the frame, just as you did before to the inner mat.

Activate the Fuzzy Select tool and click in the left outer frame area to select it. You'll notice that the top and left sides are the only ones selected because they are just slightly lighter in color than the right and bottom sides. You will need to press Shift and click on the right side to add it to the selection. Right-click, and choose Script-Fu, Decor, Xach-Effect, OK. Deactivate the selection.

Now, right-click again, and select Script-Fu, Decor, Xach-Effect. Change the x and y drop shadow offsets to -2 (minus 2). Click OK; deactivate the selection, and there you have it. The picture is matted, framed, and ready to display, as illustrated in Figure 16.18.

FIGURE 16.18

Framing an image is an excellent way to spice it up and draw attention to it.

16

Summary

The merging of images is probably one of the most enjoyable ways to let your creative juices flow. After you master the techniques you need to know to effectively combine images, you'll never look at a photograph the same! Instead, you will undoubtedly begin to visualize the possibilities that could happen with the image and your newly honed compositing skills.

Q&A

Q What if the images I want to combine are all different sizes?

A No problem. Either resize or rescale the images before you begin. Or better yet, start with a large blank image and add each of your images in its own layer so that you can rescale within the dimensions you need as you go.

Q After I cut and paste one selection into another, I can see unnatural looking jagged edges around the selection I pasted. What can I do?

A First, make sure you have the antialiasing button checked in the selection options before making the selection. Create a new layer to paste into, rather than pasting the selection directly into the other image. That way, you can use the Eraser tool to *carefully* erase those jaggies and get a more realistic look for your composite.

Exercise

I want you to see just how much fun it can be to practice your compositing techniques! Get some pictures of yourself, family, and friends and move the facial features from one to the other using what you learned in this hour. If you don't have any of your own pictures scanned in, go to some Web pages of famous people, download their pictures, and practice making composites using their features. Play the "What if they had children...what would they look like?" game. Enjoy!

HOUR 17

Photo Restoration and Enhancement

In Hour 16, "Photo Compositing," you looked at some of the different ways of combining images, but you haven't really explored the possibilities for repairing and enhancing photos that aren't quite right to begin with.

If you have ever experimented a little bit with photography or taken some quick snapshots, you know that there are many variables to be considered to get a good picture. The subject, lighting, angle, background, and camera adjustments themselves, can all affect the way a picture turns out.

Luckily for you, you have GIMP and its uncanny capability to easily correct most of the flaws and mistakes in your pictures. Just about any photo problem can be remedied with the tools at hand. In this hour, you will learn some tips on how to:

- Restore old photos
- Add enhancing touches to newer photos
- Create a cool photo edge effect

"This Photo Looks Bad! Is It Salvageable?"

Almost all pictures can be improved in some way, even pictures that are extremely damaged. In the case of old photographs, many times all that is needed is a little color adjustment. You might want to refer to Hour 7, "Working with Color," to refresh your memory on the different color adjustment tools and what they can accomplish before you begin practicing photo repair.

Tips and Tricks for Working with Old Photos

The following is a general list of some practical techniques to keep in mind when manipulating photos:

- Always work on a copy and keep it side by side with the original to make it easy to compare and decide on changes as you make them.
- The Zoom tool is invaluable for photo restoration. Use it to greatly magnify small areas that might need pixel-by-pixel editing.
- Most basic color functions in the GIMP can be accessed by right-clicking and selecting Image, Colors.
- For old photos that have yellowed, a simple grayscale conversion can work wonders. However, you might want to use the Desaturate option so that the color depth is not reduced in the process.
- Faded pictures can often be brought back to life with either the Normalize or Auto Stretch Contrast options in the Color menu.
- For photos that are blurry, try applying the Sharpen function located in the Filters menu under Enhance. If only a portion of the image is blurry, you can make a selection around it before applying this feature.

Removing Flaws

A major problem that plagues older photos is that they've been passed around a lot and haven't been properly stored, resulting in things like scratches, bends, and frayed edges.

Here you'll take a look at a couple of old photos that are in need of repair so you can see how to begin the restoration process.

The first photo (see Figure 17.1) is about 50 years old, but looks as though it has really been through the wringer. It has been badly bent, scratched, and stained.

In a case like this, where almost every part of the image needs work, the first step is to pick a starting place and zoom in on it to get a really good look at the damage, as in Figure 17.2. That way, you can work on a small area at a time to see if the damage can be undone.

FIGURE 17.1

This badly damaged photo looks as if it did some time in a wallet!

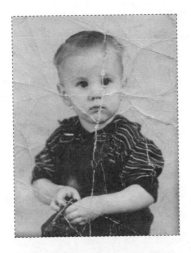

FIGURE 17.2

By magnifying the area, it's much easier to work on.

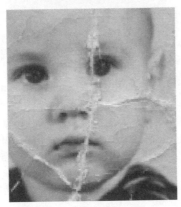

17

Reminder: By right-clicking on the image and selecting View, New View, you will open a duplicate image window that will show the same changes you make to the first window. This is convenient to have open so that you can see how the changes you are applying to a magnified area will look when not magnified without having to zoom in and out.

In actuality you can greatly repair this photo with the use of just one tool: the Clone tool.

As you might remember from Hour 3, "Basic GIMP Tools." the Clone tool is capable of picking up an exact duplicate or *clone* of an image area, pattern, or color, which can then be placed elsewhere. This works wonderfully in photo repair because you can pick up the exact colors you need to cover scratches, bends, and so on, directly from the area surrounding the damage, and then replace the bad portions with the cloned portions, perfectly blending colors and textures.

The Clone tool uses the Brush dialog box (File, Dialog, Brushes) to set the size and shape of the area, so that you can clone one pixel at a time, which is great for areas that need extreme detail. Or you can set a bigger brush size to paint in large areas of the image, which is good for filling in missing pieces of backgrounds.

Double-click the Clone tool to bring up the options, as in Figure 17.3.

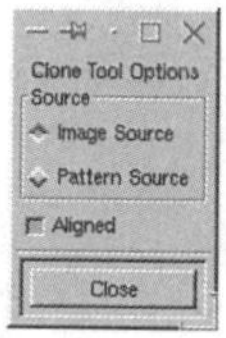

FIGURE 17.3

The Clone tool offers a few choices.

- **Image Source**—Clones a selected area of the image.
- **Pattern Source**—Enables painting with a chosen pattern.
- **Aligned**—When this option is checked, the Clone brush can create a duplicate of an entire image or pattern from the point where you begin painting. If you release the mouse button, and then begin painting again, it will pick up where you left off. In other words, it allows you to stop painting and then resume again without starting a new clone. With the Aligned option unchecked, the cloned area will be duplicated over and over again, starting a new clone area each time you release the mouse and start painting.

To clone an area, place the cursor over it, and hold the Ctrl button as you click. Then release Ctrl and left-click in the area you want to begin painting with the clone. As you can see in Figure 17.4, by using the Clone tool and a small soft brush, the bend and scratch marks are already beginning to disappear.

After you start working with this tool, you'll find you can do some major repair work extremely quickly and easily. Even with no additional restoration, the photo, shown in Figure 17.5, is already looking a lot better.

> Try using one of the artistic filters, such as the GIMPressionist, to add some texture and help hide flaws in a severely damaged image.

FIGURE 17.4

With the Clone tool, you can pick up the area adjacent to the worn part and use it to cover the damage.

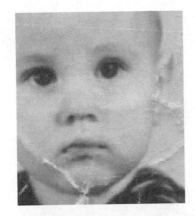

FIGURE 17.5

Just a short session with the Clone tool has worked wonders here.

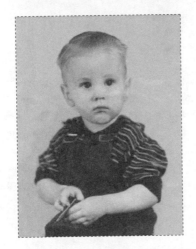

17

The next photo (see Figure 17.6) is quite a bit older, closer to 80 years old, but most of the damage is around the edges.

FIGURE 17.6

This photo suffered most of the damage on the outside edges, probably by being glued into a frame.

The first thing you'll notice with this image is that it is pretty washed out, so to begin the repair, I've simply right-clicked on the picture and selected to Image, Color, Normalize. This is an easy way to enhance the contrast in the image. Look at Figure 17.7 to see the difference it has made.

FIGURE 17.7

Because this image had a lot of contrast potential, the Normalize function worked well to high-light the subjects from the surroundings.

Now, there are two ways to go with this picture. I could use the Clone tool as I did in the previous image to easily clean up the bad edges. But, in looking at the photograph, it seems that the edges are not really necessary to the picture as a whole, and it might look better with some sort of edge treatment, so I will make an oval selection around the area with the children, and select Edit, Copy. Then select Edit, Paste to paste it into a new blank image window and give it a framed appearance. A little clean up of the few scratches that are left is all that is necessary to finish this one (see Figure 17.8).

FIGURE 17.8

By selecting the good portion out of the bad edges, this picture has a much cleaner look.

Color Manipulation

Whether a photo is old or new, there are countless ways to change the appearance by adjusting the color.

Tinting

The tint used on many older photos was the Sepia tone. Sepia toning produced a brownish-red hue to the entire picture giving it a certain unique quality and warmer appearance than a regular black-and-white picture. By reproducing the look, a newer photo can achieve a real old-time look.

To give a photo this (or any other) tone is easy to accomplish in GIMP. Open the picture you want to tint, right-click and select Image, Color, Hue-Saturation. By playing around with the sliders, you will be able to apply the hue of your choice.

Colorizing

Have you ever seen an old photo that looks as though it was painted over with watercolors? Basically, that's the method they had to use in the early days before color film became widely available. This look is also fairly easy to duplicate with only a paint-brush and a blend mode.

To begin, open the image you want to colorize.

Bring up the Brush dialog box and after choosing your brush size and shape, click on the blend mode drop-down menu and choose Color as the blend mode. In essence, this enables the original image luminance to show through while accepting the new color hue.

Choose the color you want to begin painting with in the foreground color area of the toolbox and watch your picture spring to life as you paint.

Another way you can do this is to add a new transparent layer to the image and access the Color blend mode from the Layer dialog window. By doing it this way, you also have control over the opacity of the painted layer if need be.

Red Eye

When the light from a camera flash hits the eye of a subject at a certain angle (usually when looking straight at the camera), the result is that the flash reflects off the eyes and can cause an unattractive orangy-red tinge to the eyes in the finished photo.

Most cases of *red eye* can be fixed fairly effortlessly. Usually all that is required is the use of a selection tool such as the Lasso to select the eye area, and then right-click, Image, Color, Hue-Saturation to bring up the options and adjust the hue slider until the color is back to normal.

When an animal looks straight at the camera flash, it can also result in red eye or even worse, a reflection making the eyes appear a bright green or yellow, such as happened to the pup in Figure 17.9.

FIGURE 17.9

In reality, this dog possesses big brown eyes, but the reflection of a flash bulb has hidden them.

The first step to repair the damage here is to zoom in and use the Lasso to select the eyes. After selecting the first eye, hold the Shift key, which will allow you to then add the second eye as a selection also (see Figure 17.10).

FIGURE 17.10

By using the Lasso to select the discolored eye areas, the color changes will not affect the rest of the image

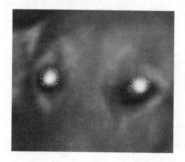

Because these eyes are reflecting so badly, there's more to do than just change the hue to brown. Right-click and select Image, Colors, Hue-Saturation. In addition to getting the right hue, I also need to get rid of the reflectiveness by greatly lowering the Lightness slider.

With those changes comes a vast improvement to the image, but because the selected area required such a major shift in brightness, the selections have now acquired jagged edges and do not blend in well with the surrounding area.

To remedy this, with the eyes still selected, right-click, Select, Grow, and set the grow option to 2 pixels. This expands the selected areas just a little (see Figure 17.11).

Then right-click and select Filters, Blur. By blurring the selections, the outer edges of the changed eyes will blend in with the image, as in Figure 17.12.

Color Enhancement

Sometimes a photo can be enhanced just by changing and brightening some of the colors. Open the burro.jpg image from the CD-ROM tutorials section and I'll show you what I mean (see Figure 17.13).

FIGURE 17.11

By using the Grow option from the selection menu, you can expand the selected area by a chosen number of pixel.

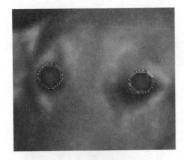

FIGURE 17.12

Now this dog looks more like herself, and less like Master Po!

17

FIGURE 17.13

A tan colored burro on a winter day doesn't make a very colorful image.

This image has only two basic elements, the burro and the grass in the background. What you need to accomplish here is a greater color differentiation between the two.

First of all, use either the Lasso or Bézier Select tool to select the area around the burro. Now, right-click and go to Image, Color, Color Balance. By playing around with the sliders, increase the red hue to make the burro a slightly darker, richer shade of brown.

Next, right-click and choose Select, Invert, to switch the selection area to the grassy background. Once again, right-click, Image, Color, Color Balance, but this time, adjust the sliders so that the grass looks green as if it were spring. With just these two adjustments, the washed out picture will gain enough color contrast to make it into a pretty nice photo.

Edge Effects

In some of the previous hours, you've learned many cool ways to apply edge effects to images by using masks, gradients, feathering, and so forth.

To wrap up this hour, you'll learn to create one more simple yet interesting edge that's fun to add to certain photos.

To start, you'll need to open an image. Use the burro from the last lesson.

What you will do here is create a look that resembles a torn and burned edge. The first step is to use the Lasso tool to select an uneven jagged area around the image so that it will appear as if it is ripped along the edges (see Figure 17.14).

FIGURE 17.14

Visualize a piece of ripped paper while you form this selection.

Right-click and choose Select, Invert, to reverse the selected area to the outside border.

Open the Pattern dialog box (File, Dialogs, Patterns) and choose a pattern to put in the selected area. I've chosen one called *pine*. Use the Bucket tool to fill in the selection with the pattern (or you can use the Clone tool set to the pattern source and paint the pattern). At this point, your image should look something like Figure 17.15.

FIGURE 17.15

By filling the background with a pattern, the image is beginning to stand out.

Now, once again, right-click and choose Select, Invert, to reverse the selection back to how it originally was.

Add a drop shadow by right-clicking and going to Script-Fu, Shadows, Drop Shadow. Make sure the Allow Resizing option is unchecked.

Now for the finishing touch, give the edges a burned appearance using the Gradient editor.

Double-click the Gradient tool to bring up the options. Change the shape option to Shapeburst Angular and choose the Custom (from editor) Gradient option.

Open the Gradient dialog box (File, Dialogs, Gradients) and choose *Coffee*. This is a gradient that goes from transparent to a dark brown.

Apply the gradient to the selected area of the image by starting in the center and dragging to the edge in any direction. Deactivate the selection and presto! Your picture will now have a ripped and burned edge, as in Figure 17.16.

17

FIGURE 17.16

Making new images look tattered can be just as much fun as restoring old ones.

Summary

This hour you looked at some of the ways GIMP can be used to really spiff up old photo albums (and newer ones too!). Tools that were once available only to professionals are now readily accessible for anyone with a computer.

Whether you want to give an old photo new life or make a new photo look as if it were a hundred years old, you'll be able to achieve some miraculous results with a little patience and a practice.

Q&A

Q I want a photo to appear just barely visible (as if in a fog) so I can use it for a background. How can I do that?

A Add a new layer in white and adjust the opacity until you get the effect you want.

Q What is the best file format to save my photos in?

A That depends on what you are planning to do with them. For Web use, JPEG is the format of choice for photos. If you want to view them on your own computer and maybe do some editing, any format that supports full color will do (BMP, PNG, TIFF). If you recall from Hour 15, "Web Graphics," the JPEG format loses image quality each time it is edited, and then resaved with the changes, so if you plan on doing anything to the images besides simple viewing, you'll want to choose something other than JPEG.

Exercise

To put into practice what you've learned during this hour, try these two assignments:

1. Get the lousiest photo you have of yourself (you know, the one where you had spinach in your teeth, or maybe that other one where your hair resembles that of a troll doll). Use the tricks you've learned and see just how much better you can make it look!

2. I know you've been dying to do this one, so go right ahead. Pull out that old, dog-eared, crumpled, faded photo of your first love that you've been sporting around in your wallet for how many years? Restore it, and then sit back and admire your work.

HOUR 18

Digital Painting

According to my dictionary, to *paint* means to "make a representation using paints or colors". It would follow then that everything created in the GIMP could actually be considered a *digital* painting.

In this hour though, you are going to explore some techniques in digital painting that are akin to *real* painting—the kind where you have brushes, easels, and turpentine (and a smock and beret if you're *really* into it!). You'll use various brushes and settings to create different looks that are similar to watercolor and oil paintings.

There are several factors that can make painting with GIMP in the digital realm even more enjoyable than painting on canvas.

- You can *undo* and start over every time you make a mistake.
- You have a plethora of tools and filters to help your natural talent along.
- You won't spill paint on your clothes and there are no brushes to clean when you're finished.

Simulating Painting

In Hour 13, "Artistic Filters," you learned about some of the artistic filters, such as *GIMPressionist* and *Van Gogh*, which can give any photo or image the appearance of a work that has been painted.

What you are going to do now is a little different. Using a tutorial approach (and assuming a familiarity with the basic program tools acquired from the previous hours), you are going to make three paintings from scratch—begin each with a blank canvas and work your way through from beginning to end until you have complete paintings. After you've finished the tutorials, you will feel comfortable using your mouse as a paintbrush handle. While painting, try to keep the following tips in mind:

- Keep the Brush dialog box open to make it easier to switch brushes and settings. You can minimize it to keep it out of the way.

- Use a new layer for each consecutive step of your painting. That way, if you're not happy with a certain section, you can delete the entire layer and start a new one.

- As with all graphics, remember to keep light sources and shadows consistent on all the objects in the painting.

- Utilize the Magnify tool when working on small, highly detailed areas.

Lesson 1—Watercolor

This first painting simulates a rose that has been painted with watercolors.

Begin by opening a new white canvas in a medium to large size. Add a new transparent layer (you'll come back to the white background layer later).

To get the basic rose shape, use one of the small plain brushes to sketch in a rough outline of the flower, as in Figure 18.1.

FIGURE 18.1

A simple sketch forms a basis to grow on.

After you have the sketch, you'll be surprised how easy it is to fill in the colors and have your painting complete. When going for a watercolor look, think how you would paint if you were using real watercolors. You would have a medium sized soft brush to spread the watery paint with, so choose a GIMP brush that would be similar to that. I like to use the circle fuzzy brushes. You might also want to adjust the opacity slider in the Brush dialog box to give the paint a transparent, watered down look. In Figure 18.2 the darker edge colors have been painted in (in a new separate layer, of course).

FIGURE 18.2

Use smooth, easy strokes to fill with color, just as you would with a real paintbrush.

Keep adding layers, and by reducing the opacity of the brush each time, you can paint in lighter, watered-down hues of the same colors to get a blended appearance, as in Figure 18.3. To give the colors a softly blended look, try using the Blur filter to apply a slight blur on each new layer of color.

FIGURE 18.3

The painting gets a softer look as each new layer of color adds highlights.

18

Because the Eraser tool also uses the Brush dialog box options, you can use it to lighten colors that have been painted too dark. By reducing the opacity in the options, it will not erase completely, but it will erase in varying degrees according to the opacity setting. Think of it as an *unpaint* brush.

After you have the flower portion finished, go back to the white background layer and color in the background. For the background in Figure 18.4, a radial gradient was used to give a little glow around the rose. Over the gradient, I used sweeping motions with a large brush (with reduced opacity and white as the color) to give the background the sort of wrinkled look that sometimes happens when painting with real watercolors.

FIGURE 18.4

With GIMP and a little planning, you can pro-duce watercolor simu-lations that appear as though they were painted with a brush on paper.

Lesson 2—Landscape

Now try a more complex image, this time giving the appearance of a more detailed oil painting.

Open a new image window—give yourself plenty of room. Don't use a sketch to start off this time, that way, you can add sketches of elements as your imagination calls for them.

Because you are doing a landscape, start off by filling in the background with a vertical linear gradient going from a dark to light blue (or color of your choice) for the basis of a sky. Add a new transparent layer and choose one of the small texture brushes to begin a white cloud formation, as in Figure 18.5.

FIGURE 18.5

To begin the clouds, dab in a line of white using a texture brush, such as the Galaxy, small brush.

To fill in the rest of the clouds, choose a very light shade of the sky color and a fuzzy brush tip. Use the Airbrush tool to give the clouds some shape using small circular motions (see Figure 18.6). After the shape is there, blur to soften the clouds.

FIGURE 18.6

With few wispy clouds here and there, the painting has a start.

This painting is screaming for mountains, so add a few of those too.

To form the mountains, you'll need a simple custom brush with a flat tip, similar to a fan brush used in oil painting. To make this brush, open a new, very small image (around 15 × 10). Draw a thin straight line horizontally across the center of the image. Right-click, and select Script-Fu, Selection, To Brush (in the description option, name it something such as *fan brush* or *line brush*). If you check in the Brush dialog box, you'll find the new brush waiting for you.

Take the new brush, reduce the opacity a little, and use quick downward strokes to put in the basic shapes of mountains. By having the opacity reduced, you'll see that overlapping the strokes causes the mountainside to automatically gain cliffs and ridges, as in Figure 18.7. You might want to add a few lighter colored strokes to highlight one side of the mountains as if the sun were shining on them.

Now that you have a start on the mountains, you'll need a nice tranquil lake in front of them. Use the Rectangle selection tool to select the mountains and a large part of the sky. Then copy and paste it into a new transparent layer. Use the Flip tool to perform a vertical flip on this new layer and place it so that the foot of the mountains meet on both sides to form a reflection. Use a 180 degree motion blur on the reflection layer and reduce the opacity a little to give a more realistic effect, as in Figure 18.8.

18

FIGURE **18.7**

A custom horizontal brush makes quick work of building mountains.

FIGURE **18.8**

The Flip tool saves you the trouble of painting in a reflection.

Now, back to the mountains. Use the horizontal brush again to bring the mountains out into the water a little more—maybe forming a little cove to one side.

Switch to a tiny circle fuzzy brush, and with white as the foreground color, begin to paint in some details along the ridges, giving the mountains an icy look.

As long as you have the white paint out, use the Airbrush tool to spray a frothy line along where the water meets the base of the hills (see Figure 18.9).

This painting still needs a little something—perhaps a tree would do it.

Use a dark grayish color and a soft, medium-sized brush to sketch in the basic shape of a tree on the right side of the image, as in Figure 18.10.

For the finishing touches, use a tiny brush and lighter shades of gray to fill in the details of the tree trunk, in the same way the icy details were added to the mountains (see Figure 18.11).

Figure 18.9

A little ice and frost on the mountains help define the shapes.

Figure 18.10

A tree on this side of the lake will add a touch of interest.

18

Figure 18.11

The more detailed the tree bark has, the rougher it looks.

Last but not least, to really turn it into a work of art, apply the canvas filter by right-clicking and selecting Filters, Artistic, Apply Canvas. This lends a texture to the painting, as though it was painted on canvas. Place a nice frame around it, and it's ready to hang in your gallery (see Figure 18.12).

FIGURE 18.12

Who says you can't oil paint with a mouse?

Lesson 3—Spacescape

In this lesson, you'll create a really quick-and-easy painting of the final frontier.

Open a new canvas in a very dark *spacey* color such as black, dark blue, or deep purple.

The first thing to put in is a star field. Set the foreground color in the toolbox to the color you want for the stars. Use small brush tips to place many random, various sized specks throughout the image. (I like to make tiny x's and cross shapes, some with a white speck in the center for brightness.) To give them a glowing, far away look, apply a Blur filter.

On a new layer, add a cluster by placing a denser gathering of tiny random specks. Add a small supernova in the midst of them by right-clicking, and selecting Filters, Light Effects, Supernova (see Figure 18.13).

To make a vortex effect, form another dense star cluster, select it, and apply the whirl and pinch filter to it by right-clicking, Filters, Distort, Whirl & Pinch, as in Figure 18.14.

Use a textured brush tip, such as one of the galaxy brushes, and the Airbrush tool to spray in a little interstellar gas and maybe a nebula here and there, as illustrated in Figure 18.15.

Use the Gradient tool in selected circular areas with a Radial gradient to add some closer bright stars, as in Figure 18.16.

FIGURE 18.13

The basic elements of a space scene. Now you need some details.

FIGURE 18.14

A vortex forms with just the click of a filter.

18

FIGURE 18.15

With the textured brush tips, space painting in GIMP is just too easy. Here I combined the galaxy small and confetti brushes to paint, and then I blurred the layer.

FIGURE 18.16

The Gradient tool once again rises to the occasion.

Okay, you've almost got it. All that's lacking are the planets. You're going to love this.

Open a new image window to create a planet. Here you will make the planets as separate images, and then paste them into the space scene.

Use the Bucket Fill tool to fill in the image with the base color you want for the planet. Then activate the Airbrush tool and use sweeping motions to spray in some white areas of texture, as in Figure 18.17. This will be the planet's texture.

FIGURE 18.17

The texture is the first element to form for the planet.

Now, right-click, and select Filters, Map, Map Object. This great filter (see Figure 18.18) provides the capability to map any image to either a sphere or a plane and has a lot of different options available, including lighting direction, source type, and source color. Tinker around with the options until you get your planet the way you like in the preview window, and then apply the filter. Make sure you have the Transparent Background option checked because you will be moving the image into another one.

FIGURE **18.18**

The Map to Object fil-
ter offers an easy way
to create spheres and
planes.

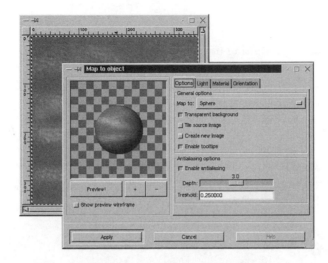

After you've made the desired planets using the filter, copy and paste them into the original image to complete the spacescape, as in Figure 18.19.

FIGURE **18.19**

The planets complete
the scene.

18

Summary

This hour, you looked at a few of the many ways you can utilize the brushes and other
GIMP tools to create paintings that simulate real-life art. These days, with the advent of
so many fine computer graphics programs to choose from that perform such neat tricks,
you only have to possess the imagination and desire to become an artist. Just think what
Da Vinci could have accomplished with the tools available today!

Q&A

Q **When I paint using the Airbrush tool, it sometimes comes out too faint. What am I doing wrong?**

A Remember, the Airbrush functions just as a real live spray can would. The slower you paint or the longer you hold it in one spot, the more paint is deposited there.

Q **I want to achieve a brush stroke that appears to run out of paint, just as a real one would. Can I do this?**

A You can if you are using the Paintbrush tool. Double-click the tool and set the Fade Out option. (Refer to Hour 4, "Using Brushes and Patterns in Depth," to refresh your memory on how this option works).

Exercise

Practice, practice, practice! Work on your painting techniques. Try to make your own original paintings from scratch using the methods described in this hour. You might also want to practice painting by opening up some simple images—try some of that drab clip art or black-and-white line art!—and then seeing if you can find the right brushes to turn them into masterpieces.

Hour 19

About Plug-ins

In Hour 12, "Using Filters to Improve or Distort Images," you learned a little about plug-ins (in the form of graphics filters, specifically), and how to use them to alter your images directly. Now you will spend some time learning about how GIMP interacts with plug-ins, what exactly they are, and how you can use them to augment your GIMP experience.

So, What Exactly Are Plug-ins?

The GIMP relies on plug-ins for its internal operations. In fact, almost *everything* you do in the GIMP is the direct result of a plug-in at work. This is way GIMP was designed.

Because it's an Open Source application, development on the GIMP is taking place at a mind-blowing pace. New features and elements are being added all the time. Therefore, in order to satiate the end user's appetite for new functions and features, and to make things easier for the developer, GIMP was designed from the ground up to be a *modular application*. This means that many things, such as graphics filters, file types, small internal applications, can be added to GIMP. They can be written as plug-ins, and can enhance the GIMP directly without the need to reinstall or recompile the entire application, at least most of the time. As often as new things are added to the GIMP, continually recompiling would be a pain.

This modularity has many benefits. For one, a developer with knowledge about a certain kind of application can extend the GIMP relatively easily. For the end user, this is fantastic because it means he or she can immediately enjoy new benefits without the need to recompile the application or wait for the next release. (In the traditional commercial arena, being able to use an added feature or function means waiting for another release of the product or purchasing an upgrade.) Therefore, an added feature such as support for a new file format, a new type of filter, or even a sophisticated internal application, can be enjoyed with little trouble. And, official release development of the GIMP can concentrate on improving and stabilizing the internals of the application itself, providing a faster and more secure environment for these plug-ins to run in.

This also means that it is relatively easy for a large number of people to contribute to the GIMP project. And the more that people contribute, the more robust the application will become. (It's only at version 1.0 now; imagine how robust the GIMP will be a couple of major revisions from now!)

A WORD ABOUT GIMP DEVELOPMENT

If you are a little daring and want to try your hand at contributing to GIMP development, there are a few things you can do.

- From the end user standpoint, if you run into a bug or find something that doesn't work quite like it's supposed to, you can always submit it to the GIMP bug report mailing address. Fill out Zach Beane's bug report form at http://xach.dorknet.com/gimp/news/bugreport.html.

- Writing plug-ins is the easiest way to contribute to GIMP development, because it adds features and functionality without tinkering around in the core source tree. It also doesn't require *official approval* from the GIMP developer community at large. You simply need to write your plug-in, and then submit it to the plug-in registry at http://registry.gimp.org/. The end user is your quality assurance team—if your plug-in doesn't live up to it's expectations, it can be deleted without affecting the rest of the GIMP installation. However, if your plug-in is good enough, there is a chance that it will become a staple of any good GIMP distribution in the future.

- If you want to dig a little deeper, you can always download the latest developer's core source tree and muck around in it for a while. The latest, *unstable* developmental releases are available from the GIMP CVS (Concurrent Version System), which is a method of version control for software products. Please read http://www.gimp.org/devel_ver.html carefully for more details. You should also check out the GIMP developer FAQ at http://www.rru.com/~meo/gimp/faq-dev.html.

- Of course, if you do start creating your own patches for the core GIMP development tree, you will want to start communicating with other GIMP developers and get your fantastic patches accepted into the official distribution. This is handled through the GIMP developer mailing list. You can subscribe and unsubscribe from the GIMP mailing lists at http://www.gimp.org/mailing_list.html. The GIMP development community is composed of many different people from all areas of life, each with their own ideas about how things should work. The GIMP, inheriting the strongest and most practical ideas from this pool of knowledge, grows and evolves like a true Darwinian organism—it thrives on developer dissension and rivalry. It really is exciting stuff, even if you only sit back and watch it all happen.

This is somewhat different than the concept of plug-ins in Photoshop. In that application, plug-ins are mainly filters and other similar apps that alter and create images. In the GIMP, a plug-in is *anything* that can be added to the GIMP without affecting the core source tree. This makes the GIMP infinitely more scalable, but perhaps a bit more obfuscated at times.

Yes, there are many things that are internally native to the GIMP itself that are not plug-ins. These include the color models, the basic tools, the GTK interface, the Plugin API, the base Script-Fu interface, and the core functions such as layers, undos, masks, antialiasing, core dialog boxes, and so on. *Everything else* is handled by a plug-in of some sort. This includes all the filters, extraneous tools, file formats, interfacing applications (for scanners, printers, email, and so forth), and many other things.

How to Obtain and Install New Plug-ins

19

In order to install a new plug-in, you will need to find and compile its source. (No binary distributions here!) Note that a few of the plug-ins are version-dependent and as such they will only work in versions 1.0 or 1.1 of GIMP. This is because the plug-ins must communicate with the GIMP directly, and the internals can get drastically altered between releases. If you do encounter such a plug-in, its documentation should tell you everything you will need to know. With smaller, less complex plug-ins, you can almost always get away with using it with any relatively recent version.

Why Compile?

Again, *compiling* is the process by which source code is translated into an executable binary. And yes, while it would in theory be simpler to distribute plug-ins as binaries, this would not quite be in the Open Source tradition. Source code does offer a few benefits: It allows for the easy installation on any number of operating systems and processors (not everyone runs Linux or uses an Intel processor), and it makes for easy patching and bug fixing in the public arena. Trust me, compiling is a good thing, and even the non-coding newbie can get the hang of it after a few tries.

Installing the Easy Way

After you have the source downloaded, you can begin compiling. As mentioned earlier, GIMP provides a remarkable tool for accomplishing called `gimptool`. You can use this tool to compile and install the plug-in only if the source only has one .c file. This applies to most of the simple filters you will encounter. Of course, you should read the READMEs that come with any source distribution, but the procedure is usually as follows:

- `tar -zxvf foo.plugin.tar.gz`   (decompress)
- `cd foo`   (cd to directory)
- `gimptool —install-admin foo.c`   (compile and install)

`gimptool` takes care of compiling, installing, and relocating the plug-in for you. The preceding example illustrates the steps needed to install a plug-in system-wide, which should be done as root. Otherwise, if you want to install the plug-in locally only in your own .gimp/plug-ins directory (not system-wide) all you need to do is give `gimptool` the `—install` argument. For any other functionality, the `man gimptool` page should give you the answers you need.

Otherwise, if the plug-in is more complex, that is, has many .c source files, makefiles, and so forth, you will need to take a more traditional installation route.

`./configure && make && make install`

If you're familiar with UNIX, the preceding headline phrase should be a mantra for you by now. One thing you should know is that after your binary is compiled and relocated, on the next startup the GIMP registers the plug-in in your local *pluginrc*, which is the way the GIMP keeps track of which plug-ins are available and their preferences. It is located in your .gimp directory (.gimp/pluginrc). The system-wide one, of course, is installation-dependent, but is traditionally in /usr/share/gimp/1./. However, if you should ever find that one of your plug-ins is acting weird, sometimes deleting this file in your local directory will fix it. (GIMP will automatically create a new one on startup). In any case, editing this file is probably not a good idea.

When installing complex, involved plug-ins with more than one source file, there is really only one rule: Read the README or INSTALL documents, and follow the directions. Depending on the author, the documentation can range from informative to terse or nearly non-existent. Usually, though, a little perusal through the directory will turn up something, and after you've done a few, it seems that most of them install pretty much the same way. If you do have problems, feel free to ask the world's most responsive technical support team—a newsgroup, a mailing list, or that 12-year-old Linux hacker down the street. You should be back in business in no time. Also, it might be good to hit up the GIMP newsgroups and mailing lists; they tend to be very helpful.

- **Newsgroup**—`comp.graphics.apps.gimp`
- **Mailing list**—`http://www.gimp.org/mailing_list.html`

The DB Browser

This plug-in keeps a browseable database of all the available installed plug-ins, extensions, and internal functions in the GIMP. It can tell you the author, the version and build date, and other such information. It can be very helpful when you're trying to determine what your GIMP installation has available, or at least it serves as something to look at now and then just to get a slight glimpse into what makes GIMP tick (short of looking at source).

You can find DB Browser under Xtns, DB Browser. It might take a moment to initialize, but once you have it open, you should see something that resembles what is pictured here in Figure 19.1.

FIGURE 19.1

The DB Browser gives you a searchable list of everything that is registered in the GIMP

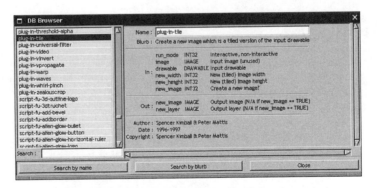

19

You have two options here: You can browse the database to find what you want, or you can use the Search by Name (refer to Figure 19.1) or Search by Blurb (see Figure 19.2) functions to find what you're looking for. Simply enter a search by plug-in name or function (for example, *blur*), and you should be able to find what you're looking for—as long as you do actually have the target plug-in installed and running.

FIGURE 19.2

*Search by Blurb gives
you instant access to
everything in the DB.*

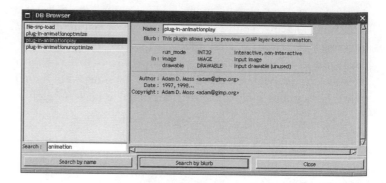

As you can see, after you find your listing, the DB Browser lists everything about the
plug-in in question. Finding this kind of information can be very useful for many things,
including finding an author's email so as to pose a question, make a suggestion, point out
a bug, or suggest a bug fix. (I do not encourage bothering these authors with questions
that can easily be answered elsewhere, however.) You can also use it as a scriptmaster's
tool by searching for a particular function that a Script-Fu script is calling, which is great
for finding out what exactly those scripts are doing behind the scenes or for finding new
things to try out with the GIMP.

In any case, the database browser makes finding information pertaining to your GIMP
installation a snap.

Summary

Now that you have the resources available, you should have no problems getting GIMP
to do more than it had done before. Go to the GIMP Plug-in Registry (`http://
registry.gimp.org/`) and download and install as many good plug-ins as you can.

When you play with this stuff, keep in mind that your directory structure might differ
than the one illustrated in this book (that is, your administrator might have installed it in
/usr/local or even /opt…). Also keep in mind that some plug-ins might have special
needs, such as file dependencies or they might need to be installed as root. Therefore, I
cannot stress this enough: README is your friend.

Q&A

Q I get an (`insert error here`) error during the `make` stage. What do I do?

**A Make sure that the gtk and glib libraries are the latest available compatible version,
and make sure that the plug-in version is the latest available as well. If these two
criteria are met and you are still having problems, it might be that your `makefile` is**

looking for libraries that aren't in their proper location. You should compare notes between what the `makefile` says and where files are actually located. Otherwise, you might have a good question for GIMP gurus to answer.

Q My source has no `makefile` and no good instructions! What do I do?

A You can either try a straight compile, or create a `makefile`. This is a little beyond the scope of this book, and it can be a little disconcerting to those with little or no programming experience, but doing this once or twice will make the process a more bearable.

If you do run across a source package like this and you still want to pursue it (fortunately most packages are packaged a little better), the best thing to do is to get online and ask questions. You will find someone willing to help you. There are also many good tutorials and references for this situation. Be forewarned that the few plug-ins packaged in this manner tend to be new and experimental, so you are somewhat on your own. (But then again, life on the bleeding edge can be rewarding in and of itself).

Exercise

In the next hour you will do a little exploring into some of these more complex plug-ins. After that, I have little doubt that you will be inspired to find, download, and compile as many of these great plug-ins as you can. Remember that for every plug-in you touch on, there are at least 10 more out there that are just as neat, if not better. Go get 'em!

As with anything, the best way to approach this if you've never done it before is to start small and simple. Go to the plug-in registry online and find what would look to be simple, uncomplicated filters. Use `gimptool` to compile and install them. Do this a few times, moving up the ladder to some of the larger and more complex plug-ins, and before you realize it, you will soon have installed every GIMP plug-in there is.

19

Hour 20

Using More Plug-ins and Extensions

In this hour you will acquaint yourself with some of the more complex plug-ins that behave differently than mere graphics filters, and I will illustrate just how beneficial they can be.

The plug-ins in this hour can be found in the Filters, Render menu, as well as in the Xtns menu. They are like mini-applications embedded in GIMP, and can therefore achieve a level of complexity like no simple filter can.

The main difference between these plug-ins and those labeled as filters is that these do more than just alter images. In fact, many of them will help you create new images and patterns from scratch, among other things. Other than that, though, they work in much the same way as anything else you will encounter in the GIMP.

Gfig

Gfig is a *very* interesting application, and a very well written one. Gfig is a robust, nearly self-contained drawing program used for the design and implementation of perfect geo-metric shapes and patterns. It was inspired by the popular UNIX application Xfig. Working with this tool within the GIMP environment is much more useful and conve-nient, in my opinion.

To invoke Gfig, go to the right-click menu from any (preferably clean-slated and layered) image and find Filters, Render, Gfig. You will now see the Gfig interface, as shown in Figure 20.1. Now this is where the fun begins! To render a simple shape, select a preset pattern from the left in the Shapes list item box.

FIGURE 20.1

This is the initial view from within Gfig. As you can see, it is an apparently complex plug-in.

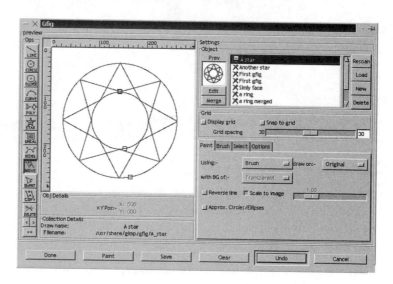

Looking at the dialog box, you will see a drawing area on the left and an Object area to the right. This Object area is where you can load and save custom objects. You don't have to save your pattern after you paint it onto your image, but if it is good, you might want to so you won't have to duplicate it in the future.

Drawing common shapes in Gfig is a snap. The first thing to do is to get a clean palette in the drawing window. You do this by clicking New in the Object area. There will now be a highlighted area indicating your unsaved object. Double-click it to name and save it (they are saved as files in ~/.gimp/gfig/). Later, if you want to work on it some more, you can find it in the list. Right-click and select Edit (or click the Load button for figures not in the ~/.gimp/gfig directory). You can also merge two objects into one image by finding an object, clicking Edit, and then finding another good drawing and clicking the Merge button.

Now then let's say you want to draw something simple, such as a star. All you need to do is start with a clean slate and select the kind of shape you want to draw from the panel of choices in the Ops toolbar. Obviously, you would select the one that says Star. Now, if you click and drag over the preview window, you will see a star take shape (refer to Figure 20.1). This is much easier than simply drawing it by hand!

These tools on the left have many options as well. For example, you do not want to be stuck with a four-sided star but want to draw a six-sided one. To take a look at all the available star options, all you need to do is double-click the Star button. This will bring up a dialog box with all available star shapes, as shown in Figure 20.2.

FIGURE 20.2

Gfig has more options for each function than you will probably ever use. (How often do you need to draw a 100-sided star?) It's still great to have it available though!

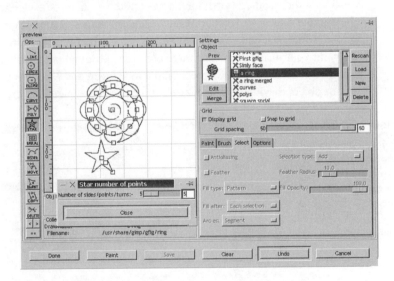

After your shape is drawn, you might want to move and resize it to get it just so. If you look at your shape, you will notice little hollow rectangles placed on the outline. These are your *control points*; they enable you to control the size and position of your object. By clicking on the Move button, and then positioning your cursor over a control point, you can now move the shape anywhere you want. Likewise, using MvPnt will move only one point at a time, thereby resizing and reshaping the object. Using the Copy option will create an exact duplicate of the object, which you can drag into any position. The control point behavior is a little different for each shape. For example, a star usually has three control points, one in the center for moving, and two others, each corresponding with the outer and inner points in the star.

20

If you need to get a closer or more removed view of what you've just drawn, you can use the slider next to the Scale to Image option in the Paint tab to zoom it in or out (You need to uncheck the option first). You can then recheck the Scale to Image button to restore the original view.

After you draw your shape, you can paint it onto your canvas. Gfig uses the standard GIMP brushes in order to do this. Go to the Brushes tab and select the brush you want to use. (Click the Paint button to draw the shape using the FG color and brush you selected. (Make sure to save your object in the Object list if you want to use it later).

There are a few more options to consider when painting your image. In the Paint tab (shown in Figure 20.3), you can set the tone for the way in which Gfig paints your object. The Using drop-down menu determines what sort of drawing you will have. Brush uses the standard brush method to outline your shape; selection will turn your object into a selection. Selection+Fill will paint your selection according to the Select tab options, which resemble the Fill tool options. Furthermore, the Draw On option will let you paint your image on one of three canvases: Original paints the object directly onto your image, New paints the object onto a new layer, and Multiple paints each single part of your object (having unique control points) onto a separate layer.

FIGURE 20.3

You can manipulate the size, shape, and position of your object by using control points.

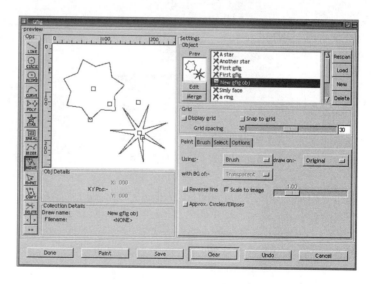

If you do use one or more extra layers when painting, the With BG Of option enables you to choose between Transparent, Background (your BG color), White, and Copy, which duplicates the background image on each new layer.

It is easy to use these simple shapes in concert with each other in order to come up with something a little more complex. As an example, you can use the Bézier curves in combination with a slanted brush to create something with a calligraphic look and feel to it, or tweak around until you come up with a representation of a real object outline (see Figure 20.4).

FIGURE 20.4

A few variations of the same painted object. You can use Gfig to automate tasks that take a little longer to do by hand.

You aren't limited to drawing simple, dark lines with this tool. The Fade Out option (see Figure 20.5), in the Brushes tab enables you to create lines and shapes that fade like brush strokes, to create something similar to a sumi-e painting. You can also select the Reverse Line option in the Paint tab to reverse the direction of the paint.

Finally, the Options tab gives you access to a few settings for Gfig, such as whether to show ToolTips, control points, the background image, the number of Undos within Gfig, and the grid. Grids can be useful when trying to precisely position something.

20

FIGURE 20.5

Gfig gives you full control over the look and feel of your brush strokes by using the Fade Out option.

GUASH

GUASH is a simple file previewer program made to run within GIMP. It enables you to preview your images by way of ordered thumbnails and open selected files accordingly in the GIMP, if you so choose. Using GUASH is a very convenient feature when dealing with directories that contain *many* graphics files, which in turn saves time by eliminating the need for hide and seek when you can't seem to remember exactly what you named that particular image you're looking for.

Starting and using GUASH is simple: select Xtns, GUASH, and you're ready to go. You will see the initialization screen, and then a directory listing of the directory you're in (see Figure 20.6). Navigating GUASH is as straightforward as any modern graphical file manager. Click the folders to view that particular directory, open graphics files, and so on. You can also move, rename, and delete files from within GUASH.

FIGURE 20.6

Using GUASH gives you an easily browsable graphical representation of your file tree.

After you encounter a directory containing many files, GUASH might take a few seconds rendering the thumbnails, depending on the number and size (and the machine you're working with). It will then display the thumbnails in alphabetical order. After you find what you're looking for, double-click the file to open it in the GIMP (see Figure 20.7).

In my opinion, GUASH has one shortcoming: The plug-in might crash when attempting to view files contained on a neighboring FAT16 or FAT32 partition (Windows). This might not be an issue by the time you read this, but be forewarned.

FIGURE 20.7

GUASH is useful for keeping track of your images, and it also gives you some simple options for managing your graphics files and directories.

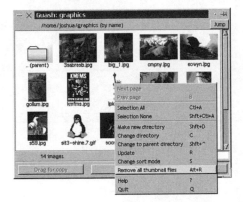

IfsCompose

This truly remarkable plug-in lets you render *fractals* on-the-fly. Fractals are mathematical principles, composed of complex types of geometric shapes that usually exhibit the property of self-similarity (snowflakes are a good example of this). You can use this tool to create complex, yet realistic and natural (or unnatural) patterns, textures, and objects by manipulating three or more triangles in 2D space. (The initial interface is shown in Figure 20.8)

Your fractal starts out with three isosceles triangles. To create a unique pattern, all you need do is start manipulating these triangles with your mouse until it appears to your liking. You can rotate, move, stretch, and resize them to any proportions. It's really not all that difficult, and you might be surprised at what you can come up with. For example, many organic objects, such as trees, feathers, corals, molluscs, leaves, landscapes, and so forth can be very closely approximated by fractal shapes. Using this tool, coupled with a little experimentation, can be useful in replicating these kinds of objects (see Figure 20.9).

20

FIGURE 20.8

This interactive fractal generator, although quite mundane looking at first glance, can help you do some truly amazing things.

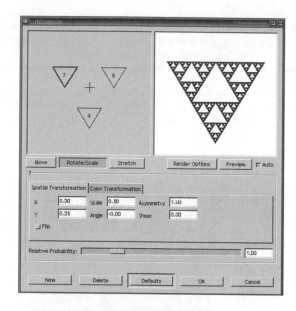

FIGURE 20.9

Just a sample of what is possible with the wonderful world of fractal geometry.

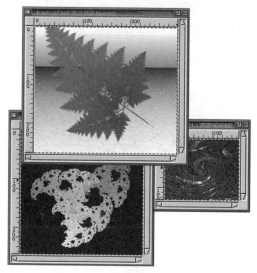

To render a pattern, you need to start the plug-in on a clean canvas. Now you can begin playing with those triangles. As you can see, any slight movement in one triangle can drastically alter the entire image quickly (see Figure 20.10). This is a delicate instrument.

Rendering a pattern isn't nearly as difficult as you may think. Although this tool is based on mathematical principles that are way beyond the scope of this book, using it to achieve a certain graphical effect is really a matter of tweaking. As an example, if you want to create a neat-looking complex pattern, you would have to follow only a few steps.

- Start with a transparent layer over a clean slate or an image that you want to use as a background.
- Open IfsCompose.
- This is where the fun begins. First, click the Rotate/Resize button underneath the preview window. Then drag over the selected triangle. You can see that just the simplest movement of that shape can affect the entire composition quite easily. Be subtle here (see Figure 20.10)

FIGURE 20.10

You can see by experimentation how one small alteration in a single triangle affects the composition.

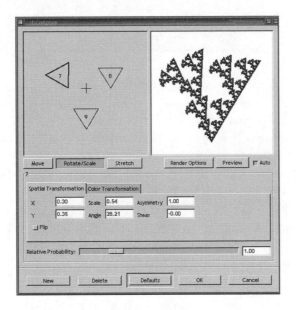

- Now do the same to the other triangles in order to get the basic pattern sketched out (see Figure 20.11).
- In addition to rotating and moving the shapes, you might also want to alter their shape to add some more texture to your pattern. This is where the Stretch button comes into play. Used like the Move, Rotate, and Scale buttons, this one will actually change the aspect ratio of the triangle to a more angular position.

FIGURE 20.11

Adjusting all the triangles brings the shape into focus.

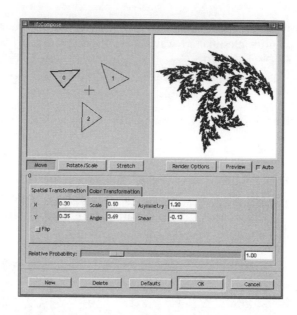

- Now that your pattern is pretty much how you want it, you might be thinking about colorizing it. Go to the Color tab and you will see two options for coloring your fractal image: Simple and Full. Simple changes the color of your selected fractal (see Figure 20.12). So for example, if you choose the color orange (by clicking in the right-hand box by the Simple option and bringing up the GIMP Color dialog box), the image in the preview window will be colored orange in a pattern corresponding with the triangle's position.

- By contrast, using the Full coloring function lets you create more sophisticated coloring schemes within your pattern by setting the influence of color from the other fractals. This is a good tool for experimentation, and it can create some pretty strange (or realistic) coloring effects.

Now that you have your pattern looking more or less how you want, click OK, and the pattern will be drawn onto your palette. As you can see, this is much more efficient (and within the realm of possibility) than attempting to draw these kinds of things by hand.

This tool has a few more options. The Relative Probability value changes how much impact each fractal triangle has over the entire object. Altering this can affect your fractal in subtle but noticeable ways. Subdivide determines how much detail goes into drawing each fractal. Raising this value will usually not affect the image very much except in the case of larger images, but it can slow down the render process quite a bit.

FIGURE 20.12

The Color Transformation tab. Altering the colors here can create some nice looking gradient transformations, and in turn make your object appear even more complex and interesting.

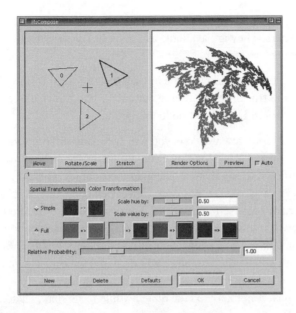

Fractal Explorer

Fractal Explorer is, if nothing else, a great time-killer. This plug-in is just plain cool (see Figure 20.13). It lets you browse through a list of predefined fractal designs and draw them into your image. It's a quick-and-easy way to come up with some really intense designs and textures.

FIGURE 20.13

This is definitely one of the plug-ins you will want to have available for demonstration purposes.

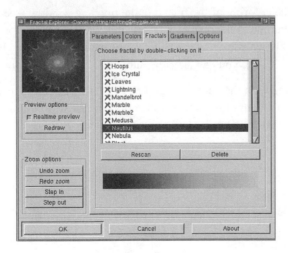

20

You have many fractal designs to choose from, such as the Mandelbrot set, Julia, and many, many others. They are available as option boxes near the bottom of the dialog box (under the Parameters tab).

You will see a preview window to the left where the fractal resides. You can zoom in on any portion of the fractal by dragging your cursor into a rectangular area over the image. Clicking the Unzoom button will undo this action.

To the right of the preview window, you will see many different variables that affect the composition of your fractal. I will not get into the mathematical implications of these sliders, but suffice it to say that by changing their values, you alter the fractal in new and unusual ways, by way of size, position, viewer perspective, and so on. The iterations slider is important because it defines just how complex and detailed your fractal will be, and in turn how it looks and how long it will take your machine to render it. Because a fractal is nothing more than a repeated pattern, the iterations variable determines just how many times *down* your computer will draw the pattern. The maximum on this is 10,000, which is way more than you will need and unless you're lucky enough to be running a nice Alpha, it is likely to take quite a while to render. (Thank goodness for that Cancel button!)

If you click on the Fractals tab (refer to Figure 20.13), you will see a whole list of presets, some of which are truly amazing! I implore you to take some time and browse through them now.

Neat, eh? Okay, now that you've done that, go ahead and click the Gradients tab. Here you can choose from a list of gradients taken from the Gradient editor, plus a few custom ones, to alter the coloring of the fractal in the preview window (see Figures 20.14). You are bound to stumble onto some neat effects this way, but remember that this activity alone can quickly whittle away the hours, so be careful! Also, by clicking on the Colors tab (see Figure 20.15), you can alter the individual colors more precisely.

If, after tinkering with the sliders in the first tab and with colors in the third, you happen to come up with a pattern that is just too cool, you can save it as a preset. Just click the Save button and let the plug-in do the rest (see Figure 20.16).

FIGURE 20.14

Using custom gradients is a quick-and-easy way to alter a fractal's tone.

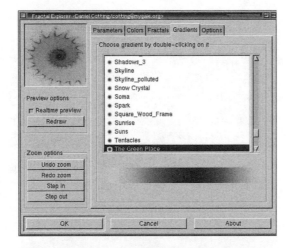

FIGURE 20.15

Tweaking the colors can not only drastically alter the look of the pattern, but leaves you with full control to develop the perfect color scheme.

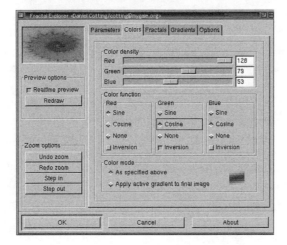

20

FIGURE 20.16

Some quick examples of cool things accomplished with fractals. Take my word for it, they look sharp in color.

Screen Shot

You've spent hours and maybe days putting together the world's greatest X desktop. You've worked hard putting together a great Enlightenment theme, made some great rxvt pixmaps, found the perfect background image, tweaked your GTK theme, and now you want to show it off. This plug-in (see Figure 20.17) lets you do just that, quickly and easily. Using this plug-in is easy. Select an option between single window and full screen, set a delay if you like, click OK, and when your PC speaker beeps, you'll have a screen shot.

FIGURE 20.17

This plug-in provides convenience by allowing you to work with screen shots from within the GIMP.

Inroot

Having this plug-in, from a right-click, File, Inroot will set the active image as your X background image (known as wallpaper in Windows nomenclature). This will not set the image as the permanent background on startup—that is usually handled by your window manager—but it is an easy way to preview an image as your desktop background (see Figure 20.18).

FIGURE 20.18

Setting an image as a temporary root window image.

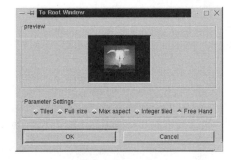

Crypto Tools

Yes. You read that correctly. Crypto. The GIMP has a few great plug-ins that allow for the encrypting and embedding of files within graphics. Real spy type of stuff. You might not have a real need for this, but they are still really cool plug-ins nonetheless.

Encrypt/Decrypt

This plug-in (right-click, Filters, Crypto, if you have it installed), does exactly what the name implies (see Figure 20.19). It will use a phrase key from you to encrypt your favorite image into what appears to be pure garbledygook. And, of course, only the sup-plied phrase can decrypt it back into recognizable form. I will not supply you with any ideas as to what this can be useful for, but I will say that to my current knowledge this GIMP filter is the only application that can effectively decrypt these files (well, without a fight, anyway).

FIGURE 20.19

As you can see, an encrypted image leaves no visible clues as to what is hidden inside. This is almost as cool as my old Captain Crunch decoder ring!

20

One thing to note with this plug-in: You should encrypt something only after you have finished making any changes to it, and then you should only save it in a non-lossy graphics format. Yes, this means no JPEGs. (GIFs, TIFs, PNGs, BMPs and so forth should work just fine, though.)

This plug-in is not the strongest or most secure encryption formula out there, so don't count on it keeping your secret counterrevolutionary blueprints out of the reach from the CIA or NSA, but it is powerful enough to keep them safe from the probing eyes of your little sister.

Stegano

Stegano provides a way to embed other files within a graphics file. It's simple enough; just startup this plug-in, click the Browse button, and use the dialog box to locate the file you want to embed. Click the Write button, and then save it in your favorite non-lossy format (see Figure 20.20).

FIGURE 20.20

Using Stegano is an easy way to transfer one type of file hidden inside another. How you would want to use this is entirely up to you.

To view a hidden file, open the graphic and this plug-in, click the Read button, and it should write the hidden file into your directory.

This filter will not embed a file that is too large in proportion to your graphic. If you get a message that says your file is too big, you will have to use a smaller file or larger graphic.

Summary

Now you've played with some plug-ins that do a little more than just distort pictures—they allow GIMP to do things it wasn't really planned or designed to do. And it only keeps getting better. It is a good idea to keep your eyes on the GIMP Plug-in Registry because there are always new plug-ins, extensions, and filters being added.

One fun thing to do is to find new uses for these plug-ins. In others words, for many of these plug-ins, you often have a solution looking for a problem. (How often have you had the need to render fractals in the past, for example?) Keep with it, and you might be surprised at what is possible with these things—you never know just when they might be useful.

Q&A

Q When using Gfig, I find that the image I painted does not look very smooth, but instead looks somewhat choppy. What can I do?

A In the Brushes tab, make sure that you have the brush spacing set to 0.

Exercise

Now that you have had more exposure to many of the good plug-ins in the GIMP, your task now is to try to determine your favorites and find as many possible uses for them as you can. For example, many of these applications can be used in concert with such things as special effect images, Web graphics, and photo manipulation. Keep you eyes peeled and whenever you apply a technique, try and think if there as an easier and more appealing way to accomplish the same thing using one of these fancy plug-ins. (For example, I frequently find Gfig to be a worthy substitute of the Bézier tool.)

20

Hour 21

What the Heck Is Script-Fu?

Script-Fu adds a tremendous powerhouse of additional functionality to GIMP by enabling you to automate and group together some of your favorite and most often used effects into GIMP-executable scripts. This is a very useful feature, especially if you happen to have a favorite effect that requires the application of a number of various steps (that take a while to do by hand).

If the effect is cool enough, the benefit of writing a script is two-fold. First, you won't have to go through every step to re-create the effect again, and second, in the open source tradition, you will probably post your fantastic scripts on your home page for the entire world to download and use. This is where the power of Script-Fu is most easily observed: By becoming a Script-Fu collector, you will gain a potentially massive library of quick-and-easy effects that can be remarkably complex in nature and difficult to reproduce otherwise.

Script-Fu scripts are generally written in a language known as SCHEME. However, if you are more comfortable in another programming language environment, the GIMP also has plug-in interfaces available for the use of Perl and a few other languages for your scripting needs. Given a little fortitude and patience, there's almost nothing you can't accomplish with a well-written script!

Because Script-Fu employs the use of a fully-fledged scripting language, the possibilities that this tool gives you are almost limitless. These scripts appear in the GIMP not as files with a few sequential instructions, but with a graphical front-end in the GIMP style. In fact, without the knowledge of what exactly Script-Fu is, these scripts appear to the end user just as any GIMP plug-in would. They truly are a blessing.

Using Script-Fu

Now that you know a little about what Script-Fu is, you can start using some scripts. By default, GIMP comes with a plethora of great scripts to start messing with right away, but of course you will want to download and try out new ones. The first thing to know is that Script-Fu scripts are stored in simple text files with an SCM extension. Therefore, installing a new script is as easy as downloading one into your ~/.gimp/scripts directory. Depending on what the script is supposed to do, it should then be categorized somewhere either under Xtns, Script-Fu in the Tool dialog box (or Script-Fu from the right-click menu). The general rule of thumb is that scripts that alter an existing image are usually stored under the right-click menu, whereas scripts that generate new graphics from scratch are stored in the Xtns menu. If you are wondering where to acquire more of these scripts, gimp.org has references to many fine Scriptmaster's resources.

Script-Fu Examples

The first few scripts you'll try out will generate new graphics from scratch, so you can really see how they work. One of the best things to use Script-Fu for is text effects, like those used as Web page headers and so forth; and Script-Fu has gained quite some measure of notoriety for its utility with just this purpose in mind. By setting a few variables, such as font properties, color, texture, background, and so forth, you can use these scripts to whip up some awesome text logos with absolutely no work. Script-Fu is indeed the Lazy Webmaster's dream tool because you can come out looking like a real pro in just a few seconds. Is it considered cheating to use this method to create difficult looking logos with little effort? Well maybe, but it sure is fun nonetheless.

Text Effects—Quick and Easy

To use your first Script-Fu text logo, try out one named *Basic 1*, because it is one of the simpler effects.

First, go to Xtns, Script-Fu, Text Logos, Basic 1. You'll see the dialog box pop-up now, as shown in Figure 21.1. You can then choose the appropriate options, such as font size, color or pattern, effect depth, etc., whatever the script offers you. Now simply click the Ok button to see what this one does. This illustrates just how easy it is to create a simple logo. You can now merge layers, reduce color depth, and save as a GIF for a quick and easy header. That was easy. Let's go ahead and try another one, then.

FIGURE 21.1

The Basic 1 dialog box and result. It's as easy as that.

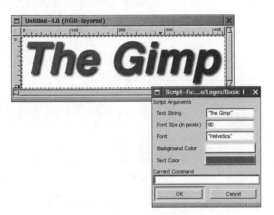

This next one, named *Starscape*, creates a slightly more complex logo. The steps in creating this one are exactly the same as before. After running this script, you should have a result similar to Figure 21.2.

FIGURE 21.2

This logo is a little more complex looking, but just as easy to create.

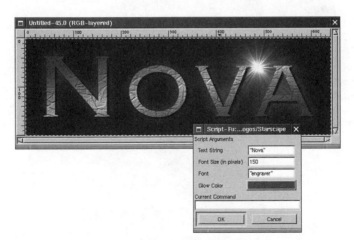

You could stop there and be happy with what you've got, but one of the great things about Script-Fu is that it frequently leaves you with an image that is still in a layered format. This is nice because it leaves you free to alter and enhance the resulting image as

21

you see fit. In this example, the image background and some colors and textures were altered, and whammo! The end result is something that looks quite different from the original (see Figure 21.3).

FIGURE 21.3

Most scripts leave the image layered and ready for more tweaking by hand.

For the Script-Fu example, try the named *Glossy*. It's a little more sophisticated, and it happens to be one of my personal favorites.

The first thing to do is to open the Glossy dialog box by going to Xtns, Script-Fu, Text Logos, Glossy (see Figure 21.4). After Glossy does its magic, it creates a neat embossed logo effect (see Figure 21.5).

FIGURE 21.4

The Glossy Script-Fu dialog box. As you can see, with Script-Fu it is possible to define any number of variables that can enrich the script and make it that much more versatile.

Script-Fu:...oolbox>/Xtns/Script-Fu/Logos/Glossy

Script Arguments

Text String	"Galaxy"
Font Size (in pixels)	100
Font	"Eras"
Blend Gradient (text)	"Shadows_2"
Blend Gradient (outline)	"Shadows_2"
How big outline?	5
Background Color	
Script Toggle	Use pattern for text instead of gradient
Pattern (text)	"Electric Blue"
Script Toggle	Use pattern for outline instead of gradient
Pattern (outline)	"Electric Blue"
Script Toggle	Use pattern overlay
Pattern (overlay)	"Parque #1"
Script Toggle	Default bump-map settings
Script Toggle	Shadow?
Shadow X offset	8
Shadow Y offset	8
Script Toggle	Flatten image?

Current Command

OK	Cancel

FIGURE 21.5

The effect after having defined some fairly standard variables. With Script-Fu, sharp logo creation is almost too easy.

You might have noticed that the Script-Fu dialog boxes have no drop-down menus or preview boxes in reference to fonts (like the Text tool does). This isn't so bad, except that you might not remember all the fonts installed on your system, or you might just want to browse the fonts to see what suits your fancy.

Actually, this is not a problem because there are many good third-party font previewers to choose from. For example, if you're running a standard Linux setup, you probably already have a program called *xfontsel*. This program is okay if you have a few fonts and are running at 1280 × 1024 resolution or above, because the font list tends to scroll *way* off screen. For the rest of us then, there are two good options.

If you are a KDE user, there is a program in the distribution called *kfontshow*, which is a very handy application.

Otherwise, there's a similarly good program that complements the GNOME project called *gtkfontsel* (see Figure 21.6). I like this program. You should go ahead and snag it from `http://glade.pn.org/fontsel/` right away (along with the rest of the GNOME distribution, while you're at it).

Another thing to keep in mind is that many scripts require some pretty involved font information from you, such as foundry, weight, and so on. Not only is it difficult to remember which foundry each font belongs to, but some fonts have different ideas of weight—some use normal whereas others use medium, for example. This is another situation where one of these font utilities will come in handy.

Fortunately, future versions of GIMP (what's in development right now) will include an implementation of Script-Fu with more robust Font, Pattern, and Gradient dialog boxes.

You probably observed that the application of this script involves many individual steps. As it renders the effect, you can observe each plug-in referenced from within the script doing its thing. So, the script did nothing you couldn't do by hand—it simply performed these actions for you.

21

As a quick demonstration, I will use this same script, but this time change the variables more drastically, thereby showing just how versatile these things can be (see Figure 21.7).

FIGURE 21.6

Gtkfontsel is a handy program for previewing and managing your fonts. I regard it as an indispensable companion to GIMP and Script-Fu in particular.

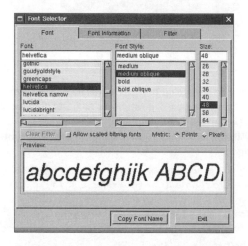

FIGURE 21.7

This effect has now taken on an entirely new personality.

Script-Fu—The Art of Web Graphics

Of course, Script-Fu is useful for much more than logo creation. One of my favorite things about Script-Fu is the simplicity it brings to Web creation. Under the Xtns, Script-Fu, Web Page Themes menu, you will see a few scripts grouped together that will help you create matching sets of logos, banners, icons, buttons, and things. In Hour 15, "Web Graphics," you learned about GIMP in relation to making Web site objects, but I did not mention that you can *cheat* and make this stuff easily with a few parameters and a click of the mouse. It really isn't that hard to do. Find a look you want, plug in the font, textures, and so forth, and a Web site is made. The GIMP comes with three of these Web page themes by default, one of which emulates the look and feel of gimp.org—with a little tweaking, you can create something new and unique with ease. There are also more of these available for download if you look around a little. As a quick demonstration, I used a Script-Fu Web page theme to create a simple Web page, as illustrated in Figure 21.8.

FIGURE 21.8

Script-Fu can make the art of creating Web sites quick and painless.

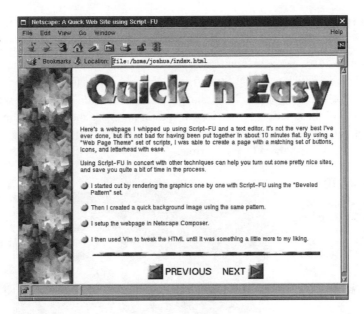

You can also draft some quick buttons for the Web site, as shown in Figure 21.9—Script-Fu has covered this as well. Under Xtns, Script-Fu, Buttons, a script can be found that will generate a beveled button with text according to any specifications you choose. You can even make matching pressed buttons if you like, which is great for those JavaScript mouse-overs. Be careful, though—this filter does require pretty thorough font information.

FIGURE 21.9

Making matching buttons is now a simple task. It's a good idea to save that background layer as a template for other buttons, so you can make a perfectly match set if you want.

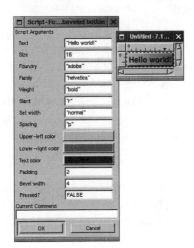

21

Other Effects

Script-Fu can also be used to create many other things besides simple text. Among other things, they can render patterns, fractals, geometric shapes, and many other odd things, some of which you might find useful. You can find many of these scripts under Xtns, Script-Fu, Patterns and Xtns, Script-Fu, Misc. I haven't gone into much detail here, as each of these scripts has their own special purpose, and some of these are merely *proof of concept* exercises more than anything. Figure 21.10 illustrates some of the possibilities available with these type of scripts.

FIGURE 21.10

Some of the patterns and textures produced by Script-Fu.

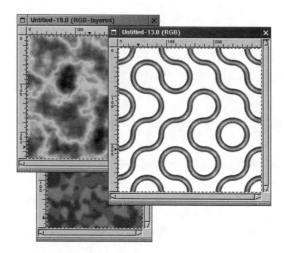

Script-Fu to Alter Images

Now come some of the other type of scripts—those that alter images and behave like a filter. Remember that most of these scripts can be found from the right-click menu under Script-Fu. Unlike their counterparts, these kinds of scripts require the presence of an open active image on which to do their work. And their effects on your image are limited only by the scripter's ingenuity. Alas, I have encountered scripts that do little to an image, and others that leave it in a completely unrecognizable state. That's part of what makes playing with and trying new scripts so fun.

Drop Shadow

The first example illustrates a simple, yet very helpful utility: the Drop Shadow. No more hassling with blurring and offsetting here—a simple execution of a script can give your object a nice, clean, antialiased drop shadow in a matter of seconds. This will lend your image a nice, simple, 3D look and feel.

In order to use this script, you should work with a layered image, preferably with the object you want to shadow on its own transparent layer.

First, you will want to make sure your image is selected, and then you execute the drop shadow script from (right-click, Script-Fu, Shadow). A few variables and seconds later, you will have a nice shadowed object on your hands (see Figure 21.11).

FIGURE 21.11

Drop shadowing adds a touch of realism to your image.

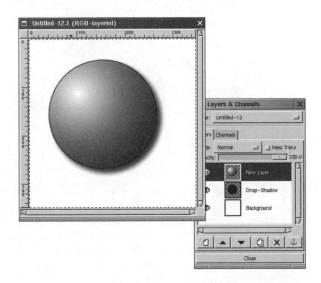

Sometimes this script has a habit of leaving the drop shadow on the top layer, so you might need to lower the layer to directly below the subject's layer from the Layer dialog box.

Perspective Shadow

The Perspective Shadow is like the Drop Shadow but with a touch more sophistication. It enables you to create a shadow with a much more realistic 3D perspective from any angle.

From the same menu as the Drop Shadow, the Perspective Shadow dialog box gives you some important options. The most important of these is *Angle*, which is to the direction of the shadow itself (see Figure 21.12). You can effectively change the direction of the shadow by means of this control. You can alter the opacity, color, length, and horizon distance as well. As before, you will need a separate, layered selection, and then you can execute the script. Your shadow should then appear.

21

FIGURE 21.12

Quite realistic for a quick shadow.

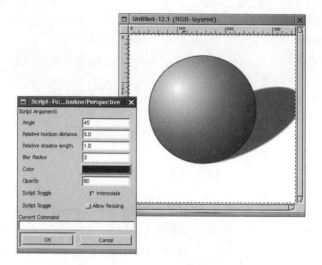

When dealing with shadows, borders, glows, and other such effects, I find it handy to render the effect onto its own layer. Instead of trying to find the perfect luminance from within the plug-in or script itself, I will make the effect at full darkness (or lightness), and then adjust the effect's depth by moving the Opacity slider for that layer in the GIMP Layer dialog box. That way, I can avoid guessing the perfect shade beforehand, and therefore avoid redoing the effect if I find it too light or too dark for my liking.

Add Bevel

Under the right-click menu, select Script-Fu, Decor, and you will find a few scripts that add an aesthetic touch to your image, and therefore act as effective filters. One of my personal favorites is Add Bevel. This by far supercedes doing bevels by hand—even if it does limit your options a little—and is indeed a fantastic time-saver. Again, as before, you will need a selection, preferably on a separate layer before you execute the script. The script simply creates a bump map and renders your object with a groovy beveled 3D edge. And, of course, this effect is most useful on text headers in combination with a drop shadow (see Figure 21.13).

Sometimes it's useful to adjust the brightness and contrast of a freshly beveled image in order to add a little more depth.

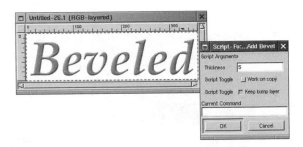

FIGURE 21.13

Beveled logos are classic and now fairly simple to create.

Line Nova

As a quick example of some of the more radical things scripts are good for, I present to you one called Line Nova. It creates a bunch of concentrically centered pointed lines. It's pretty simple and pretty cool. See Figure 21.14 for an example of what I am talking about.

FIGURE 21.14

Notice that by adding this to the background layer of the image and increasing the brightness ever so slightly, this text logo takes on an entirely new look and feel.

The options on this script are pretty easy to figure out. In any case, this script is one that is fairly simple in concept, and yet would be tedious and nearly painful to reproduce by hand—especially more than once.

Old Photo

Last but not least, here's a neat script that can come in handy from time to time. Old Photo uses a few subtle distortion techniques to replicate that old time photo look. Why spend so much time and energy making those old photos look better when you can make them look worse? Believe it or not, this effect can have some surprisingly pleasing results. And those unrecoverable photos can benefit from this script as well (see Figure 21.15).

21

Under the right-click menu, select Script-Fu, Decor, and the dialog box for this script will give you four distorting effects to choose from, including Sepia (that old photo orange tone), and Defocus, the addition of a fuzzy border and mottle.

FIGURE 21.15

The lion now appears as if he had this picture taken a long time ago. This effect adds character and tone to a photo.

Summary

In this hour, you were introduced to the wonder that is Script-Fu, and looked at a few examples. There were no tutorials in this hour, but don't worry, the next hour will uncover some more Script-Fu secrets!

Because this is a brief primer, I did not cover all the scripts. There are simply too many out there already, and to attempt to do so would be an effort in futility. (And the GIMP is such a young program!) For every script that I touched on, there are at least 10 more that are of equal or greater utility and coolness factor. Each script has its own unique behavior and purpose, and these can best be understood by direct contact with the scripts. Script-Fu encompasses a lot of different functions, and therefore can be used for many things that we probably haven't really thought of yet. We really are living on the bleeding edge of development and experimentation, and I can think of no better environment for doing this in the graphical realm than the GIMP and Script-Fu.

Q&A

Q **When I try to execute a script, I keep getting a *Procedural Error* and the script exits. What does this mean?**

A This means that the script ran into a variable whose value was non-existent for some reason, and the script therefore could not continue. For example, this frequently happens when the user references a font that is not installed (or is mis-spelled, as has often happened to me), a numeric value that is invalid or out of range, or the script internally references a GIMP plug-in that is not installed. In all practicality, 99 percent of all Script-Fu errors are a result of faulty font informa-tion, either from non-installed fonts, misspelled fonts, or entering wrong font infor-mation (using *normal* where the script expects *medium*, for example.) This is precisely why having a font viewer utility nearby is of great use to anyone using the GIMP extensively.

Q I downloaded a script into my .gimp/scripts directory, but it's not showing up.

A Make sure to click Refresh from the Xtns menu any time you add a script.

Exercise

You touched on some pretty interesting scripts in this hour, but there are still many, many scripts to be explored. Because you probably now have a pretty good idea how to get around in these scripts and where they go, you should play with every single one of them. And I strongly recommend that you pay a visit to `gimp.org` and find places to download as many new scripts as you can. I urge and implore you to find and collect more scripts than you can handle. You never know what kind of effect, texture, logo, or utility you'll bump into.

21

Hour **22**

More with Script-Fu

Script-Fu is a powerful tool; using it effectively can entail a lot more than simply running a script. This hour is meant as a brief introduction into the wider world of Script-Fu and development, if you should opt to traverse that path. Overall, it is really quite a complex topic that deserves in-depth documentation of its own, which is beyond the scope of this book. This hour introduces some of the more specialized uses of Script-Fu.

Using Script-Fu in Combination with Your Own Effects

When you execute a script from within the GIMP, you are doing nothing more than issuing a sequence of commands for GIMP to execute. Needless to say, there are probably some scripts that don't quite fit in exactly with what you are trying to do so, it would be nice if you could take what that script has produced and do a little tweaking. Well, there is absolutely nothing stopping you from doing so! In fact, most scripts in the GIMP leave their output data in layered format so that it is easy to take what has been produced and create some alterations and customizations.

Dissecting the Image

Because many of the output images of these scripts are still layered, it is really a simple matter of taking a look at these images and deciding on any alterations you might want to apply. For example, the Glossy script uses a few layers; the top layer has the screen Blend mode property, which allows the lower layer to show through. In this example, I manipulated each layer individually to create a completely different effect. By filling the second layer with black, blurring it, and changing the properties of the top and bottom layers, this image now has a completely different tone (see Figure 22.1). I more or less used the output of the script as a template to help create an effect I wanted.

FIGURE 22.1

Just because Script-Fu gives you a result doesn't mean that you have to be stuck with it. Having the finished product in a layered format gives you a lot of flexibility.

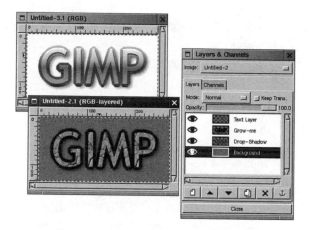

As another example (see Figure 22.2), I used the Engraver script and merged the text layers into one by right-clicking, Layers, Merge Visible Layers, making sure to unclick the Eye icons on layers I did not intend to merged. Then I used Bump Map with a copy of the text layer (filled with white and Gaussian blurred at 7) as a map, added a drop shadow, and again, the result is drastically different.

FIGURE 22.2

Sometimes it's fun to alter the effects by hand when the standard results get a little worn.

Script-Fu as a Tool

Script-Fu is not meant to be used alone; it is meant to be an aid to augment your graphics techniques. They can, in fact, be great tools for assisting you in creating the effects that you routinely encounter and for becoming just one step in the entire image creation process. The following examples are meant to give you some ideas as to how scripts can fit in as a tool, not just a filter or simple image generator. (Which is really helpful in respect to those amazing animation scripts that are covered in Hour 23, "Animations.")

Brushes Revisited

Want to make a brush quickly? Earlier in Hour 4,"Using Brushes and Patterns in Depth," you learned how to create a brush by hand out of any image. The Two Brush script that greatly simplifies this task. After you have an image open, right-click, go to Script-Fu, Selection, To Brush, and whatever you have selected in your active layer will be saved in your ~/.gimp/brushes directory as a brush. This script, then, is a tool for convenience (see Figure 22.3).

FIGURE 22.3

Creating a GIMP brush is a snap with the assistance of this script.

Rounded Selections

Sometimes you might want to create a shape that is neither a rectangle nor a circle, but instead a shape that lies somewhere in between. This shape is a little difficult to perfect by hand, but is a breeze with the magic of scripting.

- First of all, you will want to create a rectangular selection that approximates the desired selection area (see Figure 22.4).

- Then right-click, and go to Script-Fu, Selection, Round. Voilá! Your shape takes on a more elegant form (see Figure 22.5)

FIGURE 22.4

Selecting the general area.

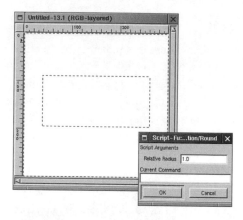

FIGURE 22.5

The selection becomes a little more distinct. This is actually more difficult to do by hand than it might appear.

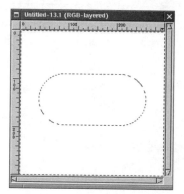

- Now that you have the shape more or less in place, the rest is up to you.

  In this example (see Figure 22.6), a nice, Web header was created using the Gradient tool as a base texture, the Bump Map filter for depth, the Text tool, (again, with Bump Map, and the Screen Blend mode), and the Drop Shadow script. In essence, the script was used to help enhance script output.

FIGURE 22.6

After the shape is in place, adding the refinements is a matter of taste.

22

You can use this tool, with the acquisition of many more shapes in your selection, to come up with more *organic* shapes, which are great for things such as logo planchets and Web navigation consoles.

Script-Fu—A Look Ahead

Now that Script-Fu use is becoming pretty familiar, taking a look at what makes these things tick internally can be a worthwhile endeavor if you have such an inclination.

If you are a developer and want to mess around with interfacing with GIMP, chances are there is a supported language that you are familiar with. Some of the interfaces include

- Gimptcl (TCL/Tk)
- GimpJava
- Gimple (GNU Guile)
- GIMP-Perl
- GIMP-Python

I'm sure there are more that I neglected to mention. And, of course, some are bound to be more steady and stable than others based on their relative stages of development and completion. As always, you can find and download these options from `registry.gimp.org`.

> One caveat: If you do opt to develop scripts with one of these other interfaces, you should keep in mind that sharing them with others might be a little more difficult to do because many people might not have all the required components needed in order to run your scripts. This, of course, depends on the release of the GIMP they have installed, and how diligent they are on keeping up with the latest plug-ins and patches. Nonetheless, if you are already a Perl guru, for example, then it might be an easier task for you to draft up some scripts for GIMP.

Developing scripts themselves, while not necessarily an easy task, can be a rewarding one if you aren't uncomfortable with programming and scripting already. One of the easiest ways to get started is to open up some of those SCM files with you favorite text editor and take a peek. Looking at other people's code, talking to other script writers, and reading some SCHEME materials should set you on your way to writing high-quality scripts that everyone can enjoy. If you are itchin' to start writing scripts for GIMP, I suggest that you pay a visit to a fantastic site: Mike Terry's Black Belt School of Script-Fu, at `http://www.soulfry.com/script-fu-tutorial/`. This is an excellent beginner's resource for the would-be scripter.

Procedural Database

This will probably only be of interest to you if you are a scripter. This plug-in is a testbed interface for SCHEME development (see Figure 22.7). Select Xtns, Script-Fu, Console. I won't get into its subtleties here, suffice it to say that it is a wonderful loopback device for the developer to tack in some test strings. (For an example, try entering (**+ 3 5**) and see what you get.)

FIGURE 22.7

This is a great interface for the GIMP developer testbed.

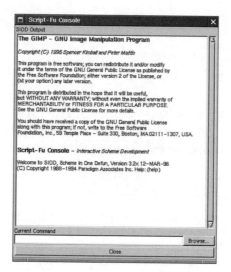

Net-Fu

Net-Fu is something that has some interesting possibilities for the future of GIMP utility. It is an interface that lets GIMP accept commands from over a network. Net-Fu lets you work remotely within the GIMP and still come up with some interesting effects. This can be useful if, for example, you are trying to create some images remotely on a non-UNIX machine; although truthfully Net-Fu is for the most part something that can be fun to play with from the developer's perspective. I mention it here to illustrate some of the things GIMP will likely be capable of as more developers lend their support. Net-Fu is at this point in time more of a *proof of concept* than a useful application. It will be exciting to see what kinds of clever applications people come up with in the near future. GIMP has a lot of room to expand into areas not previously considered.

For a good, real-life example of Net-Fu in action in an application, check out
http://www.cooltext.com/.

It is possible to set up Net-Fu to accept remote commands and create a Web-based, Java-based, or even a native front end to Net-Fu (see Figure 22.8). Be forewarned, however, that this is not an easy task to achieve, and is definitely not for the faint of heart! To quote the Net-Fu README. "Installing this stuff is not fun!". But if you do want to set up your machine as a Net-FU server and do some experimenting with the possible client/server applications that GIMP can handle, there are some good resources at cool-text.com to help get you started.

FIGURE 22.8

Telling GIMP what TCP port to listen to for remote connections. At least that part is easy.

Summary

Using Script-Fu as a tool in combination with your own graphics techniques is something that will just kind of bump into you when you're looking to create that certain effect and a script seems to fit that purpose perfectly. Keep at it! Don't forget to check up with gimp.org often to keep track of any new scripts that might be out there for you to devour.

Q&A

Q Can I get a script to run from the command line without X?

A Yes. Of course, this is a difficult task; it is only really good for scripted tasks and requires a coder's touch, (for now). Read the Net-Fu documentation for details. If you're looking for a way to convert image formats in batch mode, for a number of unattended files, a better way is to use the ImageMagick suite of utilities, which complement GIMP nicely. The ImageMagick man pages can point you in the right direction.

Exercise

Begin on an image project that will be somewhat intense and heavily layered. See if some scripts can fit in there somewhere to make the steps, and consequently, your entire project, a little easier. Sure, necessity is the mother of invention, but sometimes inventions are created with the specific purpose of looking for a problem to solve. And in looking for such problems, it is easy to come across new ways of doing things that might not have previously been considered, but are later regarded as indispensable.

Also, if you want to forge ahead into the prospect of tinkering with script internals, again, the best way to do this is to tinker with other people's scripts. For example, if there is a text logo script that you'd like to behave a little differently, chances are you will find it relatively painless to alter the script itself to do what you want—even if you are a non-programmer—simply by studying the syntax and context.

HOUR **23**

Animations

Animations are one of the more entertaining aspects of working with digital graphics. Creating an image that appears to move is a little eye candy that can enhance any project. (For instance, what would the Netscape/Mozilla browser be like without that cute little animated lizard?)

You probably have noticed what impact a simple movement can have on a Web site. A scrolling banner or small, animated button can make quite a difference and can enhance the site considerably without a lot of effort. (Wilber's eyes on `gimp.org` or the title graphic on `opencontent.org` are good examples of animation used well.) Sure, it's frivolous, but people like things that add a little life to something that is static and motionless.

Likewise, a Web page with way too many animated GIFs can be distracting and can look downright goofy, and thus detract from the entire experience. It is obvious that these frivolous animations, if used, can enhance or break a site altogether. (I'm sure you have run across sites built by newbies who got carried away with animated GIF fever. It is sometimes difficult to avoid the temptation not to overuse a new technique.) Therefore, it is easy to see just how much impact these animations can have.

The GIMP in particular lends itself well to creating graphics for use on the Web, and animations are no exception. In this hour, you'll learn a few techniques for creating some simple animated graphics for the Web and otherwise, as well as optimizing them for use in low-bandwidth situations.

Creating a Simple Animation

As you probably already know, an *animation* is a visual effect created by layering different frames of the same subject in motion, and then cycling through them at a speed that is high enough to fool the human eye. (You probably made those little animated flip books in elementary school.) Well, making animations digitally is really no different. You start out with many different images, or frames, which represent a continual flow of motion, and you then pile them one on top of the other, and play them in sequence to create the illusion of motion.

Creating an animation in GIMP is really a easy because working with the individual frames of an animation is really the same as dealing with layers. The Layer dialog box in this case doubles as a frame manager. The only real difference here is that the layers must have a specific name in which the timing information is stored. An example of this is shown in Figure 23.1.

FIGURE 23.1

If you can use layers in GIMP, you can build an animation.

To build an animation, you need to start with a clean canvas, and then add a layer for each subsequent frame. This is really no different than drawing a cartoon, altering the subject ever so slightly in each frame to achieve the illusion of motion.

You will, however, probably want to build your frames more or less separately, and then combine them into your final animation. When building animations, the Layers dialog box becomes a frame manager, and works pretty much the same, except that animation frames do *not* support varying degrees of opacity, as with many layered images. Animations support full transparency and full opacity with no variations. If you create an animation with pixels that allow shades of the image behind to show through (as with drop shadows), such pixels will be effectively converted to a solid or transparency when saving to GIF89a.

In this example, I will build a simple text logo animation so you can get a feel for it. This one replicates a spotlight effect and was made with the gradient editor, used on layers with protected transparencies, and with the added assistance of Script-Fu. It was created with detail in mind as opposed to size. It is included on the CD-ROM so you can take a peek at it if you want (for a proof of concept as to how animations basically work).

- The first thing you'll want to do is start by creating the first frame of your animation onto the first layer (see Figure 23.2). Name this *Frame 1*. (Or *Frame 0*, if you're real picky like me).

FIGURE 23.2

An animation has to start somewhere.

- The next step, as you've already probably guessed, is to create your next frame. You do this by creating a new transparent layer in the Layer dialog box. You will need to name it *Frame 2*. In this example, I have already prepared all the individual frames from separate images beforehand, so I am merely pasting each frame onto a new layer (see Figure 23.3). This is usually the most convenient way to approach animations that aren't too terribly complex.

- Continue in this fashion until all the frames are created and the movement proceeds in an endless looping fashion (unless you want a play-once animation). When all the frames are in place, you can then test your animation by right-clicking the image and going to Filters, Animation, Animation Playback. After clicking Play, your animation should spring to life (see Figure 23.4).

At this point, a preliminary animation is built, but there is still some work to be done. For one, you might have noticed that your animation is a little choppy—that is, there is a delay between frames. Fortunately, you can change the delay between frames. In the GIMP, the timing for the frames is reflected directly within the frame naming convention. It might be a little disconcerting at first. So for example, if you want frame two to appear for only 100 milliseconds, you rename it to *Frame 2 (100ms)*. (No space between

100 and *ms*.) Likewise, for half a second of time, you would use *Frame 2 (500ms)*, and for a full second you would use *Frame 2 (1000ms)*. Reducing the time on all the frames should speed up and smooth out your animation. All frames default to 100ms, or 1/10 of a second, if not specified otherwise.

FIGURE 23.3

The animation starts to take shape. You can probably already see where it is going.

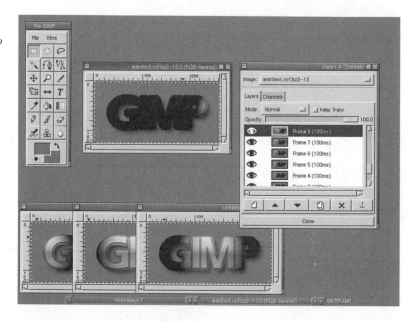

FIGURE 23.4

Playing back the animation to see if it was sketched out well enough the first time. Sometimes if the animation is too choppy, more frames will need to be added to smooth out the effect (or subtracted to save space).

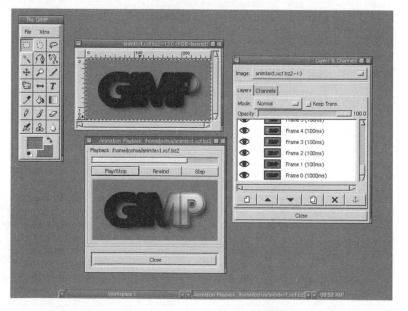

When building an animation, you'll want to try and make it as smooth as possible, within size constraints. How smooth your animation will be depends on a few factors, such as the timing in milliseconds for your frames, as well as the amount or subtlety of movement of the animated elements between the individual frames. Obviously, for a smoother animation, you would use more subtle movements, more frames, and less time for each frame. But there is also a balance to be achieved by accounting for file size and build time. (For example, 100 subtle frames with a movement of 1 pixel apiece at high speed might be a little more than is practical to build.) Each graphic is different, but a good rule of thumb to remember is that if the animation starts looks choppy with the frame speeds set at ~100ms, you'll probably need to build a few more intermediary frames to tighten the movement.

23

If you don't have size constraints, that is, you're not making it for use online, there is little reason to avoid going for detail—a little more time spent building more frames at higher speed, each with smaller changes in movement, can result in a much cleaner image.

Building Animations for the Web

As you can see, building a simple animation is relatively painless. There are a lot of little effects you can use—pixelization, noise transition, banding and blinding effects for text logos, blinking, pulsating, and color transformation effects for small objects such as buttons. These things are easily created with a few copies of a single image to work on and a little patience. But there are a few more things to consider when building them specifically for the Web.

GIF89a is pretty much your only choice for use on the Web, especially because it is the only animated format that GIMP supports for *saving* at this time.

A Word About GIF89a

When you have finally built, timed, and tweaked your image, you should of course save it! When you save an animated GIF, remember that first of all you must reduce the color depth, just like any other GIF. Then go to the Save As menu and name your file with a GIF extension. The GIMP automatically recognizes that you are about to save a GIF89a animation and gives you a few more options in the Save As dialog box (see Figure 23.5). *Loop* allows you to determine if you want the animation to loop endlessly or play one time through. *One Frame per Layer (Replace)* forces each frame to cover up each previous frame in its entirety (traditional flip-book animation style). And *Make Frame from*

Cumulative Layers (Combine) enables you to show each new frame on top of each previous frame (used with the optimization techniques outlined next, this saves space, and is similar to using a separately painted background image on top of which your subjects interact—like how LooneyTunes and other such cartoons were made before computers came into play).

FIGURE 23.5

The Save As GIF dialog box adapts itself to dealing with animations.

Size Issues

When building animated buttons, banners, and such for the Web, there are a few things to take into consideration. Most importantly, *bandwidth is everything*. Not everyone has the luxury of a T1 line. (You'd be surprised just how much your world-view changes when moving from the campus fast Ethernet back to a 28.8 modem)

This is especially true for advertisement banners. If you are faced with making one of these remember that people did not come to the site to look at banners specifically, and they tend to get real cranky when a bulky ad banner detracts from the load time of the content they came to see. If you want to increase banner click-throughs, a small, simple, non-bulky banner is usually best. You can even sacrifice on color-depth and detail a little more as well (as long as you still antialias your fonts), because you do not want to overimpose your presence on the site on which you are advertising. Keywords here are *small* and *optimized*!

For example, the banner shown in Figure 23.6 consists of only two frames (to emulate the flowing water effect) and is therefore quickly downloaded, but the effect is still eye-catching, and it gets the point across.

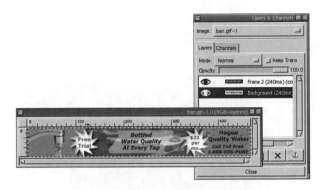

FIGURE 23.6

Banner ads help pay for Web space, but a small, less-detailed, quick-loading banner makes for a more enjoyable browsing experience.

Optimizing Animations

When you build an animation, there are a lot of elements in the picture that are repeated within every single frame. This is extremely wasteful, as repeating the same portions of the animations takes up valuable space and eats bandwidth. The way to counteract this is to use only the information that changes from the previous frames in each new frame.

You can improve your animation efficiency by hand simply by cutting out the obvious unnecessary information. Figure 23.7 illustrates this with the example of a simple, traditional 88×31 animated Web button. Eliminate the unnecessary by cropping away everything that was not within the animated portion after the first frame, which is confined to a little square area in this example. The animation is then saved with the Make Frame from Cumulative Layers option, which allows the background frame portions to show through in each frame. This saves a lot of space.

As you can see, this is fairly simple to accomplish when dealing with an animation in which you know that all altered portions are taking place within the confines of a small square (or whatever). But what if the animation has things going on throughout the entire image, as in Figure 23.8? Obviously, it would be a bit more difficult to determine exactly what is static and cut it out from the successive frames. Fortunately, there is a wonderful plug-in that can take care of this for you named *Animation Optimize*. This plug-in is great because it can find *every single pixel* that is static after the first frame and cut them all out! This not only can cut out a few extra kilobytes (or many more, depending on the file), but can also make it possible to drastically slim down the more complex animations by reducing them to only the elements that are absolutely necessary, right down to the absolute value (see Figure 23.9). In this example, I was able to reduce the animation's size after experimenting with the color depth as well as using the Optimization plug-in. (155k is still definitely not a good size for a Web graphic, but it does illustrate the point.) Some animations in fact often have greater file size reduction as well (up to 50 percent).

Although it looks a little strange in Layout view, in playback it is indistinguishable from the original. Using this tool with Web graphics is a must. This would not be possible by hand in most circumstances.

FIGURE 23.7

By cutting out the fat, you achieve the same look, but save your Web clients precious time by conserving bandwidth. This particular example was reduced in file size by a factor of three by reducing many of the repeated elements.

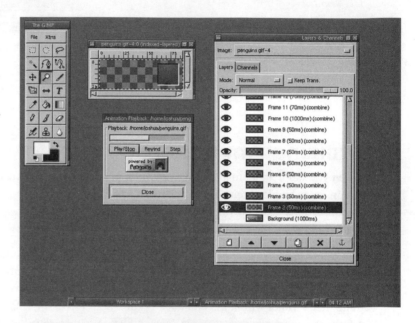

.**FIGURE 23.8**

Before running Animation Optimize, each frame has a lot of duplicated information. This particular animated GIF weighed in at 214k. Not very good if you happen to be browsing with a 28.8 modem.

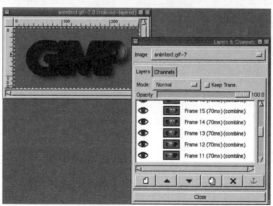

Using this plug-in is simple: Prepare your animation, pull up Animation Optimize by right-clicking and going to Filters, Animation, and then sit back and let the plug-in do its thing. Pretty soon, you will have an animation that plays exactly the same, but has a fraction of the file size! Optimizing your Web animations in this way can let you save bandwidth, and by doing so allows you to go ahead and cram a little more information into your graphic for higher detail and smoother playback.

This plug-in creates a new duplicate when optimizing, so as not to disturb your original composition. (Better safe than sorry.)

FIGURE 23.9

By contrast, the exact same animation, after optimization has been applied, takes up a mere 155k of space total.

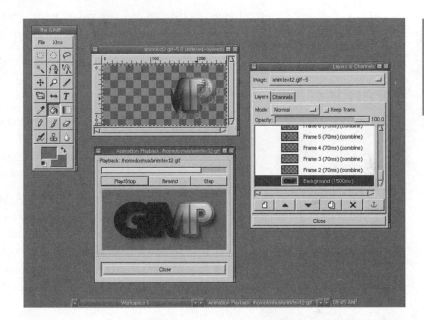

23

Summary

Animations can lend enhancement to any project, but keep in mind that anything used in excess can detract from a project more than if it hadn't been used at all. So *subtlety* is key here (most of the time). Also, if you are going to use animated GIFs for whatever reason, you should take into consideration that some browsers (Microsoft Internet Explorer, specifically) might play some of your GIFs at a slightly different speed (a little faster) than you might have intended, depending. It tends to roundup the frame speeds at times.

Q&A

Q I have changed the duration of each frame, but I want some frames to stick around longer than others. Can I do this, or do all frames have to be the same?

A Fortunately, each frame can have its own individual frame speed. This enables you to have more freedom in creating custom animated effects, including momentary pauses in motion.

Exercise

A good thing to do when creating Web animations is to play around with optimization techniques, such as color depth reduction, dithering, and so on. The smaller you can get the file size, the more room you'll have to play with—to use for more animation detail or to ease download time.

In this hour you covered the animation basics—setting up and creating a few simple animated GIFs by hand—yet the GIMP is capable of handling much more sophisticated animation work. If you want to move beyond simple animated GIFs and into some of the more complex motion graphics, I encourage you to check out the *GAP* suite of plug-ins (`registry.gimp.org`). These plug-ins are quite involved and do require a patching and recompilation of the entire GIMP source tree, but if you are into high-quality animations and want to move beyond simple animated GIFs, it might be the thing for you. It is included with the CD-ROM as well under *plug-ins*.

HOUR **24**

Using Peripherals with Linux

Well, after all the techniques and tutorials outlined in this book, you have acquired a basic understanding of how GIMP works, and you have a competent knowledge of manipulating digital graphics with it. But, for all that, something this still missing… how to get all those digital imaging devices to communicate with the GIMP. Using the GIMP is even more fun when digital scanners and cameras are involved.

For what it's worth, the quick tips outlined within this hour are pretty Linux-centric in nature. If you happen to be running another UNIX variant, the steps illustrated here are probably mostly valid there as well, especially if you are using Intel-style hardware, but I can make no guarantees that everything will apply exactly the same.

Digital Scanners

Ah, yes, the digital scanner. I don't know what I'd do without one. The scanner makes using your hand-drawn and painted work a snap—not to mention making collages and photo manipulation that much easier to do!

So now you are faced with the challenge of attaching your scanner device to your Linux box. If you are in the market for a good digital scanner, there are a few things to keep in mind if you want to maintain Linux-compatibility.

- A SCSI interface is your best option. Some parallel scanners are supported, and you can, at least in theory, get one of those SCSI-to-parallel setups to work, with luck and a lot of hacking, but if you want to keep your sanity, make sure that you get a good SCSI card to accompany your scanner.
- You should take a look at the *SANE* compatibility list. SANE is the scanner interfacing software that is fast becoming the most frequently used and is the one this hour will be dealing with. You can find the list at `http://www.mostang.com/sane`.
- Don't be afraid to spend a little extra money. The added quality you will gain by spending a little more on a higher end scanner will be well worth it. The reason: besides scan quality and durability, there is also the issue of user-adjustable scan resolution. You will want a scanner that will let you change this easily, otherwise, you might be stuck with RAM-intensive scans at $1800 \infty 1600$ resolution for something like your small driver's license photo. This can waste a lot of time.

There are actually (not surprisingly) a lot of choices when faced with using a scanner with Linux. However, the SANE package offers the widest variety of supported devices, as well as easy expandability and good networking support. Scanner device support is still in its developmental stages in Linux, so you will definitely want to check the compatibility list before purchasing a scanner to use explicitly with Linux.

After you have chosen, purchased, and wired your scanner, getting it picked-up under Linux isn't too difficult, provided that you do have a fairly standard scanner attached to a SCSI interface.

The first thing to do is to download the SANE distribution from `www.mostang.com/sane`.

After untarring the distribution, follow the directions as outlined in the README (`./configure && make && make install`), and you should be all set. Then you will want to start sane with the `xscanimage` command. This brings up the Sane dialog box, as shown in Figure 24.1. You can also use it via the command line with the `scanimage` command. (Consult the man page for more details.)

By going to scanner interface in the dialog box and selecting your scanner interface model, you will be ready to scan something, as long as there are no difficulties.

To scan, turn your scanner on, load your source image into the scanner, select the proper scanner interface from within xscanimage, and press OK. Your image should appear onscreen shortly (see Figure 24.1). You can also use the Preview function to get a quick overview of the appearance of your scan.

FIGURE 24.1

Using a scanner device isn't too terribly difficult with the GIMP and SANE.

Scans frequently come in at a larger size than you want to use for your final image. This is actually a good thing because editing your image, and then reducing the image size usually results in a higher-quality image than if you had simply scanned it in at the desired size to begin with.

You can now use xscanimage as a GIMP plug-in by making the following symlink:

```
ln -s /usr/local/bin/xscanimage ~/.gimp/plug-ins
```

It should now appear in the GIMP's Xtns menu.

Sometimes the scanned image, if taken from a book or magazine, might look a little grainy. This is due to the inks printed on the medium not translating well to screen. This can be counteracted by tinkering with the options in the NL Filters plug-in. You can use this, and the Sharpen tool, to make quick work of those grainy lines. Also, doing this at a larger size, and then reducing the file dimensions will also lessen the grainy effect. The SANE package also has support for some functions for the improvement of image quality, such as color intensity and gamma. You should play with these settings to find what effect looks best.

SANE also comes with a command-line client, *scanimage*, which has a plethora of useful, if not cryptic features. You might want to read the man page or get a listing of options with *scanimage –h*.

Digital Cameras

Getting digital cameras to work with Linux is a little more straightforward. There are packages for many different types of video and tuning devices under Linux. As long as you have a good parallel port interface, you can get many of them to work.

You can find a listing of compatibility client applications for Linux at http://roadrunner.swansea.uk.linux.org/v4l.shtml.

If you're using something such as the Quickcam, you can use the application gnomovision (available from gnome.org) or something similar to capture and save video snapshots.

Color Printers

Fortunately, printers connected directly to the printer port are one of the easiest peripheral devices to get working under Linux. In fact, there are only a few obscure models that are *not* supported (beware of Winprinters!) The GIMP print plug-in uses a straight PCL/PostScript printing interface with regular UNIX lpd, so this plug-in should give you no trouble whatsoever.

After you have your printer plugged in, you can set it up one of two ways. 1) Use the Printer Setup utility that comes with Red Hat Linux (on their CD-ROM), or 2) Set it up by hand. Both methods are relatively painless, pending a standard printer setup.

If you set up Red Hat Linux, start the program printtool as root, as shown in Figure 24.2. This will give you a nice, friendly little TCL/Tk interface to printer configuration. Scroll down the list of printers, pick one, and try out the Print a Test Page function. If this doesn't work right away, there are a few things you can try.

Otherwise, if you do not want to use printtool, you can do this by hand. You can consult the Printer Howto, which should either be in /usr/doc, or you can find it at the Linux Documentation project Web site: http://metalab.unc.edu/LDP/index.html.

The next thing to take care of is the GIMP print plug-in (see Figure 24.3). This should be installed by default, but if not, it is easy to do with gimptool. After you have that taken care of, start the GIMP, open an image, and try printing it. Right-click and select File, Print; then choose the print resolution and layout and press OK.

Sometimes, printing something in the GIMP, even on a nice color printer, will not turn out as nice an image as appears onscreen. This is due to the limitations of the printing parameters, print resolution, and the differences between monitor and printer gamut. These topics are a little complex, and are not covered here. But, with a keen eye and a little patience, you can usually get your inkjet printer to print out pretty close to what is shown onscreen (This might take a few test prints). If the image isn't quite what you expected color-wise, you may want to tweak with the Hue, Saturation, and Luminance settings until the result is a little closer to what you expect. Also, it might be good to print out something with a distinctive color that you are familiar with as well, in order to get an idea of the amount of difference between monitor and screen, which makes for easier adjustments. This isn't a perfect solution, but should suffice for average home printing. If you require a more professional job, talk to your local print shop and find out what they require as far as image format goes. They are experienced with complex color issues and should know what to do.

FIGURE 24.2

Setting up a printer with Red Hat Linux.

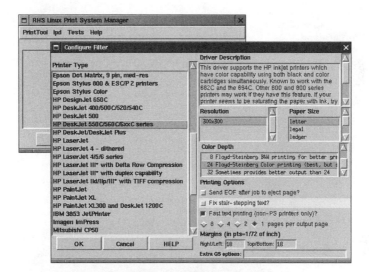

24

FIGURE 24.3

The GIMP print plug-in makes printing from within GIMP a breeze.

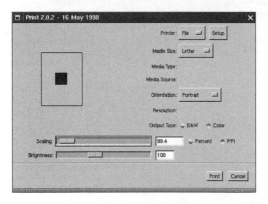

Wacom Pens and Other Pointing Devices

Using Wacom pens is a matter of getting the device recognized by X. You must have the XFree86 module `xf86Wacom.so` available in order for this to work. It comes with most distributions of Xfree86, otherwise, you can get it from `http://www.levien.com/free/linux_intuos.html`. You will need to make sure that it is in your modules path, which is probably /usr/X11R6/lib/modules.

In order to get Xfree86 working with another pointing device, you will need to edit you /etc/X11/XF86Config file. Add is the module in the modules section of the config file, like this:

```
Section Modules
    Load xf86Wacom.so
EndSection
```

Then, X will need to set some parameters for using the module. These are set in the Xinput section, as in this example:

```
Section "Xinput"
        SubSection "WacomStylus"
            Port "/dev/ttyS0"
            DeviceName "Wacom"
            Mode Absolute
            Suppress 15
        EndSubSection
        SubSection "WacomStylus"
            Port "/dev/ttyS0"
            DeviceName "WacomCore"
            Mode Absolute
            AlwaysCore
            Suppress 15
        EndSubSection
        SubSection "WacomCursor"
            Port "/dev/ttyS0"
            DeviceName "CURSOR"
            Mode Absolute
            Suppress 15
        EndSubSection
        SubSection "WacomCursor"
            Port "/dev/ttyS0"
            DeviceName "CursorCore"
            Mode Absolute
            AlwaysCore
            Suppress 15
        EndSubSection
        SubSection "WacomEraser"
            Port "/dev/ttyS0"
            Mode Absolute
            Suppress 15
```

```
        EndSubSection
        SubSection "WacomEraser"
            Port "/dev/ttyS0"
            DeviceName "EraserCore"
            Mode Absolute
            AlwaysCore
            Suppress 15
        EndSubSection
    EndSection
```

Of course, this might need a little tweaking from the example listed here, and the device setting will depend on how your device is set up. If you are using one of the pens that share a PS/2 port with your mouse, /dev/mouse should be a safe bet. Likewise, if it uses a dedicated serial port (recommended), you will need to use /dev/ttyS0.

After this is in place, you will need to make sure that the GIMP supports Xinput. This is actually done through GTK, so you might need to patch it. (The latest releases of GTK have this built in.) You can grab patches for GTK here: http://www.gtk.org/~otaylor/xinput/patches.html. You will need to recompile GIMP after applying the patches.

24

A Word About Video Editing

Video editing in the GIMP is now in its infantile development stages, but it does promise to be quite powerful feature in future releases. Nonetheless, you can get started playing with video now—with a few tweaks.

As of yet, you cannot use the ATI All-In-Wonder card with Linux, although there is work now being done on this. Stay tuned, this could change pretty quickly.

There is right now another developmental branch of GIMP development that is singularly dedicated to further improving interoperability with the GIMP and professional video editing equipment. This series is not yet ready for prime time, but if you are so inclined, you can learn more about it at http://film.gimp.org.

Summary

Using peripherals in order to help acquire and manipulate graphics with Linux is usually not a difficult task, but it can be a process that can require a little digging. Sometimes certain devices (especially scanners) might have support from specific software packages. Some of them are only commercially supported. Any good Linux resource or search engine inquiry, should land you some good results. There really aren't that many PC devices that aren't supported by Linux in some way. The trick is to do research. Chances are, no matter how obscure you device may be, if more than 500 people have one, at least one of them has gotten it to work under Linux.

Q&A

Q I have a USB device. Can I use that?

A Perhaps. USB support in Linux is really in its infancy, but it is there. USB support does require you to patch the kernel. Because this is life on the bleeding edge, you might be successful at getting the device to work. But if the device is a pretty cutting-edge, standard one, there is no reason why it would not work. Therefore, although I wouldn't recommend buying a USB device explicitly for use in Linux at this point in time, expect this situation to change *quickly*. In any case, full USB support should work its way into standard kernel releases after it has proven to be reliable enough. (By the way, if you happen to be an iMac owner, you're a perfect candidate to help test and debug USB support in Linux.)

Exercise

Well, honestly, if you have such a graphics-related peripheral device, chances are you want it to work in Linux, so that isn't much of an exercise, really. Your assignment then, now that the end of the book is at hand, is to try and surpass everything you have learned so far. At this point, if you have followed the tutorials diligently, you have acquired a base of understanding that will enable you to create stunning digital graphics with a little effort and creativity. But the journey is far from over. One thing that I have encountered often in my many pursuits is the simple, yet true, popular pontification: "The more I learn, the more I find out that I don't know as much as I thought I did...". As you have probably found, this maxim is especially true in the realm of computers. So, with that in mind, keep at it! And remember that the fun you have had learning what you know so far pales in comparison to what lies ahead. You ain't seen nothin' yet!

INDEX

Other Related Titles

**Sams Teach Yourself
Linux in 24 Hours,
Second Edition**
Bill Ball
ISBN: 0-672-31526-2
$24.99 US/$35.99 CAN

**Special Edition Using
Linux, Fourth Edition**
Jack Tackett, Jr.
ISBN: 0-7897-1746-8
$39.99 US/$57.95 CAN

**Linux Unleashed, Third
Edition**
Tim Parker
ISBN: 0-672-31372-3
$39.99 US/$57.95 CAN

**Red Hat Linux
Unleashed, Third Edition**
Bill Ball
ISBN: 0-672-31410-X
$39.99 US/$57.95 CAN

**Complete Idiot's Guide
to Unix**
Bill Wagner
ISBN: 0-7897-1805-7
$16.99 US

**Sams Teach Yourself
Photoshop 5 in 24 Hours**
Carla Rose
ISBN: 0-672-31301-4
$19.99 US/$28.95 CAN

**Sams Teach Yourself
Paint Shop Pro 5 in 24
Hours**
T. Michael Clark
ISBN: 0-672-31362-6
$19.99 US/$28.95 CAN

**Inside Adobe Photoshop
5, Limited Edition**
Gary Bouton
ISBN: 1562059513
$55.00 US/$78.95 CAN

**Complete Idiot's Guide
to Adobe Photoshop 5**
Robert Stanley
ISBN: 0-7897-1769-7
$16.99 US

**Photoshop 5 Artistry
Photoshop 5 Artistry**
Barry Haynes
ISBN: 1-5620-5895-9
$55.00 US/$78.95 CAN

**Complete Idiot's Guide
to Linux**
Manuel Ricart
ISBN: 0-7897-1826-X
$19.99 US/$28.95 CAN

**Sams Teach Yourself
KDE 1.1 in 24 Hours**
Nicholas Wells
ISBN: 0-672-31608-0
$24.99 US/$35.99 CAN

**Sams Teach Yourself
StarOffice for Linux in
24 Hours**
Nicholas Wells
ISBN: 0-672-31412-6
$24.99 US/$35.99 CAN

SAMS

www.samspublishing.com

All prices are subject to change.